SCHMUCKS with UNDERWOODS
CONVERSATIONS with HOLLYWOOD'S CLASSIC SCREENWRITERS

M A X   W I L K

APPLAUSE
THEATRE & CINEMA BOOKS

Schmucks with Underwoods:
Conversations with Hollywood's Classic
Screenwriters
by Max Wilk

Art direction: Michelle Thompson
Book design: Kristina Rolander

Library of Congress Cataloging-in-Publication Data:
Wilk, Max.
Schmucks with Underwoods: conversations with
Hollywood's classic screenwriters / Max Wilk.
p. cm.
Includes index.
ISBN 1-55783-508-X
1. Motion picture authorship.
2. Screenwriters—United
States—Interviews. I. Title.

PN1996.W398 2003
808.2'3—dc22
2003015771

British Library Cataloging-in-Publication Data
A catalog record of this book is available from the
British Library

APPLAUSE THEATRE & CINEMA BOOKS
151 West 46th Street, 8th Floor
New York, NY 10036
PHONE: (212) 575-9265
FAX: (646) 562-5852
EMAIL: info@applausepub.com
INTERNET: www.applausepub.com

Sales & Distribution
NORTH AMERICA:
  Hal Leonard Corp.
  7777 West Bluemound Road
  P. O. Box 13819
  Milwaukee, WI 53213
  PHONE: (414) 774-3630
  FAX: (414) 774-3529
  EMAIL: halinfo@halleonard.com
  INTERNET: www.halleonard.com
UK:
  Roundhouse Publishing Ltd.
  Millstone, Limers Lane
  Northam, North Devon Ex 39 2RG
  PHONE: (0) 1237-474-474
  FAX: (0) 1237-474-774
  EMAIL: roundhouse.group@ukgateway.net

DEDICATION

HEREWITH ARE INTERVIEWS WITH SCREENWRITERS WHO HAVE LABORED IN and out of Hollywood, from the silent film days until these DVD days.

Their wisdom and wit has been assembled since 1972, which, alas, means that most of the talented people whose memoirs are included here are no longer with us except in the films they wrote.

But their agonies and their ecstasies, their quips and their comments, accumulated over the years, still remain.

Their interviews are but a sampling of the authors and writers and playwrights who trod the weekly Hollywood treadmill, who partook of the bread of David Selznick and Sam Goldwyn, Darryl Zanuck and Harry Cohn, Jack Warner and Louis B. Mayer, and danced to their tune. And who created, out of their angst, an organization called the Screen Writers Guild, for which we all owe them a debt of gratitude.

It seems only fair that this book be dedicated to them, so that they may have the credit they've all earned.

And if their names are not exactly above the title—Jack Warner, as usual, has that billing—these writers come pretty damned close!

CONTENTS

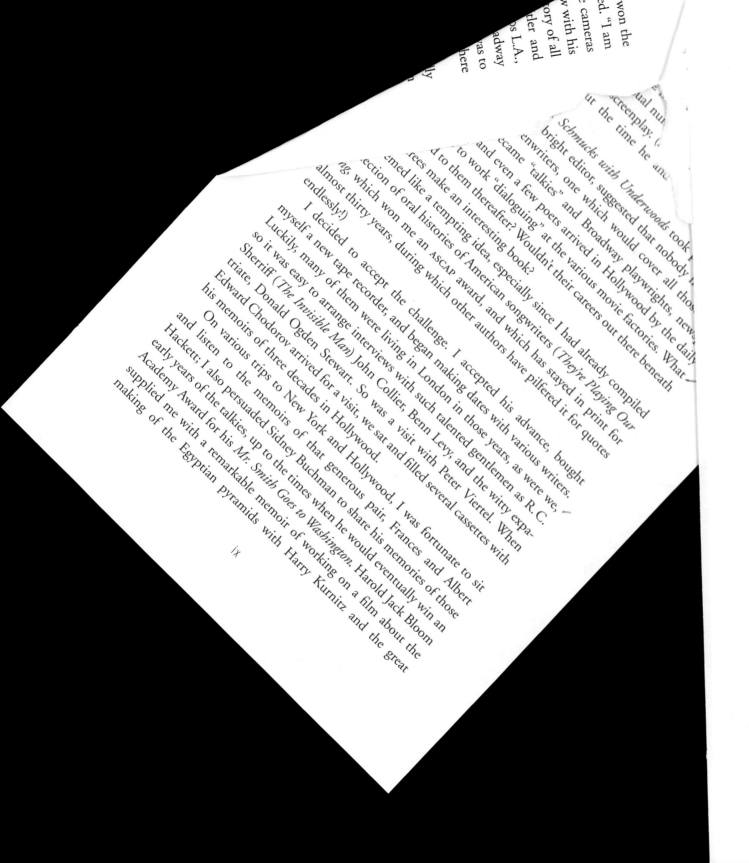

ACKNOWLEDGMENTS

AND NOW FOR THE AUTHOR'S THANK-YOUS. PLUS LOW BOWS TO A BATCH OF generous people who have helped me make this book a reality.

For starters, I thank Edward Sorel, Dana Fradon, James Stephenson, Robert Andrew Parker, Arnold Levin, Frank Modell, and Arnold Roth. Who could ask for anything more than their remarkable contributions?

To Kevin Brownlow, for his contribution to the silent film title–writer chapter.

To Karen Pedersen, of the James Webb Memorial Library, who has spurred this project on from Day One. To Linda Mehr, of the Motion Picture Academy Library, another enthusiast. To Joel Raphaelson for generously providing me with "Freundshaft." David Goodrich, who provided photos of his relatives, and many thanks to Leslie Epstein, for the photo of both his father and his uncle, Phillip and Julius Epstein, neither of whom can ever be replaced. To Larry Gelbart and Michael Tolkin, and to Marian Seldes, the keeper of the Garson Kanin memoir library, and to Hal Kanter and Dick Fleischer, and Cy Feuer, and to the late Alan Rivkin, who got me started on all this history search years ago, and to Stanley Rubin and Walter Doniger, and all the other writers who helped me learn screenwriting as part of the First Motion Picture Unit, Army Air Forces, Culver City, California, and to Roger Mayer and his staff at Turner Classic Movies, who each day treat all those antique Warner, RKO, Universal, Paramount, and MGM films as if they were treasure ... thank you. And to Charles Champlin, of the *L.A. Times*, who was working this turf years before anyone else did, and to Mark Glubke who liked my proposal from the day we first talked about it. To Marsha Scarborough, a damned good writer, and to Curt Akin, of Syllables, who brought me kicking and screaming into the 21st century, and to Coleen O'Shea who knows how to negotiate a good deal, and Kallie Shimek who knows how to edit a good book.

To son David, who's always there to help straighten out this damned computer, and a low bow to that ever-patient proofreader, who has never wavered, ever since I handed her my first finished manuscript, all those years ago — my dear wife, Barbara.

And last, but far from least, someone I a[...]
deserves the final bow. Back in 1921, he w[...]
Selznick film studio in Fort Lee, New Jers[...]
was another Wilk, my late father Jacob[...]
special bond of kinship. May I pay[...]
lovely drawing of Sidney Buchman, bu[...]
a great talent and a true friend.

The late, great Al Hirschfeld. *Ave, atque*[...]
you, dear Louise.

William Faulkner. (Yes, you read correctly, the same[...]
Nobel Prize!) I wanted to interview I.A.L. Diamond, h[...]
operating on our new script, removing half an hour befo[...]
roll," he explained. However, he did agree to arrange an interv[...]
longtime partner, Billy Wilder, who was an authority on the his[...]
those European refugees (himself included) who had fled H[...]
managed to make it safely to Hollywood in the mid-1930s. In 197[...]
I spent hours recording Albert Lewis, who had migrated from Br[...]
to Hollywood in the 1930s and went to work at Fox, where his task w[...]
lure playwrights out to that newly established sound film factory[...]
"dialoguers" were so necessary to supply words and plots.

All of this remarkable material was captured safely on tape, carefu[...]
transcribed, and put away, along with other material I had amassed fro[...]
tion of Darryl Zanuck and Arthur Caesar, the famous Hollywood wit (his descrip[...]
Harry Kurnitz was "From Poland to polo—in one generation!").

But after a year or more of amassing material, I discovered, to my
dismay, that two other books were due to be published on the subject of
writers in Hollywood. One of them dealt at great length with the unfortunate experiences of such legends as F. Scott Fitzgerald, Dorothy Parker,
John O'Hara, and of course, Faulkner out in L.A. And another one dealt
with Herman Mankiewicz at great length—and with John O'Hara and
Dorothy Parker.

It seemed to me, and my editor agreed, that those books might be
causing a glut on the market. Temporary or not, but still a glut.

So we decided to postpone the history of all those Hollywood figures
I'd captured on tape; we shifted gears. I would spend the next two years
working on yet another book, one that dealt with the pioneers of the early
days of "live" television, a subject that I knew quite well, having supported
my family for many years by writing scripts at CBS and NBC. It would be
The Golden Age of Television, which also became a useful text for other
writers.

But what about those audio tapes? And the transcriptions thereof?
The tapes went into a fireproof safe in my closet, and the transcripts
were stored away in a large cardboard box, also safely sequestered. Over the
next few years, there they all sat, while I worked on various other projects.
But one afternoon, while I was visiting Hollywood again, my old friend

Karl Malden, then the president of the Motion Picture Academy, took me on a tour of that organization's remarkable new library. When I mentioned the steel box at home, so packed with oral Hollywood history, it was decided then and there that such important memorabilia be properly stored away in the archives of the Academy Library, which is where they are now safely sequestered for students, scholars, and film fans.

All of that took place over a decade ago.

Then two years back, while searching for some other material, I unearthed that large cardboard box upstairs; scrawled on its lid was "HOLLYWOOD WRITERS." And when I opened it, I found, nearly thirty years after they'd been stored away, the sheaves of all those transcripts, the oral histories I'd recorded, those voices, which had patiently been waiting their turn for so many years, to be heard.

It suddenly seemed important to me that I should share their memories, their accumulated wisdom, the gags and the angst of that long-gone period.

Time to bring them out of the wings, where they'd been waiting so patiently for all this time, to center stage, where they could truly take bows. And I could also add to their oral histories the various comments of other such talents as the acerbic Ben Hecht, the playwright S. N. Behrman, Raymond Chandler, and the producer Leland Hayward. Also Paddy Chayefsky, Nunnally Johnson, and Michael Tolkin, all of them with their memories and comments on day-to-day toiling in the Hollywood vineyards.

I could also take a tape recorder over to visit my close friend Evan Hunter, who has spent the past three decades in and out of various film projects, some of them adaptations, others such classics as the Alfred Hitchcock film *The Birds* and his own, *Strangers When We Meet*. And I can also share with you the hilarious reminiscences of my older pal, Edmund Hartmann, who went to work in the Universal salt mines back in the 1930s to serve time with W. C. Fields, Abbott and Costello, and Lucille Ball, and finally to write a series of hit films with Bob Hope, Hal Kanter, and other such talents.

It's my pleasure, and I'm sure it will be yours, to have them all join the party.

So here it is—a collection of *le temps perdu*—a little late, but I can promise you, worth the wait. I've spent the past year and a half assembling all of these memoirs to provide future generations a sense of what it must have been like to be hired by one of the studios, way back when, to work and rewrite and struggle to do one's best to craft a screenplay which would end up being made into a decent picture—one which would entitle its author to yet another assignment. One which perhaps you might even see tonight in that 24-hour wonderland of Turner Classic Movies, where writers, going back to the silent days—even such as the title wizard, Ralph Spence—customarily receive the credits they deserve.

Remember, none of those pictures on Flix, American Movie Classics (AMC), or Turner Classic Movies (TCM) would exist, to be shown to you again, if someone hadn't sat down with the blank yellow pages and spent hours filling them with the story line, the dialogue, and the overall work which turned the pages into a screenplay.

Jack L. Warner, whose grinning face on the cover of this book lined by Edward Sorel, may have enjoyed referring to his cadre of writers as "schmucks with Underwoods," and some of you may find his epithet hilarious—while other find it offensive. But I must ask, if you were one of those writers who worked away on the Warner Burbank lot, punching the time clock in the morning and punching it out each night, how would you feel, knowing exactly what your boss, the Colonel, thought of you?

Especially if you knew that J. L., of whom it was usually said, "The guy who'd rather tell a bad joke than make a good movie," was not at all kidding about his writers!

So here it all is, for avid film fans, for the French cineastes, and especially for all those weekly artisans of the press who list the current movies which are playing, old ones and new ones, and who persistently manage to credit such films only to the director.

Better, always, to close with a laugh. One which will put a proper button on the subject.

It was when Darryl Zanuck, producer and co-founder of 20th Century Fox studios, was running a new picture and invited George Jessel, then one of his henchmen, to share the projection room with him. When it was over Zanuck turned to Jessel. "How did you like it?" he demanded. "Be completely frank."

"Okay, Darryl," said Jessel. "Frankly, I think it stinks."

"Who the hell are you to think it stinks?" demanded his furious boss.

"Who the hell do you have to be to think it stinks?" replied Jessel.

This is from the same Jessel who would later say, "When I die, I want to be cremated, and you should take my ashes and throw them all over Darryl Zanuck's driveway, God forbid he should ever skid."

Okay, boys, roll 'em!

1. OVERVIEW:
WRITERS in HOLLYWOOD

"Film Daily Product Guide," List of Available Writers, 1937:
Samuel Hopkins Adams, Peter Arno, Franklin P. Adams, Bugs Baer, Rex
Beach, Roark Bradford, Bessie Breuer, Heywood Broun, James M. Cain,
Erskine Caldwell, Leslie Charteris, Irvin S. Cobb, John Collier, Padraic
Colum, Marc Connelly, Frank Craven, Kyle Crichton, A. J. Cronin,
Russel Crouse, Clemence Dane, Elmer Davis, Owen Davis, Theodore
Dreiser, John Drinkwater, Ashley Dukes, Lord Dunsany, Walter D.
Edmonds, John Emerson, James T. Farrell, William Faulkner, Rachel
Field, F. Scott Fitzgerald, Gilbert Gabriel, Paul Gallico, Wolcott Gibbs,
Michael Gold, Dr. Isaac Goldberg, Rube Goldberg, Louis Golding, Paul
Green, Milt Gross, Emily Hahn, Albert Halper, Alvin Harlow, Moss
Hart, John Held Jr., DuBose Heyward, Sam Hoffenstein, Paul Horgan,
Richard Hughes, W. W. Jacobs, Will James, Elsie Janis, MacKinlay Kantor,
Sidney Kingsley, Jack Kirkland, Arthur Kober, Claire Kummer, Wilton
Lackaye, Noel Langley, Emmet Lavery, Meyer Levin, Newman Levy,
Victoria Lincoln, Joseph C. Lincoln, Anita Loos, William McFee, Mary
McCarthy, Horace McCoy, St. Clair McKelway, J. P. McEvoy, H. C.

(Sapper) McNeill, Albert Maltz, Joseph Moncure March, Edwin Justus Mayer, Christopher Morley, Ogden Nash, J. C. Nugent, Elliott Nugent, John O'Hara, Dorothy Parker, John Patrick, S. J. Perelman, J. B. Priestley, Ayn Rand, Quentin Reynolds, Damon Runyon, Adela Rogers St. John, Irwin Shaw, R. C. Sherriff, Upton Sinclair, Booth Tarkington, Wilbur Daniel Steele, Gertrude Stein, G. B. Stern, Deems Taylor, A. E. Thomas, James Thurber, Carl Van Doren, John Van Druten, Alec Waugh, Evelyn Waugh, Franz Werfel, Dame Rebecca West, Thornton Wilder, Ben Ames Williams, Harry Leon Wilson, P. G. Wodehouse, Thomas Wolfe, Alexander Woollcott, Phillip Wylie, Stefan Zweig…

…and many, many more.

Authors. Playwrights. Poets. Critics. Novelists. An illustrious list. A literary Who's Who of the past six decades.

What is the one experience all of them had in common?

It's the time they spent working (or trying to) on scripts for Hollywood producers.

All the way back to those early days when Sam Goldwyn brought his first group of Eminent Authors out, in 1919.

Eminent Authors Inc. was the title Goldwyn and his press agent gave to that noble experiment, when Sam hired Gertrude Atherton, Mary Roberts Rinehart, Rupert Hughes, Gouveurneur Morris, and Leroy Scott —all prestigious names indeed. (In retaliation, Adolph Zukor and Jesse Lasky signed up Elinor Glyn, Arnold Bennett, Gilbert Parker, and Somerset Maugham!)

After reading Leroy Scott's completed screenplay, Goldwyn said, "Mr. Scott, you are undoubtedly a great novelist but I am afraid this is not good for the movies." Goldwyn made the identical speech after reading Basil King's screenplay—and so it went with the invasion of Eminent Authors.

When it came to the great Belgian author, Maurice Maeterlinck, who had written *The Bluebird*, Goldwyn was prepared to pay out $100,000 to have that illustrious name added to his contract list. He installed the great writer in a California hilltop home, where Maeterlinck spent three months scribbling diligently away. Each day a translator took the written pages and translated the great man's work into English. Finally, the day came when his script was presented to the waiting Goldwyn. Sam struggled through it, and then—as the story goes—emerged from his office waving the pages in astonishment. "My God," he cried, "the hero is a *bee!!*"

When Sam escorted his writer to the railroad station, from which Maeterlinck was due to leave town, he patted him on the arm. "Don't worry, Maurice," he said. "You'll make good yet."

Ever since those first simple silent-film days, countless other authors and playwrights, poets and essayists have picked up their portable Underwood typewriters, climbed aboard The Twentieth Century, and headed West to serve their time in one of the various feudal domains presided over by L. B. Mayer, Zukor, Laemmle, the brothers Warner, Lasky, and the rest.

Some of them became skilled screenwriters, whose finished work actually made it to the screen. (They'd be the ones who stayed on, or commuted, shrewd enough to put aside enough savings to enable them to go away and return to their own projects.)

But the majority of them did not.

They climbed aboard The Chief and left town. Sometimes bewildered, often sadder … and perhaps a bit richer.

Over the next six decades, quite a few who'd been through the mill wrote about their own experiences.

Some of that literature survives. Fitzgerald drew heavily on his sad experiences at MGM to create his brilliant unfinished *The Last Tycoon*. Isherwood gave us *Prater Violet*, and Evelyn Waugh *The Loved One*. Aldous Huxley drew from his own studio experiences to write *After Many a Summer Dies the Swan*, and William Saroyan wrote the play *Get Away, Old Man* out of his term with L. B. Mayer. Raymond Chandler captured some of the feeling of Hollywood in various Philip Marlowe adventures, and Gene Fowler wrote biographies of some of the players.

Out of angst comes mirth. S. J. Perelman gave us a series of caustic pieces that use Hollywood as a punching bag. Ben Hecht wrote *Concerning a Woman of Sin*, and Bella and Sam Spewack turned their MGM years into the hilarious farce, *Boy Meets Girl*. George S. Kaufman and Moss Hart wrote a hit comedy about Hollywood— *Once in a Lifetime*—even *before* they went West and lived through it!

But there's much, much more that hasn't been printed.

Certainly, there's no lack of literature about Hollywood. That library stack grows wider each month. The film business and the people who populate it are a seemingly inexhaustible source of anecdote, gossip, and Rashomon-style personal history.

We've had autobiographies from actors telling us which actresses surrendered, when and where and for how long—and lately, the ladies have begun to brag about which star's Simmons Beautyrest trampoline they performed on. Every possible history has been compiled—silent, sound, and animated—from the films of Renee Adoree and Rin Tin Tin to the comedies of Our Gang and the musicals of Judy Canova. Gene Autry came down off his horse to give us The Word about Westerns, and Mr. David Selznick has been immortalized by the ultimate coffee-table book, *David O. Selznick's Hollywood*, which costs a bit more than a decent coffee table. There's a cottage industry which sprang up in the past decade based merely on one man—Groucho.

So, why another book about Hollywood?

A fair question, one that deserves an answer.

An answer from *writers*.

"Movies," Ben Hecht was to recall, "were seldom written. In 1927 they were yelled into existence in conferences that kept going in saloons, brothels, and all-night poker games. Movie sets roared with arguments and organ music. Sometimes little string orchestras played to help stir up the emotions of the great performers—*Traumerei* for Clara Bow and the *Meditation* from Thais for Adolphe Menjou, the screen's most sophisticated lover.

"I was given an office at Paramount. A bit of cardboard with my name inked on it was tacked on the door. A soiree started at once in my office and lasted for several days. Men of letters, bearing gin bottles, arrived. Bob Benchley, halooing with laughter as if he had come on the land of Punch and Judy, was there, and the owlish-eyed satirist, Donald Ogden Stewart, beaming as at a convention of March Hares."

There's more, much more in Ben Hecht's memoirs, some of it hilarious, sharp, and barbed, some of it angry and bitter, as when he recounts his political arguments with his well-paying bosses.

"Not all the talent of a good writer was discarded," he wrote. "A part of it could be used for a script—a dime's worth. And there was an occasional script you could work on with all the stops out. But that wasn't why you came to Hollywood—to do the masterpiece. You came as a pencil for hire, at sums heretofore unheard of for pencils. You brought no plots, dreams, or high intentions. If you wrote a good movie it was because you were lucky enough to get on the payroll of a classy boss. Classy or not, the boss called the shots and you did as bid. You were a sort of literary errand boy with an oil magnate's income."

"You write stinking scripts," said Charlie MacArthur, Hecht's long-time collaborator, "but you meet the people you like to be in a room with."

Read on:

"My first writing job in Hollywood was a picture called *A Woman's Face*, which starred Joan Crawford, Melvyn Douglas, and Conrad Veidt. I was the thirteenth writer, I learned in the course of that adventure, who had tackled that story at MGM. The first, I think, was Marc Connelly, of *Green Pastures* fame, my immediate predecessor was Christopher Isherwood, one of the most sensitive and articulate English writers of our time. Originally, the plot that turned out to be *A Woman's Face* was a trite, worthless play by one of Paris' hack playwrights, although it had served as a vehicle for Gaby Morlay. The Swedes bought the play, entitled *Il Etait Une Fois*, which was about the life of some English people in Hungary ... or was it the other way around? As the Swedes turned it out, the heroine, after being anti-social for nine reels, was 'saved' and resolved to turn herself into a missionary to the Lapps in the ever-frozen North ... However, MGM scouts who had strayed as far as Stockholm noticed the very young lady, whose name turned out to be Ingrid Bergman, and liked her work so well they bought the piece for peanuts. Then followed the years of re-hashing by the thirteen assorted writers, to which, in my term of effort, were added the Countess Lili Hatvani, from Budapest, and Donald Ogden Stewart, the American humorist. I cite the progress of that tale, from a French stinkeroo of a stage play to a Hollywood smash hit, to illustrate how Hollywood often upsets the usually sound proverb of 'from nothing comes nothing.' Unfortunately, in all candor, it must be admitted that, beginning with an excellent play, or novel, or original idea, the world film capital produces and spreads to all corners of the earth dull or pompous monstrosities."

That's a brief sampling of the Hollywood observations compiled by the late Eliot Paul, in a book called *Film Flam*, which is also a mother lode of first-hand reportage of Paul's adventures in the film business amid his preparation of such films as *Rhapsody in Blue* and *New Orleans*.

As Paul remarked, "I thought before I struck Hollywood that I had at least a nodding acquaintance with all the screwballs in the world. I found I had no background of madness at all."

Legends?

Over the years they've accumulated. Such famous ones as the story of William Faulkner requesting permission of his MGM producer to take the script home and work on it there — and not showing up again until his agent, Leland Hayward, had tracked him down to Oxford, Mississippi!

Or the remarkable saga of P. G. Wodehouse's term contract at MGM in the '30s, when that great factory's list of contract writers was so vast that nobody could keep track of the number of talents being endowed each week. "I bicycled to work each morning," the great British humorist recalled, "and thence home. Each week I received a fat check. Nobody ever asked me to write anything for the films, so I proceeded to write three novels of my own. This procedure went on for almost two years — until one day I made the grievous error of telling my situation to an interviewer, who promptly announced my situation in her next day's column. Within twenty-four hours, I finally did hear from the people at Metro. In a most abrupt manner, they terminated my employment contract."

Cloud-cuckoo land? Indeed. Down the hall from Wodehouse, the famous British musical comedy librettist, Ivor Novello, was serving out his time writing dialogue for the first *Tarzan* film!

Or the day when Aldous Huxley had a conference with Greta Garbo, in her dressing-room, where the great star informed him she would like him to write her a film on Saint Francis of Assisi, with one proviso — that *she* play Saint Francis! And when Huxley pointed out to Garbo that the Saint wore a beard, "Oh yes, I know," said Garbo. "But the make-up department can easily make me one."

Nobody has ever captured the lunacy of those days, even though Nathaniel West got a lot of it in *The Day of the Locust*. As did Billy Wilder and Charles Brackett in their *Sunset Boulevard*. And we have *A Star Is Born*. But the fantasy world out there engendered waves of satiric oral wit, most of it based on deep-rooted angst.

Robert Hopkins, the fabled "Hoppy"—the genius idea-man (*San Francisco* was spawned from a single Hopkins sentence: "Gable's a gambler, Tracy's a priest, MacDonald's a hooker—and they all end up in the San Francisco earthquake!") —remarked of a producer cursed with an ego problem, "They could shoot the Ben-Hur chariot race around his hatband." He also pointed a finger at a Metro executive and said, "You, Hyman, are the asbestos curtain between the audience and entertainment!"

It was a town which thrived on the riposte, and later had the company of wits capable of the best. Sam Hoffenstein, Arthur Caesar, Benchley, Perelman, Oscar Levant, Harry Ruby. And even the quips are enormously revealing.

"You make a lot of money and pay your bills," Dorothy Parker once remarked, ruefully, to Kyle Crichton, in from the East. "I'm up to about 1912 by now."

During the stormy Depression period, despite obdurate resistance from the producers, Hollywood screenwriters began to organize their own craft union, which would become the Screen Writers Guild. At one of the early organizational meetings, impassioned rhetoric echoed through the room as writers pointed out many of the obvious injustices and harsh practices that were rife in the industry. There was repeated mention of the plight of the lowest man on the salary totem pole—the so-called $75 a week writer.

Not all the writers who attended were in agreement. One of the more successful, and pompous, film writers of the day stood up and began to rebut. "All this talk about $75 a week writers," he declaimed. "Who are they?" He turned to Herman Mankiewicz, who sat next to him. "Tell me —do *you* know any $75 a week writers?"

"I know lots of them," replied Mankiewicz, instantly. "But they're all making $1500 a week!"

Cloud-cuckoo land, indeed.

Hollywood, as Joe Frisco, the comedian, once remarked, "This is the only town where you can wake up and hear the birds coughing in the trees."

"One morning," remembered the writers' agent, Mary Baker, "my partner, Sam Jaffe, came into my office very upset, to report that there was a disreputable-looking man sitting in our waiting room, puffing on a rotten cigar, and unable to speak English so that he could explain what it was he wanted. 'Get him out of here, Mary!' Sam pleaded, 'He's lowering the tone of this place!'

"I went out and spoke to the man — my German was rotten — but he handed me a folded scrap of paper. On it was written FRITZ LANG, and beneath it, BRECHT. I finally figured it out — this had to be Bertold Brecht, the great German playwright, come to see his friend, our client, Fritz Lang, the director … No matter how I explained to my partner, Sam, who exactly this great man was, he remained unimpressed. 'What kind of a playwright dresses like *that*?' he demanded."

And then there's the story of the day when Harry Cohn paid one of his early morning visits to his studio. He strode into the courtyard around which rose the writers' offices, and he noticed something which disturbed him greatly — that is, silence.

No sound emerged from the tiers of rooms wherein Columbia Pictures scenarios were produced.

"Where are the writers?" Cohn shouted. "Why aren't they working? I don't hear a sound. I am paying you guys big salaries and you do nothing. You are stealing my money!"

Suddenly, from a score of windows came the clacking of typewriters.

"Liars!" bawled Cohn.

So we should get started, pronto!

S. N. BEHRMAN on HOLLYWOOD in the '30s

WITH THE INFLUX OF REFUGEES IN THE THIRTIES, HOLLYWOOD BECAME A kind of Athens. It was as crowded with artists as Renaissance Florence. The modest living room of Salka Viertel's house on Mayberry Road was surely, in those days, the most fascinating salon in America. You would meet there Thomas and Heinrich Mann, Otto Klemperer, Bruno Walter, Leopold Stokowski, Arnold Schoenberg, the Franz Werfels, Miss Garbo, Max Reinhardt, Aldous Huxley, Fritzi Masary, Sam Hoffenstein. (The latter's *Poems in Praise of Practically Nothing* was found on the bedside of Chief Justice Holmes when he died.) These names are only a sprinkling; a full list would read like *Almanach de Gotha* of the arts. It was a Golden Era. It had never happened before. It will never happen again.

—S. N. BEHRMAN, *The New York Times*, July 17, 1966

2. HARK!
WHO is this EMERGING from the SHADOWS?
IT is the BRAVE TITLE WRITER who will SAVE US!

Silent film drawing by James Stephenson

THE TITLES?

They're what flashed on the screen in the silent movies, while the old guy behind you insisted on reading them aloud.

During the '20s, Chicago may have been roaring, but Hollywood was still silent. No one knew, or cared, that Sam Warner and some Western Electric engineers were back East working on Vitaphone, and if anyone did mention the possibility of sound, myopic executives (are there any other kind?) brushed it aside as lunacy. Why should anyone want to hear actors talk?

So silent love stories and melodramas and especially comedies all flourished. And around each comedian, be it Harry Langdon, or Mabel Normand, Charley Chase, Ben Turpin, Snub Pollard, or anyone else, there blossomed a cadre of guys who could "punch up" the scenes. Thus evolved a new hybrid of writer, the gag-man who could also provide the titles. Titles that contained puns, snappy quips, and very often, a double entendre.

The title writer had to handle every sort of situation. Even with the feature films, where reigned such mega-stars as Mary Pickford, Doug Fairbanks, Lew Cody, Blanche Sweet, and the Talmadge girls, there were

15

always title writers available to keep the plot thickening, with gags; to build the story to a climax, with gags; and bring it all to a passionate final embrace, with one final gag (probably the heroine's dog, nipping at the hero's ankles—always good for a laugh).

By the mid-1920s, such men had developed the art of title writing into a unique (and very well-paid, thank you) profession. Title writers were indispensable when it came to keeping the audience laughing: they found the payoffs, the closing gag buttons, and long before the arrival of Milton Berle and Henny Youngman, they had invented the one-line joke— minus, of course, today's inevitable four-letter word.

In Walter Kerr's history of silent screen clowns, he pays special attention to the gifts of such men by citing the example of a long-forgotten silent comedian, Johnny Hines. In 1925, Hines made three pictures, *The Speed Spook*, *The Early Bird*, and *Conductor 1492*. The special art of his title writers was to perpetuate Hines' character. "Hines never abandoned his Cohanesque brashness," comments Kerr. "He is all 'Push, Pluck and Providence,' as his opening title bragged." On would race Hines, headlong into this mad adventure or that comedic mishap, while his title writers introduced "young girls in their nicoteens," and then informed us that one of Hines' new pals is "rich enough to extend a cordial welcome—and a welcome cordial."

So who were these men who performed such constant miracles?

"You should try and find that guy, George Marion, Junior," Billy Wilder insisted, when we chatted in 1972. "He got twenty-five hundred a week for writing titles in the silents! He was the most sought after; the producers would bring him a picture with all the scenes finished—they wouldn't even know yet whether it was a comedy, very often, or whether they had a drama—until Marion finished writing the titles!

"I remember one title of his . . . just marvelous. It was about a traveling salesman. Now you have to know, in those days, when the first title comes on, before the picture even starts, and it gets a belly-laugh from the audience—well, then you know you're home. So—here is Marion's first title:

A TRAVELING SALESMAN—UP WITH THE LARK,
DOWN WITH THE GRAPEFRUIT, AND OUT WITH THE SAMPLES!

"A very famous title," said Wilder. "So famous, I can remember it after all these years!

"And then there was another title," recalled Wilder. "And this one shows just how Marion was able to cheat the guys in the Hays office. It was a picture with Norman Kerry, remember him? And the leading lady was Helen Twelvetrees. Kerry is a fugitive from jail—he's still wearing the handcuffs. And he's running to a small town, and he's got his hat over his hands, so people won't see the handcuffs. Somehow he's gotten out of jail, who knows how. Suddenly, we see him at a bungalow... he looks through the window and then he bursts through the door, comes inside, and there, sitting at a piano, is Helen Twelvetrees. Close up of her, she looks at him. Now... fade out. Here comes the great title:

WHAT HE TOLD HER, WE DON'T KNOW,

BUT IT MUST HAVE BEEN SOMETHING BEAUTIFUL,

BECAUSE, NEXT MORNING...

"And now we see the two of them, having breakfast! Isn't that beautiful?" mused Wilder.

"I remember another one," he said. "Not funny, but truly great. It's the opening title of *Greed*. We're in a gold mine—we see the big guy who plays the lead (Gibson Gowland) and guys are all around schlepping these carts up the hill. Up, up, up they go; the carts are very heavy, it's hard work. And there's an overseer standing there with a whip, you know, in case anybody starts to sink. And now comes this big guy, our lead, he's schlepping that cart, and suddenly he stops and looks down, he picks up a bird with a broken wing. And he looks at that bird... and now, since he's stopped, that entire column of the other guys behind him who are schlepping coal carts, they've stopped too. The guard sees that, takes the whip, and zap, zap! He's hitting those guys... and our guy, our hero, puts down the bird, picks up the guard, and throws him down into the abyss below— maybe 200 feet down! He comes back, picks up that crippled bird, and starts stroking it again... and now, comes the title:

SUCH WAS MCTEAGUE.

"Is that beautiful, or not?" mused Wilder. "So beautiful, in fact, that years later, I stole it!"

Exactly when and where, he would not tell.

We may not know who was responsible for many of such great titles, but we do know that the legendary Herman Mankiewicz brought forth a few nifties of his own. Walter Kerr refers to him as "the crown prince of the craft." And Richard Meryman, Mank's biographer, refers to an article in *Liberty Magazine* called "The Titular Bishops of Hollywood... The nine editorial prima donnas of the motion picture industry who roll around in high-priced limousines."

"Producers," noted Meryman, "wanted titles that 'hit the back wall' — got big belly laughs and could turn a clunker into a hit." For a picture called *Take Me Home*, Mankiewicz supplied this one:

DERELY DEVORE, THE STAR, ROSE FROM THE CHORUS
BECAUSE SHE WAS COOL IN AN EMERGENCY — AND WARM IN A TAXI.

For *Three Weekends*, he wrote: "I've got as much chance to wash in private as a six month old baby." And in another of Mank's titles, these words flashed on the screen: "Paris, where half the women are working women," and then, an instant later, added, "And half the women are working men."

Mankiewicz was also capable of hyperbole. In Josef von Sternberg's fascinating *The Last Command* (1928), which starred Emil Jannings and William Powell, there comes a scene in which Evelyn Brent, the leading lady, arrives on scene. Jannings, as a Russian officer, demands to know who she is; the aide is examining her passport. The aide speaks; Mankiewicz's title reads: "Why, she is the most dangerous revolutionary in Russia!"

"One knew she was a revolutionary," comments Walter Kerr. "But one had not quite thought she was out of a Dick Tracy cartoon."

"Title writing," observed Kevin Brownlow, "a process unique in silent pictures, was an art in itself. In those days, a fiction writer received from one to ten cents a word. A motion picture title writer could get about two dollars and twenty cents per word — not for the number of words he wrote as for the number he avoided writing... while still managing to tell the story.

"Titles, like any other creative process, depended on skill and judgment for their success. Sometimes they overweighed a picture, and caused squirms of agony rather than the squeals of delight which greeted the bon mots of the top title writers of the '20s." And which ones make it to Brownlow's list? George Marion, Jr., of course, and also Gerald Duffy, who worked for Mary Pickford, Joe Farnham, and finally, the legendary Ralph Spence.

"These men possessed a unique facility for turning out snappy, witty, epigrammatic, or atmospheric titles, which would not have seemed out of place in the works of such wits, say, as Oscar Wilde," remarks Brownlow. To which one must add, these were also the years of the '20s, when the Algonquin wits and the contributors to F.P.A.'s *Conning Tower* were out-doing themselves in smart one-liners. Certainly, the Benchley, Dorothy Parker, Woollcott, and Don Marquis remarks were making their way to far-off California, where one good joke engendered a topper, perhaps? Later on, the New Yorkers would come to L.A. in search of weekly checks. But for now, their West Coast counterparts were panning the movie gold.

Brownlow, in his extensive researches among the silents, offers us another example of how a title writer can add brio to an otherwise ordinary slate. In a 1926 film comedy, *Exit Smiling*, the young British comedienne, Beatrice Lillie, was introduced to the audience with this title:

> VIOLET, THE PATSY OF THE SHOW.
> BORN AND RAISED ON THE STAGE,
> SHE KNEW LIFE ONLY AS THE STAGE REFLECTED IT.

Someone, perhaps the director, Sam Taylor, must have decided that if he were making a comedy and had Bea Lillie on board, audiences should be made aware of the fact that she was a comedienne. As a result, Joe Farnham was called in to rewrite. His substitute text may have altered the sense of the script, but it certainly guaranteed an audience belly-laugh. The new text read:

> VIOLET, THE DRUDGE OF THE TROUPE...
> WHO ALSO PLAYED PARTS LIKE "NOTHING,"
> IN "MUCH ADO ABOUT NOTHING."

Even Bea Lillie must have enjoyed that one. And Farnham's line would do well for some stand-up comic today.

The craft of writing comedy titles was obviously much more complex than supplying "straight" narrative titles. It didn't take considerable genius to supply such dramatic texts as "Alone at last!" and "Look out behind you!" when the scenario called for it. And also the narrative lines—"Little did innocent Alice know that the friendly banker was bent on foreclosing on her grandmother's home"—any hack could handle that one. For that matter, how many variations exist for "John, dear, are you trying to tell me something?"

But there was another, subsidiary problem for both drama and comedy titleists. Over all the years they'd spent sitting in nickelodeons and the local Bijou Dream Palace, there were many avid film fans in the audiences who had become adept at lip-reading. So now they were able to know whether the title "Unhand me, you dreadful villain!" bore any relation to what the heroine had actually said, which may well have been a comment on the onions which the villain had consumed at lunchtime. If it were a Western and the cowboy hero in his white hat, the symbol of virtue triumphant, was leaping aboard a balky horse, what he was saying was certainly not virtuous. "Silent film fans often complained at the box office about what he'd actually said!" Louise Brooks remembered. "They'd read every one of his curses."

Title writer Gerald Duffy once explained what a complex problem the dramatic title writer could encounter. He'd been working in 1922 on *Through the Back Door*, for Mary Pickford, and he'd encountered one sequence which presented a major road block. "The title had deftly to insinuate that Mary was eloping—but it couldn't say it, because she wasn't. We simply wanted to deceive the audience into thinking she was. Also, the title had to suggest that her mother was contemplating divorce." Added to Duffy's chore was the fact that the last time the audience had seen America's Sweetheart, and the rest of her cast, they'd been on Long Island. "Now we were to show them in a New York hotel, and it was necessary that we establish that locale as well. Writing that title was a staggering undertaking," recalled Duffy. "But the furniture in the hotel sequence saved me."

Duffy's title read:

IF IT WERE NOT FOR NEW YORK HOTELS,
WHERE WOULD ELOPERS, DIVORCEES, AND RED PLUSH FURNITURE GO?

"Seventeen words," recalled Duffy, "told everything."

One of the classic Hollywood sayings of the silent-film era, which referred to someone's stinker—never one's own!—was: "The picture was so bad, they had to shoot retakes before they could shelve it!" And another was "When they screened it, they decided to cut it up into mandolin picks."

But if a desperate producer needed help in salvaging his stinker, he had only to turn to the *Film Daily Yearbook* of 1925, and there on page 230, he could find a full-page advertisement, cum photo, of one of the legendary title mavens—Ralph Spence. Across the bottom of Spence's portrait ran one of his titles—ALL BAD LITTLE MOVIES WHEN THEY DIE GO TO RALPH SPENCE.

Spence had become so successful by then that he could ask for, and receive, up to ten thousand dollars per film; his work was so recognized that one Hollywood theatre actually put up his name in marquee lights—"Titles by Ralph Spence."

"In an effort to be funny," Louise Brooks recalled, "old actors and actresses have spread the false belief that any clownish thing coming to mind could be said in front of the camera in silent films.... They forgot how the title writer has to match his work to the actors' speech. I remember one night wandering into Ralph Spence's suite at the Beverly Wilshire, where he sat gloomily amidst cans of film, cartons of stale Chinese food, and empty whisky bottles. He was trying to fix up a Wallace Beery–Raymond Hatton comedy, *Now We're in the Air*, and no comic line he invented would fit the lip action."

Director Eddie Sutherland would later conclude directing the same Beery-Hatton team in his first major feature, *Behind the Front*, but he felt he needed Spence's talent to "punch up" the comedy titles.

"Spence was a great man, but I could never find him," Sutherland recalled, years later. "His hobby was railroad trains, and he had a whole

21

room full of them. He was a drinking man, liked girls, liked fun, and he kept another room at the Hollywood Plaza. I found out what room he was in, and I engaged the one next to it. Next morning, as his breakfast was taken in, I went in too, with my film cans in my arms."

"Oh, you rat," said Spence. "You found me!"

"So we stayed in his room while he wrote the titles for me. He'd run my film on his little Moviola — the same machine which was used by film cutters — and then he'd ask, 'What do you want on this thing? What do you visualize, Eddie?'

"Beery and Hatton were in the front-line battlefield trenches for the first time, so I said, 'Something to show the danger that they're going into, and that they don't like it much, I guess.'

"So he wrote me a title:

LISTENING POST — WHERE MEN ARE MEN, BUT WISH THEY WEREN'T.

Obviously, it worked. And Ralph Spence's slogan on his advertisement may have been braggadocio, but he, and his other title-writer compatriots, obviously delivered the goods. Two years later, just before Vitaphone emerged, Beery and Hatton were still starring at Paramount.

One of the most telling examples of Ralph Spence's clever titles can be enjoyed in the 1926 Harold Lloyd comedy, *For Heaven's Sake*. Three writers concocted the script for Lloyd, but it is obvious that Spence was brought in to supply the opening titles. He begins with this: "Every city has two districts. Uptown, where the people are cursed with money — and Downtown — where they are cursed without it." To introduce one of the characters, a man with a mission in the slums, we see "Brother Paul, gentle soul, preaching the doctrine of love in a district where English was only used on billiard balls." Now we meet the rich young character played by Lloyd. One of his friends says, "Did you hear about Harold Manners? He bought a new car to match his white pants." Said car is promptly destroyed, so Harold buys a second one on the spot. "That fellow never worries," says the friend. "If this town had two earthquakes and a land-slide, he'd be pleased because real estate is so active!"

Young Harold inadvertently destroys Brother Paul's mission. Brother

Paul writes him a letter asking him for funds. The letter ends up in Harold's library, opened by his secretary. "His secretary was a sure shot with the wastebasket." But Harold ends up donating to Brother Paul and his lovely daughter. Now we meet the bully of the neighborhood. "Bull Brindle was so tough, he wouldn't eat lady fingers unless they had brass knuckles."

And after a fight in the local pool hall? "This guy is a one-man crime wave!" And then a fight... "Some guys is naturally ignorant—but you abuse the privilege!"

When Harold and the leading lady end up beneath a tree at dusk, beginning to make silent-movie love, the Spence title says, "During the days that passed, just what the man with a mansion told the girl with a mission is nobody's business!" And we fade out on the couple.

Ralph Spence advertisement

But when they decide to get married, we are plunged headlong into the customary Harold Lloyd chase scenes, involving wild rides through L.A. on trolleys, buses, horse-cars, and trains.

By that time, the film is well and truly launched. Spence had done what producers always came to him for: he started the silent film off with a series of solid laughs. Which is precisely why the producers always arrived at his door bearing cans of film, requesting that Spence apply his magic touch to the title—and why, eighty-odd years later, thanks to Turner Classic Movies, we can still chuckle at that sly Ralph Spence sense of humor.

Overnight, the talkies took over; just as quickly, the only titles that mattered were ALL TALKING! ALL SINGING! The talents of some of these clever writers were used by producers, especially when they'd begun importing comics from Broadway, performers who needed jokes and witty material each day on the set—Wheeler and Woolsey, Clark and McCullough, Edgar Kennedy—*all talking!* Farnham and Duffy would fade away, Herman Mankiewicz had long since graduated to features, and as for George Marion, Jr., he deftly adapted to full-time scenarios and librettos. Eventually, he made his way to Broadway, as librettist for the Rodgers and Hart 1930s musical, *Too Many Girls*, and followed that success several years later with another, *Beat the Band.*

And as for the legendary film-doctor, Ralph Spence? Until he died, many years later, he continued to utilize his considerable gifts to write comedies. Among his credits were *Poor Little Rich Girl*, for Shirley Temple, the comedy-thriller *The Gorilla*, and a batch of Fox musicals of the '30s that include *Seven Days Leave, Down Argentine Way*, and *The Gang's All Here.*

Ave atque vale, titleists. Some of their brilliant work is carefully stored away, either at the Museum of Modern Art Film Library, or perhaps out at UCLA. And who knows where some silent two-reeler or long-lost feature will turn up and remind us of an era when, strictly on his own, the title writer would sit up all night and try to repair a dull sequence, or brighten up a slow scene?

And isn't it ironic to contemplate those solo fliers, Spence, Marion, Duffy, and others who are forgotten, sitting in front of their hand-cranked Moviolas, relying on their own talent to repair the mistakes of some pro-ducer, or director—or the actors? *Alone.* No one peering over his shoulder in that tiny cubicle to tell him what to do (if he knew what to do, would he be here?); no executive calling him into conference to rewrite his rewrites; but most importantly, no set of "notes" from some cadre of junior executives fresh out of college who can't write worth a damn but can always tell you what needs fixing.

This flash back to the '20s does sound like a trip to never-never land, doesn't it?

Before we fade out on those wizards and their era, we have to provide them with a closing title.

How about—

BRING US YOUR TIRED, YOUR FLOPS
YOUR HUDDLED MESSES
YEARNING TO BE HITS.
AND WE'LL SAVE YOU, PAL,
...SO YOU CAN GO OUT AND DO ANOTHER!

RALPH SPENCE'S CREDITS:

FILMS:

The Pride of New York, 1917

The Yankee Way, 1917

A Laundry Clean-Up, 1917

Jack Spurlock, Prodigal, 1918

I'll Say So, 1918

Miss Innocence, 1918

A Camouflage Kiss, 1918

On the Jump, 1918

Never Say Quit, 1919

Smiles, 1919

Roman Candles, 1920

Sink or Swim, 1920

The Rough Diamond, 1921

Hickville to Broadway, 1921

Stranger Than Fiction, 1921

A Ridin' Romeo, 1921

The Oath, 1921

Do and Dare, 1922

Sure-Fire Flint, 1922

A Self-Made Man, 1922

For Big Stakes, 1922

Chasing the Moon, 1922

Let's Go, 1923

Six Cylinder Love, 1923

Luck, 1923

Custard Cup, 1923

A Friendly Husband, 1923

The Speed Spook, 1924

His Darker Self, 1924

On Time, 1924

Why Women Love, 1925

Classified, 1925

American Pluck, 1925

The Early Bird, 1925

There You Are!, 1926

Tin Hats, 1926

The Campus Flirt, 1926

3 Bad Men, 1926

Pals First, 1926

The Savage, 1926

Hard Boiled, 1926

It's the Old Army Game, 1926

For Heaven's Sake, 1926

Mademoiselle Modiste, 1926

Behind the Front, 1926

Too Much Money, 1926

The Gorilla, 1927

Buttons, 1927

Now We're in the Air, 1927

Spring Fever, 1927

Adam and Evil, 1927

*The Callahans
    and the Murphys*, 1927

Tillie the Toiler, 1927

Lost at the Front, 1927

Orchids and Ermine, 1927

The Taxi Dancer, 1927

Johnny Get Your Hair Cut, 1927

The Lunatic at Large, 1927

A Lady of Chance, 1928

Show People, 1928

Excess Baggage, 1928

Beau Broadway, 1928

Vamping Venus, 1928

The Patsy, 1928

Bringing up Father, 1928

Baby Mine, 1928

JOHN CROMWELL at PARAMOUNT in 1930

WHEN I FIRST CAME OUT TO HOLLYWOOD—IT WAS AT THE TIME WHEN sound was replacing silent films and the place was a complete shambles... around 1928. I'd been in a play called *Gentlemen of the Press*—we opened the week after *The Front Page*—and my contract with Paramount was contingent on my appearing in the play. After it flopped, I went out to the studio. They rolled out the red carpet for me, and asked me what I would like to do first. I said, "I want to go down to the cutting room and see what that's all about."

I stayed there about three months. Then they asked "Now, what would you like to do?" And I said "I want to act in a picture—I want to see what it feels like."

So I acted in one. Now I could see they were getting nervous, and they wanted me to get started making a picture.[1]

I found this story that some pretty good writer on the staff had done. I asked where his office was, and when I found out, I went down to this barrack-like building, long halls, little cubby holes, typewriters clacking away behind doors.

I went into the guy's cubbyhole and I introduced myself and I said, "I like your story. I want to do it as a picture."

He looked up and he said "Oh?"

I said, "Yes, haven't you heard?"

"Oh," he said, "We never hear."

Well, we talked all afternoon. I told him, "There are a lot of things in this you could improve like hell," and he helped me clarify them—he had a good story mind, very quick and constructive—and when we were finished talking, I asked him, "When do you think you could have these changes made?"

He looked at me and his face was a study in astonishment.

"You mean you want me to make them?"

"Who else?" I asked.

---

[1] The name of the picture referred to is *Close Harmony* by Percy Heath and Elsie Janis, which starred Buddy Rogers and Nancy Carroll.

"Well," he said, "when we sell a story to the studio, we take the check and kiss the story goodbye. And maybe months, or a year later, we hear that a certain story that smells like it was the one being previewed, well, we run to the preview and see what the hell they've done with it."

—JOHN CROMWELL, January 1970

3. SIDNEY BUCHMAN:
HARRY COHN'S FAIR-HAIRED BOY

New York, 1972

Sidney Buchman holding his screenplay for *The Group*. Director Sidney Lumet, standing, with cigarette, and the eight women who star in *The Group*: Candice Bergen, Joan Hackett, Elizabeth Hartman, Shirley Knight, Joanna Pettet, Mary Robin Redd, Jessica Walter, and Kathleen Widdoes. The young girl in the center is Nina Hirschfeld in her first movie. Courtesy of Al Hirschfeld.

In May of 1931, in the midst of the Depression, playwright Sidney Buchman left New York, a city where silent breadlines of hungry men in Times Square were commonplace, and apple vendors in shabby suits peddled fruit for a nickel in front of darkened legitimate theatres. In his pocket, Buchman had what was for those dire times a precious document, a contract to work for Paramount Pictures as "dialoguer." The weekly salary stipulated was small, but in those desperate days, the prospect of a paycheck each Friday was miraculous.

"The New York theatre was belly-up. Dead," Buchman recalled, years later. "Theatres closed, producers scratching for bankrolls. Actors and playwrights were hungry, out on the streets. A lot of other young fellows I knew, Dore Schary, Don Hartman, Allan Rivkin—all aspiring dramatists—but they, too, had to go West to find work. How else could we survive? Hollywood was still fairly solvent, and writing for the movies was the only paying game left."

It was then a transitional period for the studios, the era in which talkies were a new development. Gaudy banners reading All Talking! All

SINGING! draped across theatre marquees were more of an attraction to 25-cent-ticket buyers than the title of the film below.

"I hung around the Paramount lot for three days without an assignment," Buchman said. "I was told to sit quietly until they wanted me. One lunch hour, I was hailed in the dining room by the assistant to B. P. Schulberg, the head of the studio. This was an energetic young guy named David Selznick, who'd been sitting at a table in the midst of a lunchtime conference. He spotted me and said 'There's your man.'

"I was brought over, introduced to a director, a guy named Lloyd Corrigan, and I was immediately assigned by David to go to work on a picture they were preparing called *The Daughter of the Dragon.*

"This was some sort of a cockamamie project for which they'd resurrected the great silent star Sessue Hayakawa to play [a detective hunting] Fu Manchu, and to play [Fu Manchu's] daughter, they'd hired Anna May Wong. So after lunch, I go up to an office where I was introduced to another writer, this one a lady named Agnes Brand Leahy. She was what they called a 'continuity writer,' obviously a very old hand at this sort of work, and she showed me a copy of the 'continuity' for the picture."

What Buchman read was a series of numbered scenes on the Leahy pages, which described the action on screen for the film.

"It was broken down into Medium Shot, Full Shot, Two Shot, Individual Over Shoulder Shot, Close Up, and so on—and it told the story visually. After each shot, she'd left a large blank space. What they wanted from me was *the words.* I was, after all, a New York playwright, and therefore that made me the 'dialoguer.' My job was to fill in those blank spaces.

"After I'd read the story, I suggested perhaps I could take the scenes, and since ideas might occur to me, I could develop them; that way characters might develop along with my ideas. 'Oh, don't do that!' said Agnes. 'It will only make things more complicated!'"

Eventually, the new team came to a sort of compromise.

"I wrote dialogue for the scenes, and then she took them and broke up the scenes so that they fit her continuity. In essence, what she did was to cut the picture on paper. She provided the director with each day's set-ups all written for him. All he had to do was to direct those scenes with actors and get them on film. And that's how I got my first screen credit."

Most of Paramount's films of that era were written in the same manner. The star team on the lot consisted of William Slavens McNutt, a "continuity" man, who'd been teamed with Grover Jones, one of the leading title writers of the recent silent days.

"They worked together in the same way," said Buchman. "McNutt provided the story and the scene breakdown, and Jones doing the dialogue." In terms of output, the record of McNutt and Jones is formidable. In one year, 1932, they wrote five pictures for Paramount, including an episode for *If I Had a Million*.

"On the lot there was another playwright," said Buchman, "a very talented man named Vincent Lawrence. He did dialogue but he insisted on calling all his characters 'he' and 'she' — that was as far as he'd go."

Buchman progressed rapidly from his first Paramount assignment to several other dialoguer jobs on such long-forgotten epics as *Beloved Bachelor* and *No One Man*. Then, he contributed a sequence to Paramount's all-star 1932 epic, *If I Had a Million*, and was promptly assigned to work with a continuity man, Waldemar Young, on a major project, Cecil B. DeMille's *The Sign of the Cross*.

Before he went into the film business, DeMille had been an actor, so when the silent era ended, DeMille was uniquely fitted to directing sound films. "His entire background had been that of the stage," said Buchman, "and unlike other directors who weren't able to make the transition from silents to sound, DeMille was comfortable with the new milieu."

The powerful DeMille must have responded to young Buchman's theatrical background. Born in Duluth, Minnesota, educated at Columbia, Buchman had sailed to England in the early 1920s and enrolled as a student at Oxford. Stage struck, he traveled through Europe and managed to secure a job as assistant stage manager with the prestigious Old Vic Theatre company.

Upon his return to New York in 1924 he had become a script reader in the Warner Bros. story department, where he soon achieved a measure of fame for accomplishing an almost impossible task. "It seems that John Barrymore, then Jack Warner's most prestigious star, had cabled Warner from a transatlantic liner that for his next film he wanted to do Ahab, in Melville's *Moby Dick*." Buchman said. "The book was totally unknown to Warner, and he instructed his New York office to provide him with a synopsis. I was given the assignment—to reduce Melville's huge masterpiece to a few readable pages, understandable by the most untutored. Today, I'd be appalled by such an assignment; in those days I was too naïve to refuse. I took the book home and managed to do the job in a couple of days. I must have been successful, because upon Barrymore's return, Warner agreed to let him make the picture … It became *The Sea Beast*."

Subsequently, young Buchman wrote two plays. The first, *This One Man*, starring Paul Muni, was produced in 1930, and the second, *Storm Song*, featured the actress Francine Larimore. Although the reviews were respectful, neither play was a success, and when the offer to go West came from Paramount, the theatre's loss was Hollywood's gain.

"Waldemar Young stayed pissed throughout most of the DeMille assignment," Buchman said, "and so I got to write pretty freely. Not only dialogue, but characterizations and scene changes."

A typical DeMille spectacle composed of religion, sex, mob scenes, milk-baths, and stars. *The Sign of the Cross* was an audience-pleaser. Buchman stayed on at Paramount until 1934, at which point he was borrowed by Harry Cohn, the fiercely independent head of Columbia Pictures. Down on Gower Street, his first job was the script for a long-forgotten epic called *Whom the Gods Destroy*. The quality of Buchman's work appealed to Cohn, who promptly offered him a long-term contract. Their subsequent association would eventually continue for a remarkable seventeen years.

"I liked working for Cohn," Buchman observed, years later. "Around Hollywood he was famous for being a tyrant, an opinionated despot who ran a tight ship and who could often behave like a boorish bastard. But Harry was also first, last, and always a picture-maker, who had a passionate love affair with 'Class.' Remember, Columbia was the poor relative of the major studios; it had no theatre chain attached to it the way Warners, Paramount, and Metro did, in which the poorest studio production could get an automatic play-off. Cohn had to fight for his playing time, every inch of the way, so he evolved his own way of doing it. Once or twice a year, he would make his 'class' picture—something first class, either with Frank Capra, or with Leo McCarey, or George Stevens. For that picture, Cohn would pull out all the stops—pay whatever the talent demanded in order to guarantee that his 'class' picture would be a success."

Buchman's first class assignment would be with Capra, who was preparing a Damon Runyon comedy, *Broadway Bill*. Robert Riskin's adaptation needed some extra scenes; Riskin had gone off to Europe and Cohn assigned Buchman the task. From then on, the Capra-Buchman association was lasting. Both men respected the other enormously, and eventually, after Buchman had done some work on *Lost Horizon*, they would collaborate on the film that many critics consider Capra's masterwork, one which reappears, with phenomenal regularity after the fact, *Mr. Smith Goes to Washington*.

Buchman's enormous versatility becomes apparent by reviewing his other '30s credits. He turned out such class films for Cohn as *Love Me Forever* and *The King Steps Out*, but he also developed into a master of the sophisticated comedy. He did *She Married Her Boss* for Claudette Colbert, *Theodora Goes Wild* with Irene Dunne, and he and Donald Ogden Stewart collaborated on a sparkling adaptation of Philip Barry's *Holiday*, which starred Katharine Hepburn and Cary Grant. The film that earned Buchman his Academy Award was an adaptation of Harry Segall's play that starred Robert Montgomery: *Here Comes Mr. Jordan*.

"That was when I discovered what a gambler Cohn really was," Buchman recalled. "I knew it already, actually, because when Capra was preparing *Lady for a Day*, he came into Cohn's office within two or three days of starting photography; Capra knew in order to get a decision out of Cohn he had to see him alone, *without* an audience. He said, 'Harry, we've got to lock it up. I want you to remember, we're rolling three hundred grand on a picture with a leading lady who's 73 years old...Okay?' Well, Cohn really sweated that one, but he told Capra to go ahead.

"So when it came time for me to start *Jordan*, Cohn called me into his office—just the two of us. He was obviously very upset. 'Listen, pal,' he said, 'I got a problem. The Eastern office—the ones who control the dough—they *hate* your script. They say it's got three strikes against it. It's a backstage story—poison. A gangster story—even bigger poison. And it's a fantasy—they're death. They don't want me to let you do it.'

"It was a tough moment," said Buchman. "*I* sweated, too. Then I said 'Harry, every project has to be judged on its own merits. For every rule, there's an exception. That exception is something that gets you in the gut. Let me ask you one question. Did *you* get a boot out of the script?'

35

"'Hell *yes!*' Cohn said. 'Well, then, what else can you go on?' I asked him, because I knew he loved to gamble. 'You're right, pal,' Cohn said. 'That's good enough for me—we'll make it!'"

Here Comes Mr. Jordan went on to become a financial success and justified Cohn's gut reaction. But years later, when playwright George Axelrod presented Cohn with a fantasy, Cohn turned it down, insisting that fantasies were box office poison. "What about *Jordan?*" insisted Axelrod. "It would've made a lot more money if it *hadn't* been a fantasy!" riposted Cohn.

The relationship between Buchman and Cohn was not without its tempestuous interludes. Cohn insisted his writers appear on time each day and sign in and out of his Gower Street fiefdom. Buchman refused to be bound by such strictures. Often he would work off the lot, at home or holed up in Palm Springs desert hideaways. Eventually, reluctantly, Cohn ceased his demands; Buchman's output spoke for itself.

"Those were very tough times for writers in Hollywood," Buchman commented, years later. "Contrary to the accustomed legends, of the gilt-edged Metro contract lists and the Paramount roster of high-paid weekly writers, for most of the people things were very tough. At the time we all banded together in the '30s to form the Screen Writers Guild, conditions were truly rotten. Taking all the major studios—at that time, there were only 200-odd people under contract—and those were from a pool of over *1,200* available writers.

"True, the top writers, with contracts, were hired for periods of a year to seven years—forty weeks a year, with the rest unsalaried lay-off. But for the rest of the town, that pool of uncontracted writers, they were all at the mercy of the studios. Since so much of the film production came out of various sweat-shops—the B-units at Universal, or Universal, RKO, and Republic, there a writer could be hired on any sort of a deal beginning with, say, $1,500 for an original story and screenplay. And that would be a flat deal, including rewrites! Payment at the producer's whim, constant other abuses—directors and producers claiming co-credits on scripts they'd had nothing to do with writing; writers working on scripts without knowing other writers were rewriting their pages as fast as they turned them in; writers being closed out on a Friday night after one week's work —oh, it was a very bad scene," said Buchman.

"When I joined with other writers to form the Screen Writers Guild, two of the other major organizers, Mary McCall, Jr. and Bob Riskin, also worked at Columbia. We had rough times fighting with the studio heads —there was all sorts of pressure brought to bear in other studios to stop writers from forming a union. But not from Harry Cohn. He never tried anything underhanded to stop us."

Over those years many other craftsmen, playwrights, novelists, and short-story writers of high repute traveled to Hollywood to try their hand at screenwriting. Books have been written which document the profligate waste by studio executives of the talents of F. Scott Fitzgerald, William Faulkner, P. G. Wodehouse, Thomas Mann, and dozens of others, all of whom served their time in studio cubicles, mostly to no avail. Why was there so much failure?

"Screenwriting is an art," said Buchman. "Separate and distinct from good playwriting or fiction. Studios like Metro would hire big-name authors and dramatists to come out under contract and then try to find suitable assignments for them. It was a lot like trying to hitch up a race horse to a milk wagon."

"I remember once, at Metro, when David Selznick was preparing *David Copperfield*, with George Cukor as director—two very formidable talents indeed, two giants. They'd secured the services of a brilliant English novelist, Hugh Walpole, to do the script. Walpole was assigned to sit with the two of them as they broke Dickens' masterpiece down into its major scenes."

Buchman shook his head sadly at the recollection. "Now, picture this scene. Here's Hugh Walpole, a giant in his own field of work—dozens of major novels to his credit—sitting at a desk in an office, assigned to take Dickens' scenes and to work under the strict tutelage of Selznick and Cukor. What's his job? To make *bridges*—that's it! Poor Walpole—sitting there each day, struggling to be a carpenter. I walked by his office and there he was, looking like some beaten schoolboy, totally intimidated, utterly miserable. Is it any wonder he, and so many others like him, threw in the towel and went home?"

When World War II came, it brought hugely increased audiences to the box offices and also major problems for Hollywood producers. So many of the talented filmmakers went off to war that Cohn and all the other studio heads were hard put to maintain competent staff. Not drafted because of his age, Buchman remained on Gower Street and was soon pressed into service by Cohn to supervise Columbia's entire yearly output of "A" pictures. Working six- and seven-day weeks, he rode herd on literally dozens of films — "I worked my ass off," he remarked — and yet still found time to produce several scripts of his own. In 1942 there was the sparkling comedy *The Talk of the Town*, with Gary Grant and Ronald Colman. The following year he did work on, without credit, the Bogart-starring epic, *Sahara*. In 1945, he did the adaptation and produced the film of the Garson Kanin–Ruth Gordon hit play *Over 21*, and also found enough time and energy to produce his own screenplay of *A Song to Remember*, the somewhat romanticized biography of Chopin and his romance with George Sand.

"It was a period when Columbia had gone all out for class," Buchman said. "The double-feature system was slowly phasing out, and Cohn needed far more than one or two big pictures a year. It was damned tough turning out ten or twelve such productions each year, without stars, short of manpower. I remember once I told Harry we were in a Biblical fix — just like the Israelites — we couldn't make bricks without straw!"

When V-J Day came in 1946, however, Buchman was able to return to a more selective schedule. By now he had long since earned his way into Hollywood's new elite — the role of producer-writer with his own slate of films, financed by Columbia, but sharing fifty percent of Cohn's profits.

The first Buchman production to be so produced would prove to be a mammoth blockbuster. It was *The Jolson Story*, with Larry Parks playing the part of the legendary singer — vocal tracks supplied by Al himself. Buchman modestly took credit only for the original story, but the fact was that the entire film was his from day one of its conception until its gala opening night on Broadway. Over half a century later, *The Jolson Story* is a hardy TV perennial, as much of an audience-pleaser today as it was for the ticket buyers who fattened the Columbia treasury back in 1947. So astonishing was its popularity that in 1949 Cohn persuaded Buchman to attempt a sequel. *Jolson Sings Again*, done from Buchman's screenplay, defied the laws of probability and proved to be a durable money spinner. It received an Academy Award nomination for Buchman, and he went on to produce another such prestigious work, *Saturday's Hero*, in 1951. This film, a drama dealing with professional football would, however, be his last Hollywood-based venture.

For that year, at the height of the anti-Communist witch hunts, Buchman was called before the House Un-American Activities Committee (HUAC), which was holding hearings in Los Angeles. He admitted he had once been a member of the Communist Party briefly in 1938, but said it was based on his feelings that at the time the Party was the only force actively opposed to Fascism. He also testified he had left the party in 1945 because he had decided Communism was "stupid, blind, and unworkable for the American people."

When Congressman Francis Walter demanded that Buchman name his colleagues in the Party, Buchman refused to do so. He argued that most of the names had already been made public, that such people had never plotted subversion, and he added, "It is repugnant for an American to inform."

For the stand he took, Buchman was unemployable in Hollywood; he and other blacklisted writers migrated to more friendly atmospheres. For the next decade, he continued to write for the screen in England and France. During the '60s, the turbulence of the times began to rock the once predictable movie-audience boat. Ticket buyers were growing more and more rebellious; the younger generations had markedly less tolerance for the older generation's tastes for sophisticated comedy. Such escapist entertainment may have had an appeal for their parents, but a nation torn apart by the undeclared war in Vietnam had little appetite for the escapist fun and games of the '30s and '40s.

Buchman adapted to the times. He would write the screenplay for a drama, *The Mark*, which dealt with a difficult subject, that of sex crimes. Then in 1962 he and Ranald MacDougall spent long months earning joint credits for their screenplay of *Cleopatra*, that legendary spectacle which miraculously saved Twentieth Century Fox from imminent bankruptcy.

He went on to do a screenplay of the classic *The Visit*, by Frederick Duerenmatt, and *Promise at Dawn*, by Romain Gary. Both projects were at the behest of Darryl Zanuck, who had also moved to France. Alas, neither of the scripts were to reach the screen.

Buchman returned to America, where he did a screenplay based on Mary McCarthy's novel *The Group*. The film was successful; Buchman moved on to his next. For several years he had attempted to mount a production of a screenplay he'd written based on the life of young Mozart. The plan was to film it in Prague, where Western capital would join in a co-venture with local film producers. But the abrupt fall of the Dubcek government, toppled by the invading Russians, ended any hope of Buchman's capitalist venture reaching fruition.

For the man who had written and produced many fine films in all those years since he'd first signed on as a "dialoguer" at Paramount, the last next-to-closing years of Buchman's career must have been frustrating, indeed.

He shrugged philosophically when asked what lay ahead, on a winter's day back in 1972, when he'd finished reminiscing. "Ah, what the hell, you keep on writing," he remarked, with a thin smile. "I've been through enough Hollywood so-called history to know that's the only way you keep your sanity. Maybe I should write my memoirs. After all I've been through, they ought to be interesting, don't you agree?"

Buchman never got around to setting down the details of his part in that so-called history. But when in 1975 he died in France, he was still engaged in working on film scripts, one of which, *The Deadly Trap*, did reach the screen as a French production.

He'd lived long enough, however, to receive the prestigious Laurel Award in 1965 from the Writers Guild of America, that organization he'd helped found all those years ago.

And when Frank Capra was guest of honor at the American Film Institute tribute dinner a few years later, he would remark, "I had a lot of help along the way. I couldn't have done it without a lot of people who aren't here tonight ... Sidney Buchman, for one."

These days, Columbia Pictures is a satellite of the huge complex known as Sony. Harry Cohn, the tiger of Gower Street who used to boast "I don't *get* ulcers—I *give* them!" has long since departed from what was his turf.

But with comforting regularity, one of those Cohn-Buchman "classy" money spinners, which filled the Columbia coffers, is still playing on one of your TV channels, be it TCM or AMC, tonight. And new audiences are learning to love and laugh at them. Or sitting transfixed, while Mr. Smith goes to Washington, or Jolson sings again.

Which, who knows, may well be for such a talented and skillful writer-producer the best sort of an autobiography to leave behind.

SIDNEY BUCHMAN'S CREDITS:

ACADEMY AWARD:

Here Comes Mr. Jordan, 1941

ACADEMY AWARD NOMINATIONS:

Mr. Smith Goes to Washington, 1939

The Talk of the Town, 1942

Jolson Sings Again, 1949

FILMS:

Matinee Ladies, 1927

Daughter of the Dragon, 1931

Beloved Bachelor, 1931

The Sign of the Cross, 1932

If I Had a Million, 1932

Thunder Below, 1932

No One Man, 1932

The Right to Romance, 1933

From Hell to Heaven, 1933

Broadway Bill, 1934

His Greatest Gamble, 1934

Whom the Gods Destroy, 1934

All of Me, 1934

She Married Her Boss, 1935

Love Me Forever, 1935

I'll Love You Always, 1935

Theodora Goes Wild, 1936

Adventure in Manhattan, 1936

The King Steps Out, 1936

The Music Goes 'Round, 1936

The Awful Truth, 1937

Lost Horizon, 1937

Holiday, 1938

The Howards of Virginia, 1940

Sahara, 1943

Over 21, 1945

A Song to Remember, 1945

The Jolson Story, 1946

To the Ends of the Earth, 1948

Saturday's Hero, 1951

The Mark, 1961

Cleopatra, 1963

The Group, 1966

But Mummy, if Daddy loves you, why does he make you cry?

Wa-al, stranger, I ain't a-looking fur trouble, but iffen trouble comes a-looking fur me, wal, I guess I won't be too hard to find.

What are you trying to do, break up the act?

Why are you, a stranger, doing this for me?

…Thickish out, what?

…Steady the Buffs.

I say, old boy.

…Righto!

…Dessay, a lot of rot, but if anything happens —

Stout fella!

…Say pip-pip to Di, will you, like a good lad?

Righteeoh!

…Well, cheerio!

Cheerio!

(*Bang!*)

What do you care for your wife, eh? Fifi, she lofe you, too…Come, give Fifi beeg kees!

This is madness! You should never have come here!

Say, Chuck, there's a little girl in the chorus that can play that part!

Me, Tarzan. You, Jane.

Listen, Slade. You bought up the option on Lily Belle's property because you learned the railroad was going to be built through here! Well, you ain't going to get away with it, see?

Speak, Harlan, speak! If you won't tell where you were at the hour of the murder, *I will!*

Stop Marian! You don't realize what you're saying!

Harlan was with me, Inspector, in my boudoir!

Oh, how blind men are!

—NUNNALLY JOHNSON, 1938

43

4. HAIL CAESAR!
ARTHUR CAESAR in the 1930s

Poster for *Manhattan Melodrama*, screenplay by Arthur Caesar

POSSIBLY THE MOST QUOTED (AND MISQUOTED) OF THE HOLLYWOOD WITS of the '30s was the late Arthur Caesar.

Before he came to Hollywood, Caesar worked for a time as a reporter for the fabled Louis Weitzenkorn, whose newspaper activities became the basis of a Warner film starring Edward G. Robinson, *Five Star Final*. One of the stories Weitzenkorn assigned young Caesar to cover dealt with the so-called justice meted out by the lower New York courts. Several Bowery bums had been arrested for trespassing. They had, it seemed, broken into the church known as St. Marks-in-the-Bowery.

Caesar took it upon himself to plead their case. He obtained permission from the presiding judge to defend them. He appeared in court wearing an Inverness cape; after a brief conference with the bench, it was agreed by the judge that only one of the bums would stand trial, and his sentence would be applied to the other defendants as well.

Caesar and his defendant had a short conference and then proceeded to trial. He put the unfortunate wino on the stand as witness for his own defense. "Did you break into St. Mark's?" asked Caesar.

"I did," said his client.

"Why did you do that?" asked Caesar.

As if by rote, the client repeated, "For rest, meditation, and prayer."

Caesar turned to the judge, and with a dramatic flourish, he produced from beneath his cape a sign, which he had removed from the exterior of St. Mark's. "I should like to offer this in evidence!" he announced, and held out the sign.

The sign read: ST. MARK'S CHURCH OPEN FOR REST, MEDITATION, AND PRAYER.

"Case dismissed," said the judge.

One of Caesar's New York cronies was young Roger Wolfe Kahn, the son of financier Otto Kahn. Not only was Kahn a dedicated musician who organized his own jazz orchestra, but he also was an expert pilot who owned his own planes, which he kept out in the wilds of Long Island at a private airfield.

One afternoon Kahn persuaded Caesar to drive out to the field with him and join him in a quick spin. Kahn had Caesar strapped into a parachute when suddenly Caesar changed his mind.

"Take this damn thing off!" he demanded.

"What's wrong?" asked Kahn. "My plane is perfectly safe."

"Sure, sure," said Caesar. "And I can just see the headlines if anything happens. 'Otto Kahn's Son And Passenger Crash!' What the hell kind of billing is *that*? Forget it!"

Caesar once wrote a one-act play called *Napoleon's Barber*, which came to the attention of Winfield Sheehan, the head of Fox, who bought the screen rights and hired Caesar to come to Hollywood and do the script. The picture was one of Fox's first sound films and was directed by John Ford. From then on, Caesar remained a Californian.

"I used to get all sorts of offer to work in Hollywood," recalled Irving Caesar, Arthur's brother and himself a highly successful songwriter ("Swanee," "I Want To Be Happy," "Tea For Two," and many others). "But I always refused. I'm basically a city boy. To me, north of 57th Street has always been the deep woods.

"When people used to ask my brother Arthur why I wouldn't come out, he always said 'All Gaul was divided in three parts. But the U.S.A. is divided by we Caesars into two parts. From the Rockies west is mine; from the Rockies east is Irving's."

Caesar will always be remembered for his first meeting with Darryl Zanuck. It was on a weekend in Caliente, below the Mexican border, where Hollywood people went during the Depression for rest, meditation, and tequila.

Caesar was drinking in a bar with friends. Darryl Zanuck, the youngest production head the Warner Bros. studio had ever had, came in with *his* friends. Caesar examined Zanuck for a few moments and then, without any formal introduction, went over to Zanuck, who was seated on a bar stool, and gave Zanuck a swift kick in the rear.

"Say, what was *that* for?" demanded the startled Zanuck. "That," said Caesar, referring to one of Zanuck's latest and most pretentious disasters, "is for taking Noah's Ark, which was a hit for centuries, and turning it into a flop!"

Al Lewis, who was a producer at Fox during Caesar's early years there, remembers another time when Caesar became involved with Zoe Akins.

Miss Akins, who later won the Pulitzer Prize for her play *The Old Maid*, came to work at Fox. Although she had been born in Missouri, the lady spoke with a slightly affected English accent. "She was working in the writers' building," said Lewis, "and right next door to her office was Arthur's. When I first showed her the place, she said it was like a prison cell — which was true — but I persuaded her that a truly creative person could function in any atmosphere, and Zoe went to work.

"Arthur was working on *Napoleon's Barber*, but he'd already amassed a huge collection of friends all over the studio. Actors, grips, technicians — everybody would come by his office. He kept open house. Everybody loved to drop in and schmooze with Caesar, maybe have a drink, listen to him talk — he was a brilliant raconteur and he could go on for hours, never repeating himself.

"One afternoon Miss Akins came in to see me and she started complaining. She told me she couldn't tolerate that office any longer. The walls were very thin and she kept hearing things. 'You know, if there's one thing I cannot stand, it's mace,' she said. 'And there are definitely mace in those walls.'

"I figured out she meant mice and I decided to go down with one of the maintenance men and check out what was happening. We opened the door to Arthur's office and there he was, on the floor with three or four grips, and they were shooting craps, tossing the dice against the wall.

"'What's up?' Arthur asked me.

"I explained the problem that Zoe had raised, Caesar burst out laughing. He got up and went next door and went in. He bowed from the waist, 'It's not mace, Miss Akins,' he said. 'It's dace!'"

Caesar loved to travel, and he once confided to a good friend the secret of successful traveling. "Wherever you go, especially if you're in a strange town," he said, "you must always find yourself a good whorehouse to stay at—they always serve the best breakfasts. After all, when a staff has been working all night, it stands to reason they'll be very hungry!"

In the days when Caesar was employed as a writer at the Warner studio in Burbank, he found some of Warner's rules oppressive. He especially disliked the ukase that all writers must arrive punctually at 9 AM, spend a full working day in their offices, and not leave until 6 PM.

One afternoon Caesar leaned out of his office window and hailed a passer-by who was headed down the street to the studio gate. "Call my mother, will you please?" he yelled. "Tell her I'm okay—they treat you pretty well here, the food's not bad, the guards are pretty decent—but be sure and ask her if she'll mail me a carton of cigarettes!"

And there was the day when Caesar was invited by his friend Zanuck to sit in on the screening of one of Zanuck's latest Warner epics. When the lights came up in the projection room, Zanuck turned to Caesar. "All right, Arthur," he asked. "What did you think?"

"Darryl," said Caesar, "if it were mine, I'd cut it up and sell it for mandolin picks."

And another time he is supposed to have remarked, about another misbegotten Warner epic, "*That* one was so bad, they had to shoot re-takes before they could shelve it!"

One of Caesar's proudest claims was that on his first visit to London, he had decided to go and visit George Bernard Shaw at his home. He rang Shaw's doorbell, and when the great author appeared, young Caesar introduced himself as a fellow playwright from America who had come to pay a call. Might he now come in and have a friendly chat? Shaw eyed Caesar. "Go walk around the square a bit until I get used to your face," he said.

There are many legends about the parties Caesar gave (one of which was for the wives of his good friends and took place in the living room of a famous downtown Los Angeles whorehouse, where Caesar told his assembled lady-friends, "If we sit and wait here for a bit, I am sure most of your husbands will soon join us."). But the best known of all these stories concerns a costume party of the early 1930s.

Caesar had attended wearing a toga and a laurel wreath. In the early hours of the morning, he was stopped by a traffic cop as he drove himself home.

The cop eyed Caesar with suspicion. "What's your name?" he demanded.

"Caesar," said Arthur, cheerfully.

"Don't get wise — *gimme your name*," said the gendarme.

"*Caesar!*" protested Arthur.

He ended up in a Los Angeles jail.

People roared at the sign he kept on his desk: "I don't want to be right; I just want to keep on working." His comment on his pal Darryl Zanuck's social achievement was: "From Poland to polo in one generation."

Eventually Zanuck laughed at it, after it went all over Hollywood.

"Caesar's wit was never directed against little people," said Norman Krasna, who shared offices in the Warner writers' building with him. "He always took pot shots against the very big boys, the ones who were so smug about their positions and power. They were always willing to laugh at Arthur's cracks, but afterwards he found it tougher to get jobs. They'd bring him in for conferences on script ideas, and he'd take pot shots at everybody, but when it came time to *hire* Arthur, the attitude was always 'Why should I subsidize the guy to make cracks against me?'"

In 1953 Caesar died, and at his funeral, the eulogy was delivered by Charles Brackett, one of his fellow writers, the long-time partner of Billy Wilder; his words are well worth repeating.

> Ladies and gentlemen, I come here not to bury Caesar but to praise him. When you've known a man for over thirty years, either you don't

51

remember a thing about him, or the things you remember pile up in a rich, untidy heap. Arthur was a singularly memorable man. I'm going to try and sort out some of the stories and the memories and the legends in chronological order.

The first happened in a cold-water flat on Delancey Street, in the Lower East Side. Arthur took his little brother, Irving, into their parents' room, where hung a picture of their father as a sergeant in the Romanian army. "You know," he confided in his brother, "there is a King in Romania, and a Prince. If the King dies, the Prince becomes King. But if the Prince dies, they will have to send to America for Papa, and he will become King and Mama will be Queen and we will be Princes and there will be a parade down Ludlow Street. And as we go along, we will speak to all the humble people, but to the landlord and the butcher and the wholesale candy dealer — not a word!"

Funds were low and life was pretty rigorous in that flat of the Caesars in those days. Arthur's imagination did a miraculous job with the situation. He told his brother that the deprivations weren't necessary at all — they were more important than that. They were a kind of Spartan training his father had devised, to give his boys character. It was a shining lie that made it an excitement to endure tough times.

Whatever its physical discomforts, that home never lacked for love or learning. Arthur cut his literary teeth on Walt Whitman's poetry, which was his father's great enthusiasm. He was full-grown by the time he was eleven, and the passion for the theatre that was to haunt all his days had begun. He used to hang around lobbies and get intermission passes from drunken customers. It was his boast that in those years, he saw the *end* of every show on Broadway!

There's a hiatus in my knowledge now — and suddenly he's graduating from Yale. Getting through Yale at all had been little short of a financial miracle. On graduation day, the gilded youth in his class were getting fabulous presents — Mercer cars, trips to Europe, power launches. Well, Arthur's mother couldn't manage anything like that. But she wasn't going to let her son Arthur be without a present. She brought him a dozen white carnations. All the rest of his life, in memory of that gesture of hers, he wore a white carnation in his buttonhole.

Mrs. Caesar is also famous for the remark she made when her son

Irving achieved great success as a songwriter. He purchased a power cruiser, bought himself a blazer with brass buttons, and a captain's hat with a visor, then invited his mother to go with him on the first cruise. As the boat made its way up the Hudson, Irving said proudly, "Look, mama, I'm a captain!"

"Irving," said his mother, "by me you're a captain, and by you you're a captain. But by *captains*—are you a captain?"

There came a stretch in World War I, and Arthur donned a khaki suit with no buttonhole in the lapel. He took the war in the fashion of 1917—romantically. He enlisted and was in a base hospital unit in France long before the draft law was even conceived. There his ardor ran into a snag. He was a terrible soldier—sloppy in appearance, utterly lacking in military dexterity, the despair of the unit, a comedy figure. But a call came asking for volunteers who would submit themselves to experiments on trench fever, a disease which was raising havoc with the troops. The medical corps thought it was transmitted by lice, but no one was sure. They needed human guinea pigs.

Arthur was the first to offer himself. In Dijon, where the experiment took place, they put lice in the young soldier's arm and let them bite; they ground up the insects and injected them into his skin; he had to swallow them. Others who submitted to the experiment died. Arthur accounted for his own survival by saying, "Those were very timid lice. I come from the Lower East Side, where the lice are savage."

Delicate as those insects may have been, they left him with something to remember them by; a partial paralysis in one cheek. I'm glad to add he got another memento; a Distinguished Service citation, signed by President Wilson and General John J. Pershing.

Arthur's screen credits are too numerous to mention. For one piece of work, his original story of *Manhattan Melodrama*, he would win an Academy Award. It was made in 1934 at Metro and starred Clark Gable and William Powell; it was the tale of two boyhood pals from the Lower East Side who remain friends, even though one becomes a district attorney and the other a gangster ... As the years have passed, the same premise has appeared in many other films, without credit to Caesar's work.

...It is the same film which John Dillinger, the famous outlaw of the '30s, had seen in Chicago at the Biograph Theatre, that afternoon when he was gunned down by the Feds.

But it was as a personality, a wit and a philosopher, that Arthur stood forth. His comments on religion became part of his legend. "It's like a bank. Lots of doors, plenty of tellers—but only one that can okay the check," or "We are not punished *for* our sins—but *by* them."

To a Catholic friend who considered changing his faith: "Quit trying to play split weeks with religion. God won't be able to find you."

Time passed. He was saying fondly of his wife, "Mrs. Caesar has… taken up her option on me for the thirty-first straight year,"—and suddenly a terrible physical ailment beset him. He met the horror as was natural to him, with a joke. "All of a sudden my toes began turning red, white and blue," he explained to the doctor, "only nobody was playing the 'Star Spangled Banner.'"

His doctor asked if Caesar would submit to an amputation. "I don't write with my toes," he said. "Go ahead."

To calm any fears he might have about the future, his friend George Behrendt, an amputee, not only talked about how little he himself had been hampered by the loss of a leg, but demonstrated it by whirling about Caesar's hospital room. "You make it so attractive, George," said Caesar, "I'm beginning to be sorry I didn't have it done thirty years ago!"

In the days he spent at the Motion Picture Country Home, next door to his room, bedridden, was the great Polly Moran, a comedienne who is best remembered for her comedies with Marie Dressler.

"Polly was fond of delicatessen," reported Behrendt, "and she was desperate for the taste of corned beef and pastrami. So, to please her, Arthur arranged for a nearby delicatessen to deliver each night a couple of sandwiches. Arthur had me bring him a fishing rod with a long line. Delicatessen was strictly forbidden Polly, but every night Arthur would drop that fishing line out the window, the delicatessen delivery boy would attach the package to the hook, and then Arthur would reel in Polly's treat and see to it that the forbidden sandwiches got to her. She'd devour them. But then, afterwards, Polly would have heartburn. I was in his room one night, visiting, and then from Polly's room there was a sudden yell. 'Arthur, I'm dying—I'm dying!'"

"You can't die yet, darling," Arthur yelled back. "I haven't written your last lines!"

Caesar left only one instruction for his own funeral.

"When I die," he wrote, "be sure the services are in the morning, so my friends can get to the track and not lose any time they need for betting."

ARTHUR CAESAR'S CREDITS

ACADEMY AWARD:
Manhattan Melodrama, 1934

FILMS:
His Darker Self, 1924
Napoleon's Barber, 1928
The Aviator, 1929
So Long Letty, 1929
Divorce among Friends, 1930
A Soldier's Plaything, 1930
The Life of the Party, 1930
Three Faces East, 1930
This Mad World, 1930
She Couldn't Say No, 1930
Wide Open, 1930
Her Majesty, Love, 1931
Side Show, 1931
Gold Dust Gertie, 1931
The Tenderfoot, 1932
The Heart of New York, 1932

Fireman, Save My Child, 1932
The Chief, 1933
No Marriage Ties, 1933
Obey the Law, 1933
Their Big Moment, 1934
Alias Mary Dow, 1935
McFadden's Flats, 1935
Transient Lady, 1935
Along Came Love, 1936
The Star Maker, 1939
Little Men, 1940
Adventure in Washington, 1941
Northwest Rangers, 1942
The Loves of Edgar Allan Poe, 1942
Pistol Packin' Mama, 1943
I Accuse My Parents, 1944
Atlantic City, 1944
Three of a Kind, 1944
Arson, Inc., 1949
Anne of the Indies, 1951

WALTER WANGER on GENE TOWNE and GRAHAM BAKER

I HAD TWO WRITERS UNDER CONTRACT NAMED GENE TOWNE AND GRAHAM Baker. They were great idea men, and they understood films. Towne was an illiterate guy who used to say, "Bring that dame in here and she'll do this... Then she moves, and then the punk comes in." He had a collaborator, Baker, who was more dignified, to put the stuff down on paper. They would work out the action. "Oh, this stinks. Nobody will ever stand for that... etc."

They were under contract to me at about $2,500 a week. They would write every sequence on toilet paper and hang it on the wall. When they were ready, I'd go up and comment, "That seems a little too long... There might be a dead spot there."

"You're right. You're right."

They would tear off two pages of toilet paper. After we got a complete blueprint of the action, the characters, and the scenes, Towne would run around to every restaurant telling every actor he saw, "Jesus, Wanger's got a great part for you!" He'd build up the mirage. Then, when the thing was all finished to the best of their ability, I'd bring in Dorothy Parker, who would rewrite it and insert the dialogue. A great many pictures were made that way.

Later on, Towne and Baker were hired by Sam Goldwyn for a script. One morning they were called by Goldwyn's secretary and informed that after lunch, the producer would be bringing his guests down for a studio tour, and wished to drop by and show his guests where and how his writers worked.

At the appointed time, Goldwyn and guests appeared in the writers' building, looking for Towne and Baker. He was directed down the hall to the men's room. Upon opening the door, he discovered two desks, two chairs, typewriters, Towne and Baker, plus their two secretaries, all busily working on the script.

Towne was also fond of steambaths, and often insisted on taking his secretary downtown to one where, both completely in the buff, he would sit and steam and dictate.

When the partnership finally broke up, Baker, who was the more sober of the two, was heard to remark, wearily, "I finally had to get out of the Polish Corridor."

—WALTER WANGER

5. NY to LA, to NY, to LA:
A CONVERSATION with EDWARD CHODOROV

1972

Edward Chodorov by Dana Fradon

"EVERYBODY I TALK TO THESE DAYS TELLS ME THE ENTERTAINMENT business is dominated by youth," commented Edward Chodorov. "Please tell me—what's such a big deal about that? It's *always* been that way! I was twenty years old, 1932...and I was out in Burbank at Warner Bros., a writer-producer. But back in those days, *everybody* out there was young! From Darryl Zanuck on down, the studio was filled with us kids...all boy wonders!"

We were chatting in his London hotel suite in 1972: rather, I sat and listened, while the energetic and voluble Mr. Chodorov paced up and down, cheerfully reminiscing about those busy crowded past four decades during which he'd written, directed, and produced films, and all the while he commuted between the Hollywood soundstages and Broadway theatres.

"I learned very early to be totally indifferent, to tell myself 'fuck 'em, I'll go back to New York!' And I did...and it worked. They couldn't figure me out. Jack Warner once said to somebody 'Smart fella, Chodorov. He must have something!'"

"I had no fear of Jack, I had no fear of Harry Cohn at Columbia; I argued with Sam Goldwyn, and Louis Mayer, who brought shivers to everybody in town. Actually, *he* was the guy who controlled it. I told him once in his office, he was with his tough pal Frank Orsatti, who was sitting there, I said 'Mr. Mayer, if you would keep your hands out of the films, the films would be twice as good! You should stick to what you do best, Mr. M., putting up the money—but not giving people ideas about the movies and how they should be done!'

"I learned how to do that at a very early age," said Chodorov. "See, I was a very precocious kid. By the age of eighteen, I'd written my first play, *Boy Wonder*—the right title, eh?" he chuckled. "And it was being handled by a top agent, Dr. Edmond Pauker. For me, it only seemed natural to be able at that age to write a play people took seriously. I'd grown up in the theatre; my father was an actor, so I'd been hanging around rehearsals learning the business since I was about seven…

"Pauker sent my play to that mythological New York producer, the famous monster, Mr. Jed Harris. This, mind you, was in the depths of the Depression, nobody was producing anything; everybody was starving! Believe it or not, Harris buys my play, puts it on, and it gets good reviews! And all of a sudden, I am now a somebody. Not to mention that I have had my first life-molding experience. Because, believe me, if you could survive working with Jed Harris, you could certainly handle the worst tyrant in Hollywood!… Which is where I went, in 1932."

And for the next several hours, Chodorov, blessed with seemingly total recall, cheerfully reminisced about those early '30s in Hollywood, which were regularly interspersed by his journeys back to Manhattan, usually with a new play script tucked away in his briefcase. For Chodorov would turn out to be one of the very few screenwriters who could sit in a sunlit Hollywood office and sketch out a new play, and then proceed to actually write said play, eh?

"Don't forget my kid brother, Jerry," he said. "He could do the same thing, with his partner, Joe Fields. Neither of us ever gave up the theatre!"

Chodorov's later theatre credits would include such successes as *Kind Lady, Cue for Passion, Those Endearing Young Charms, Decision, Common Ground*, and in 1953, the hilarious comedy hit, *Oh Men, Oh Women!*

Oh yes, let us not forget, he also directed the last four plays.

"Which is how I kept my sanity," he insisted. "If things got tough, I could always get the hell out of Hollywood and go work in New York. I'd made up my mind never to lose the theatre. You see, I never felt I was a particularly good screenwriter—in the sense that one needs to see life and its various incidents, in what is referred to by the so-called scholars as 'cinematic imagery.' I was more of a dialogue man."

Four decades after his first trip West on the Chief, Chodorov's reminiscences as a writer-producer in those earliest days of sound films provided a first-hand insight into the rough-and-tumble '30s—and his experiences proceeded right on through to the 1960s, when that insidious little black box, in the corner of our living room, the mighty ten-inch TV set, began to undermine the Hollywood studio system and eventually cause its downfall.

So, if Chodorov's first play had been such a Broadway success, what had made him decide to go West?

"Remember, in this new era of sound, all the studios were desperately looking for playwrights to come West, because we were supposed to be the guys who could handle the *words*—dialogue," he said. "The gag in those days was that the William Morris Agency had just sent out its usual weekly shipment of playwrights!

"Anyway, Bob Rubin, who was the Eastern head of Metro, decided I must have talent and came after me to go out to his studio.

"I asked Jed Harris, 'Should I go?' And he said, 'Yes, kid, but *not for long*.' I still couldn't make up my mind."

So, what was the clincher that sent Chodorov away from 44th Street out to Wilshire Boulevard?

"Two hundred a week," he said. "Believe me, in those days, that was a lot of money. When I came out on the Chief, I spoke to some insurance man who asked me what I was making. When I told him, he was shocked. He probably made about sixty... he had four kids, and he was paying off a mortgage on his house... and here I was, a pushy young kid, making three times as much as he was!

"So there I was, at Metro. Writers all over the lot; they had a studio payroll for them... something like sixty thousand a *week!* I stayed there about eight weeks. Worked for a producer named Bernie Fineman... They put me to work on my first assignment; pretty soon I discovered they had *seven* other writers on the same script! But I didn't do much for

Fineman. Another guy, Bernie Hyman, was producing *Rasputin and the Empress*. He had Charlie MacArthur working on it ... but Charlie wasn't writing much ... he was spending most of his time partying around. So Hyman had four scenes he needed to be written; he gave me those scenes.

"I wrote them, and Hyman loved them. He raved about them ... Then, I discovered that Charlie was taking all the bows for what I'd written. I confronted him; I asked him why he'd stolen those scenes from me. He said to me, 'Listen, kid, this is the Argentine mining lode out here — you steal what you can.'

"From that moment on, I never liked Charlie. That alleged so-called pixie humor of his ... forget it. It was actually mean and selfish ...

"In those days, I never ran into anybody else who would do that. All of us young writers, we'd come out from the theatre, and we were all very generous to each other. In the theatre, if you went out of town to see a play by one of your buddies, you might stay a few days with him, trying to help him get his play right ... and you didn't expect anything in return from him except that he'd be around to do the same thing for you. It was that sort of camaraderie."

Chodorov shortly departed Metro for Warners. "Charlie Feldman, my agent, got me a deal there — *four* hundred a week! So I went over there, and after my first picture, *The World Changes*, with Paul Muni, they put me to work on a picture for Cagney, *The Mayor of Hell*. Reform school picture, which incidentally, caused an investigation of all those corrupt reform schools of the time. Sixteen states revised their systems, because *The Mayor of Hell* exposed the corruption and political skullduggery that went on in reform schools! That was the kind of picture Warners kept turning out all through the '30s — those hard-driving melodramas that dealt with the sociological problems of the time — one right after the other.... Cagney was perfect for that kind of picture. But the director, Archie Mayo, an ex-shirt salesman, did a dreadful job.

"I'd written a scene I was very proud of, about these tough little East Side kids, murderers, who'd just killed an old man who ran a stationery store for a few pennies. And they're caught and sent to a reform school. This is the first time in their lives they've been in the country. They're lying in this detention room, in bunks, side by side ... So I wrote them this scene ... They're out in the country, you see, and there are all sorts of insects, crickets, whipoorwills, things they've never heard.... And they're talking about when the guards come in, in the morning, they're gonna jump them, throttle them, stab them, and make their getaway.... And one kid says 'What's that?' and they all listen. And they hear all these insect sounds. So I wrote 'The camera pans down, we see their faces, and the kids are terrified.'"

Chodorov shook his head. "Believe it or not, I come on the set to watch Mayo shoot this wonderful scene, and I'm met with a burst of thunder! Live sound—in those days they didn't dub. It knocked me right on my ass! And then lightning, too, big lightning flashes across the set!

"I said, 'Archie, what is this thunder and lightning? Where are the *crickets?*' He said, 'I took out those goddamned crickets; I gave the kids something to be scared about!' So I said, 'Archie, they've seen lightning and thunder all their lives! Crickets, they've never heard about before.' Archie said, 'Ah, that's a lot of high-class intellectual bullshit!'

"I got a lot of that," sighed Chodorov. "I remember once when Jack Warner gave a big luncheon for William Randolph Hearst at the studio. And he called me up and said, 'Kid, I want you to sit next to Hearst—and you can give him a lot of that college-a-roo stuff! You're good at that!'

"My first picture at Warners, Hal Wallis was the ostensible producer. Darryl Zanuck, who ran the place, hated him. I was at a meeting, and Wallis sat in a corner, very quiet. Then at one point he opened his mouth and said, 'You know, I think—' and Darryl said, 'Look, when I want you to think of something, I'll let you know! That is, if you're capable of thinking. Otherwise, keep your mouth shut!'

"He went out into the hall afterwards, and I said, 'Mr. Wallis, I'm terribly sorry.' No use. I don't think Hal ever forgave me for watching him being put down like that." Chodorov sighed. "I'll tell you something. You mustn't be associated with a guy's worst flop...and you must *never* be around for his humiliation...

"I did about eleven pictures at Warners," he continued. "First writing, then producing. Zanuck left; he resented that whole incident in 1933 when Warner tried to get everyone to take a fifty percent cut in salary. Sure, things were very tough, but Darryl didn't believe they were that tough, so he used Jack's salary cut as an excuse to quit Warners and go over to start his own company—Twentieth Century. Now Jack was left with two pro-

ducers, Henry Blanke and Bob Lord. Somebody had to do the pictures—
that's when I got to be a producer!

"I remember once I had Jerry Wald writing on a picture called *Living on Velvet*. One day, I said to him, 'Jerry, for Chrissake, you talk like an absolute idiot, and you write even worse. But every morning you come in with a beautiful scene or two. *Who's writing 'em?*' I'll say this for Jerry, he didn't try to lie. He said, 'A couple of fellows called Epstein. Twins.' I asked him what he was paying them—he said fifty a week. I said 'You're getting two hundred, you're giving them half. Why don't you bring 'em in here, and I'll put them on salary for two hundred for the both of them... you keep yours, and everybody's doubling their money!' So he brought in Julius and Phil Epstein, and do I have to tell you the rest of *their* story? Up to, and including *Casablanca*?

"About *Living on Velvet*—it was very good, way ahead of its time. Kay Frances and George Brent... very much like a post-Impressionist painting.... Two people meeting on a transatlantic boat, falling in love, neither knowing when the ship docks they're both doomed, for different reasons...

"Years go by, and I'm in Paris, and there's a real film aficionado there— you know how the French are all nuts about *le cinema*... He asks me, 'What was that picture you did with Frank Borzage, the director?' I told him I'd never done one with Borzage. He said 'Ah, but you did.' We went to look it up, and it's *Living on Velvet*, and I said, 'My God, I completely forgot it!'

"You see, in those days, directors went from picture to picture on short notice, sometimes over the weekend. There was none of that nonsense about *auteurs*—all that high-art stuff that has developed over the years. In truth, I cannot tell you how many times I had to throw a director off the set and then went in and finished the picture myself—*and*, left his name on it... Because I didn't want to do the guy any injury, but he was simply not getting the stuff in the rushes which we wanted!... It was all part of the job, you see. In those early days, you turned your hand at everything, all over the lot!

"Out of a certain amount of desperation, I got tired of working on other peoples' scripts, and I began to work on a film biography of Louis Pasteur. I thought his story about discovering the presence of germs in food and drink would make a terrific drama. Because everybody opposed him, at the time…

"So did Jack! Warner said 'Nobody *ever* heard of Pasteur.' I told him to ask the girl who runs the green room — where we all had lunch every day. 'Ask her if she's heard of him.' Warner sent me back a note, 'I just asked her, and she never heard of Pasteur. *Forget it!*' So I sent him back another note, 'Ask her if she ever heard of pasteurized milk!' …Which, of course, she had! This went on back and forth, and Warner was really afraid to stop me finishing the script, because if he tried, and I walked off the lot, he'd have only two producers left!

"I thought Louis Pasteur would make a great vehicle for Paul Muni. He'd done *I Am a Fugitive from a Chain Gang*, and I'd done one with him called *Border Town*, in which he had a young actress playing opposite him …Bette Davis, remember her? Anyway, from the first, I knew Muni was perfect for Pasteur.

"You know how we got Muni to make it? Muni had one of those insane contracts; in Warner's desperation to keep Muni under contract, he'd agreed to a contract in which Muni had an approval clause. They could offer Muni three scripts to do. If he rejected all three, then Warners had to make the fourth, whichever Muni wanted to make. Can you imagine such a deal? Absurd! But Warner really needed Muni; he was his class act.

"So I brought my script to Muni's brother-in-law, Abem Finkel, a lovely sweet guy and a good writer. Muni's reaction when Finkel showed it to him was, 'You want me to play a man with a *beard?* With *germs* in his beard? *Are you crazy?*' …A great actor, but difficult. What the hell, most of them are…Anyway, Abem and I worked on him, and finally we penetrated into that great actor's head, and he agreed to do it…Wrote on the cover of the script 'I agree to do this. Paul Muni.'"

Chodorov grinned and shook his head, remembering. "Well, when Jack saw that script cover, he went right through the ceiling. He wanted to know how the hell Muni had gotten the script, and when he found out it was me — that I'd gone behind his back — we got into a terrible row. He threw me off the lot. Remember, in those days, there was no such thing as a Screen Writers Guild to protect my rights. And my Pasteur script belonged to Warners; I'd written it on company time."

Warner, faced with Muni's acceptance, had to proceed. He assigned

Chodorov's script to Henry Blanke, who brought in two other writers to do a "polish." "A guy named Pierre Collings, an old timer, and a very nice guy named Sheridan Gibney," recalled Chodorov. "They had no choice but to take on the assignment…they were on the payroll; how could they afford to turn down the job?

"Okay, so Charlie Feldman put me to work at Samuel Goldwyn's company—now I'm getting fifteen hundred a week! Charlie was really a damn good agent. One day, we're lying on the beach at Malibu, and Charlie told me about a package deal idea he was planning to do…He was the first guy who ever figured out how to do that, his idea was to get a writer, a director, and the stars—all of them his clients—and to put them together, and selling 'em all as a package—where he could take the profit off the top…plus a piece of the picture! That was Christmas, 1933…it took him a long time to pull it off, but it finally happened…How far-sighted he was!"

And what about the legendary Sam Goldwyn?

Chodorov shook his head. "A *very* difficult man to work for—almost the worst I can remember. You know, there's that legendary story about me and Sam? It went all over town…He had some play by Rachel Crothers; he wanted Miriam Hopkins to star in it. So he brought me in to discuss that project, and after I read it, I told him I thought it was a terrible script, and it would make an even worse picture. He kept after me, but I turned him down.

"But Sam was a very stubborn guy. Dug in his heels and had to prove he was right. Made the picture. When the picture came out, a couple of years later, sure enough, it was a dead germ. Nothing you could do to that story would improve it!

"…Anyway, a few years go by, and now I'm over at Metro, and Charlie Feldman is in a meeting with Goldwyn, and Sam has a project he needs a writer-producer for, and Charlie suggests to Goldwyn that he hire me for it. And Sam yells, 'Eddie *Chodorov*? I wouldn't have him on my lot!' And Charlie wants to know, why not? And Sam says 'He was connected with my *worst flop!*'"

Back to the saga of Louis Pasteur.

"I didn't pay much attention to it, but they made it…and suddenly, this picture that Jack Warner had fought so bitterly against, and tried to kill—and *fired* me because I'd gotten Muni—it's now a major event!" says Chodorov, shaking his head. "Suddenly, would you believe, they're nominating it for an Academy Award, and on the night of the Awards, H. G. Wells comes all the way over from England to present the Oscar!...And now, it's a great big thing! A *monument!*

"But I didn't pay too much attention...My brother Jerry said, 'Not one of those sons of bitches, *nobody*, Warner, Disterle, Muni, Blanke, Gibney...nobody's even called you up! You should've at least been invited to the Oscars!' I said, 'No, I don't believe in prizes, and I'm not going!'

"But after his pep talk," he said, "I began to feel terrible. And I went to sleep feeling terrible. Next morning, the doorbell rings, it's a Western Union telegram. It said 'IT'S REALLY YOUR PICTURE!' And it was signed by Muni, Disterle, Blanke—and the two writers! No Warner, of course."

He grinned. "And then I got a second wire—this one was from Herman Politz, a little guy, one of the Warner relatives. He worked as a tailor on the lot. It said, 'Dear Mr. Chodorov, I'll never forget how when I was making you that suit, the terrible fights you were having over the telephone with Mr. Warner about Pasteur. *Congratulations*! Herman, the Tailor.' That made me feel good. Almost better than winning...

"But in the aftermath, there was such an irony. Collings committed suicide, and Gibney went downhill. And both of them were so broke they were forced to hock their Oscars...That was before they passed the rule —before you were awarded one, you had to sign a paper promising never to do such a thing...

"After a while, I heard from Muni, through our mutual friend, Max Siegel, the producer. Muni felt miserable about the whole affair, so miserable he couldn't tell me directly. Eventually, we made up...but it was never the same. But you know something funny about me and Warners? After Jack threw me off the lot, they never took me off the payroll. They kept sending Charlie my weekly checks. I went to New York to do a play, when I came back, Charlie had a whole drawer of checks waiting for me!"

What was the play Chodorov brought to New York?

"Oh, that was *Kind Lady*," he said. "An entirely different sort of suspense thriller. I'd carried the first act around in my briefcase for a couple of years...finally finished it. It was the first of a whole new genre of plays, like *Night Must Fall, Ladies in Retirement, Uncle Harry,*...they were the kind of plays where the mystery is not *who* does it, but *how* it gets done or doesn't. The suspense in my play was based on this nice old lady in London being held captive in her own home by a bunch of rotten people whom she'd taken in and befriended ... Will she get away? It worked very well ... Years later, it ended up being made as a movie with Ethel Barrymore."

After his play opened, Chodorov returned to Hollywood. "Charlie got me a job producing a picture called *Craig's Wife*, based on a very good play by George Kelly, about a woman who's obssessed with possessions ... I wanted a woman director; I figured she'd have more intuition into the major character ... so we hired Dorothy Arzner, who was terrific.

"Harry Cohn, the boss, budgeted this picture at two hundred and twenty-five thousand. Tops. Then he went away on a vacation. So we gave Billy Haines, the actor who'd turned into an interior decorator, one hundred and eighty thousand just to do our set! But that's because the set —Harriet's home—was the most important part of her entire life. So we didn't have much left for the actors. I borrowed a young girl from Metro ... Rosalind Russell. Nobody knew her; she'd been in a picture for five minutes with Jean Harlow. Opposite her, John Boles, a guy they gave me, who'd been a musical comedy star.

"Roz didn't want to do that picture; a drama about a domineering woman, when she wanted to be a comedienne. I was in Louis Mayer's office when she told him, 'I'll go to jail before I play this part!' So L. B. nodded and said, 'Then you'll go to jail. But you'll play the part.'

"It took three weeks before Roz would even talk to me. But she was great. Became a star. Right there in Glendale, when we previewed our picture. A very hot night, and the theatre was loaded with shirtsleeved kids, out with their girlfriends ... And on came *Craig's Wife*, with a cast of totally unknown people and based on a very adult subject ... By the end of the first five minutes, it's very quiet, and I knew we'd gotten them interested. And then the picture got to them.

"We came out of the preview, and Harry Cohn, who'd been away while we made the picture, said, 'I don't understand one damn scene in this picture. I don't know what the hell we made it for! I don't know what it's all about, but you're not going to have that ending on it, where the girl walks around her empty house!' ... See, Harriet's husband has left her, and she's alone in her beautiful house, the one she's so crazy about, she's tearing up flowers, and trying to keep from going to pieces … Very dramatic. '*Forget that!*' said Harry. '*Get another ending!*'" Chodorov shook his head. "We had ourselves a terrible fight, right there. One of the worst we ever had."

How was it resolved?

"Next day, Harry has everybody in Columbia up to his office — writers, directors, executives — to have a vote on whether or not we should change the ending. And everybody says, 'Leave it the way it is.' So he had to give in. But before he did, he screamed at me, 'You went around since last night and proselytized them!'"

The rough-and-tumble Cohn was capable of such a flowery expression?

"Harry was not so dumb," said Chodorov. "I'll tell you how he worked. I could do a script for him, then he'd read it. Next day he'd call me up and say, 'Eddie, get up here.' He had the script on his desk. He'd say, 'Get 45 pages out of this shit, and get it out fast.' That meant he was crazy about it, and it would start shooting the next week. Because if he didn't like it, didn't want to do it, you'd never hear a word about it. But he had a very shrewd instinct about what would work — and what wouldn't.

"I remember one day Cohn called me and Sidney Buchman into the projection room and ran off some footage, and then he said, 'Now all you fellas come from the theatre, really, you playwrights have theatre in your brain! Now look, here you show a man coming through a door, and then you have to cut around and show him *closing* the door! *Why?* This, guys, is the *movies!* If he opens a door, then you can now pick him in *Tibet!* Do you understand what I'm saying?'

"Harry was trying to explain jump cutting to us, twenty-five years before it became fashionable. Somehow, he knew … But we didn't understand him; we laughed at him. We called him Harry the Butcher…"

Chodorov shook his head, "He was way ahead of us. Today, the cutting he was telling us to do, that's how everybody makes pictures. Jump cutting. He couldn't explain it; he couldn't make us see it. The directors who knew it, they didn't have to be told about it. They shot instinctively. Take a guy like Frank Capra. He couldn't explain why he shot certain sequences the way he did, no way, he just did it. Intuitive. That goes for all of the great ones. John Ford? Take the scene in *Grapes of Wrath*, where the little Okie guy has his outburst, and he says, 'You can't take this land away from us!' And he gets down, and holds some of the soil in his hand, and you don't see his face. Ford can't tell you why he told his actor 'Keep your head down, I don't want to see your face …' Another director would have shown the face. Not Ford. And he didn't know why, he just did it!"

It seemed appropriate to ask Chodorov to amplify the subject of the migration of writers to Hollywood. Since he had been present throughout the years when so many creative people came West to try their hand at working in the studios, could he explain why so many of the novelists, playwrights, and others proved to be unable to write successfully for films?

"It sure as hell wasn't that they didn't have the talent," said Chodorov. "Most of them, at least. But they weren't able to hold off those men — the so-called producers — who were assigned to make the decisions for them. That's true of the directors, as well. Look at Dorothy Arzner. She worked with me on *Craig's Wife*, and if I may say so, in me she had a very sympathetic and understanding producer. But the minute she went over to Metro, say, to work, she had guys who produced pictures with one motto — 'Get the goddamned stuff in the can!' Results, nothing else to write home about…

"Believe me, most of the writers who were around, whom we know couldn't cut it, were perfectly capable. They just never had the chance to write anything as well as they might because you had guys producing — I could give you plenty of names — who *didn't know!* Those so-called producers were foremen on assembly lines, who had no time to listen to what a writer or a director might have to say.

"You have to know how to treat an artist. Damn it, you have to know how to speak to people," sighed Chodorov. "I worked with all sorts of guys, and believe me, I could count on the fingers of one hand the executives who knew how to deal with creative people."

Who were…?

"Zanuck," he said, promptly. "Darryl was the best man to work for. Whatever else he had in his life, as an executive he had no vanity. He could talk to you for forty-five minutes about some marvelous idea he'd just gotten — you know, he started his career writing plots for Rin Tin Tin at Warners — and he'd go on and on, and finally, when he was finished, he'd ask, 'Well, what do you think?' And you'd say, 'Darryl, I don't like it.' And you told him why, in two or three minutes, maybe, and if you made sense, he'd say, 'Okay, forget it.' No vanity, Darryl didn't feel he could lose face if you corrected him. He knew you had talent; that's why he had you there in the first place! Believe me, in the picture business, he was rare.

"Joe Cohn had none, either," Chodorov continued. Cohn was a top-rank Metro executive for many years. "I remember, he'd be reading a script I'd brought in, and Joe could say, 'Eddie, I don't understand this crucial scene here. Read it to me.' And you read it to him, and he'd say, 'I don't know, I still don't understand it.' Then you looked at it, and you saw that you hadn't done the job. Or, maybe Joe would tell you, '*Now*, I understand it!' He was the kind of executive who brought out the best in me, when I went back to Metro."

The same studio from which he'd once fled?

"Sure, but when I went back, it was on my own terms, as a writer-producer. Not doing any of those big 'A' pictures…because I didn't want to be a messenger boy between the front office, which was Mayer, and whatever director was doing the picture. There was only one way to do that, and that was to make the kind of low-budget picture that they didn't care about. Big-budget pictures, those they worried about. I used to go up to Mayer's office and tell him what I wanted to make, maybe a Sidney Howard play like *Yellow Jack*—about the yellow fever plague in Panama, a wonderful play they had, but they hadn't gotten around to making it, and I'd try to explain to Mayer what a terrific job I could do…And Mayer would say, 'Eddie, I don't know about yellow fever, it doesn't sound like anything, but if you want to make the picture that much, make it!'

"So I went ahead, and mostly did pictures I wanted to do. Four in one year, all of them successful. That was a terrific time; they left me alone. I found some talented young guys I used as directors…I brought in Leslie Fenton, he was making shorts. I also brought in Sylvan Simon, he'd been a test director at Universal. Guys I had faith in. Not old-timers like Jack Conway, guys who'd been around movies since 1922…Those troglodytes wouldn't listen to you, paid no attention to what you wanted them to do. Say you had a conference with Howard Hawks, he listened and he nodded. Then he went out on the set and did exactly what he wanted to do. Sometimes he'd be right, others, he'd be wrong…but there was no discussion.

"I did one picture that year *Rich Man, Poor Girl*, directed by a wonderful German refugee, Reinhold Schünzel, a guy nobody wanted to use. He'd been very big in Germany, but he'd fled the Nazis so late they figured he probably *was* a Nazi, can you believe it? Anyway, we did the picture on a seventeen-day schedule, which for Metro was peanuts. Schunzel couldn't even speak English, I had to put an interpreter on it with him, down on the set!

"That little picture turned out to be a big hit! Made Metro *three* stars! Lana Turner ... she'd been hanging around the studio when Mervyn LeRoy brought her over from Warners. Did nothing much, just leg-art and bathing-suit photos. I told them I wanted her as the lead; they didn't believe I could do such a thing! Leading man? I remembered a young guy who'd played the lead in *All Quiet on the Western Front*, then he faded away. A forgotten actor, living in a fleabag hotel downtown ... I had to fight for them to agree to let me use him; finally, Joe Cohn got them to agree. They had another actor sitting around, nobody was using him much, so I cast him ... Robert Young. And then there was a girl named Ruth Hussey; she became the best second-lead actress Metro ever had."

"Did you ever hear of a 'B' picture that made *four* stars?" he asked. "*Rich Man, Poor Girl* went to the Capitol in New York and played there seventeen weeks! ... They paid me seventy-five thousand to write and produce it. Does that seem so enormous now? I made them Lana Turner and Lew Ayres, two major stars!

"And I had a helluva good time doing it," he added.

Chodorov shook his head. "You know, those days were really amazing. You walked down the hall at Metro, you saw names ... Maugham, Faulkner, Huxley ... It was like looking at Western literature of the 20th century! Sam Behrman, Ivor Novello ... Sid Perelman, George S. Kaufman, Dorothy Parker ... they were all there, trying to turn out scripts that would satisfy producers, who didn't understand what the hell they were reading!

"Then you'd go out to dinner at somebody's house, and you'd be sitting at a table with people whose books you'd read and admired, whose plays had been hits, and maybe even won a Pulitzer ... and all evening long, they'd be bitching about the lousy assignment they'd been handed." He grinned. "At a very fat salary, of course."

74

Wasn't it the same way at Goldwyn's studio? "Absolutely," said Chodorov. "Sam bought famous names like pieces of jewelry. What a collection ... Robert E. Sherwood, Lillian Hellman, Sidney Howard. Did that for years. You know, once when I was working on a script for Sam, and I was late ... instead of telling him the truth, which was simply that I needed more time, I concocted some cockamamie story about what had happened to me, and Sam looked at me and said, 'You know, Eddie, Maeterlinck tried that on me.' And I suddenly realized that Maurice Maeterlinck, that great Belgian, the guy who'd written *The Blue Bird*, had once been out in Hollywood working for Goldwyn!"

And hadn't Goldwyn, when he read Maeterlinck's attempt at a screen story, run out of his office to call out, in horror, "My God, the hero is a *bee!*"

Chodorov nodded. "That was Sam," he said. "I remember another time when he called me in to tell me that Thornton Wilder was bringing in a script for a conference. He had Wilder working on some classic work, I think it was something by the Russian playwright Andreyev. Never got made, of course. In comes Wilder, very gentle, professorial. And Goldwyn said, 'The trouble with the script, Mr. Wilder, is the character of the Baron.' Long pause. Silence. It got embarrassing, and Wilder finally said, 'Well, you see, Mr. Goldwyn, the inherent ... inability of the Baron relates back to his behavioral attitudes...' '*No, no, no*, Mr. Wilder,' said Goldwyn. 'The Baron, Mr. Wilder, is a man ... well, he's a ...' Long pause. Wilder tried again. He said, 'Would you concede, Mr. Goldwyn, as I feel myself, that the integral basic value of the essential psyche of the Baron —' 'No, no, no, no, Mr. Wilder! Let's get to the point. The Baron is a *horse's ass!*'"

"That, Goldwyn could understand," said Chodorov.

And Wilder?

"He found other employment, of his own," said Chodorov. "A simple little masterpiece of a play he called *Our Town*, which had no Barons in it..."

Obviously Wilder and Chodorov had one thing in common. When the Hollywood scene became too much to deal with, they returned to the theatre.

"Amen," sighed Chodorov. "Every time I got an idea for a play, back I went. After *Those Endearing Young Charms*, which was a hit, I came back and did it as a movie. Then I had a contract with Darryl Zanuck to write and produce one picture a year for Fox.

"That year, I think Fox turned out 38 pictures, and only two of them made any money. One was *Gentlemans' Agreement*, and the other was a picture that I wrote and produced, called *Roadhouse*. Which may be the only picture I did that I'm ashamed of. I only did it because one day Darryl said to me, 'Eddie, I've got to start shooting in three weeks, with the following contract people: Dick Widmark, Ida Lupino, Cornel Wilde, and Celeste Holm. Can you get me a story for those four people?' And I said, 'Darryl, we'll start shooting in three weeks.' And believe it or not, we did. With half a script! Made the rest of it up as we went along!...That was the other money maker of the year. Go figure!

"After that, I did *The Hucksters*, and Metro remade my *Kind Lady*, and I went back to New York and did another play, *Oh Men, Oh Women!* A big hit comedy...and that got made into a movie too..."

Formidable they may have been in their time, those presiders over their own feudal fiefdoms, Mayer, Zanuck, Goldwyn, Cohn, Wallis, and Warner, have all faded away into chapters of film history, assembled by prowlers through the elephant graveyards.

"All those guys I used to go to the mat with..." sighed Chodorov. "All gone. Nowadays, there are cadres of corporate-type 'suits,' followed by 'bean counters.' People I talk to out in L.A. tell me getting a picture made today is a long-term project. One guy I spoke to said 'Eddie, *any* picture that gets made today is a miracle...

"There was one guy left, Sam Spiegel. He was the last of the old timers. Finally, I had to leave him because I was running a 102 fever. Anyway, a couple of years go by, I'm in Paris, working on a play. He calls me. He's got a script for a picture, *Nicholas and Alexandra*, about the Russian Czar. He's been working on it for almost three years. Now, all of a sudden, he's got to start shooting in five weeks, and the script is no good. It lacks class...I tell him I'm busy writing a play, but he insists 'Eddie, you've got to do this for me!'

"So he sends me the script, and I read it, and it was a totally conventional nothing. Worse than nothing. It was a story about a young boy with hemophilia...and absolutely no point of view. I could see what had happened. Sam took it into his head at the beginning, years back, that this was going to be a love story... and it didn't work; there was no love story, it was just silly. But Sam just persisted, stubbornly went on, following his own vision of what it should be. And now he was desperate."

Did Chodorov accept the assignment?

"No," he said. "I didn't want to go back to running that 102 fever. When I left Sam, I said 'I'm leaving you, Sam, because you've changed your role. You were a great man to know whom to throw the ball to, and to let that guy run with it. But now you're dictating scenes, interfering in concepts... and you do not understand that you may wake up in the middle of the night thinking of something great, a wonderful scene, except that if you use that scene in the beginning of the picture, the first half, there's no second half. You do not understand the architecture of writing. It's very difficult!'

"Sam loved a painter, a guy called Vertes. Collected him all the time. I said, 'Would you stand behind Vertes, or even some lousy painter, and say, "A little more red there, please, a little more green here?" Damn right you wouldn't. So how can you do it to a writer? Do you think it's easier to write a script than it is to paint a picture? There are thousands of good pictures in the world, but very few great pictures! Or great plays!'

"...So Spiegel offered me an awful lot of money for five months work, and I must say, to my shame, I turned it down. We were going to go on his yacht, we were going to work on it together, and so on. Later on, I wrote him a four and a half page letter telling him what I thought had to be done, if he could get somebody else to do it. No use. He got an English playwright, Edward Bond, to do that."

And the result?

"Nothing! What could they do? They were trapped. Trapped by Sam's original vision. The picture ended up with those ludicrous sort of scenes — 'Lenin, my name is Trotsky, I want you to meet Stalin.' That sort of stuff."

Chodorov shook his head sadly. "Later on, I saw Sam again, and we started talking about it, and I asked him why he hadn't let a writer bring him *his* vision of the story first, and take it from there... And Sam finally said, 'Eddie, do you expect a leopard to change his stripes?'

"Well, the stripes gave me an out, and I said, 'Sam, it's not stripes, it's *spots*, you made a mistake!' But what Sam was saying was—he would rather make a half-assed picture and do it, and *he's* responsible for it, than make a great picture and *you're* responsible for it."

A simple question of ego, then?

"Exactly," said Chodorov.

"But think about this," he said a moment later, "a genius like Fellini, he has had a bunch of writers working for him for twenty years. Smart guys. They write a script, they bring it in, then he takes over. He doesn't have any ego problem; he knows when the lights go down, the film hits the screen, there'll be only one man, and that's Fellini. If it's good, fine. He does not try to win any victories in script conferences. He's much smarter than that."

To add to Chodorov's assessment, I must add the tale that was told to me by Ennio Flaianno, one of Fellini's faithful cadre of writers, when the subject of the great film *8½* came up in one of our discussions.

"We worked for many weeks on the subject of the agonies of a screenwriter, as he prepares a script," Flaianno said. "We created our entire story based on that one single idea. Obviously," he smiled, "we all knew what we were writing about. Then, when we had finally finished with our script, we brought it in to Fellini. It was the first time he'd seen any of it. He took it home overnight. Next morning, we all assembled in his office, obviously, very anxious to know his reaction. Fellini came in, beaming. He said, 'You have all done a wonderful script. *Grazie!*'

"...Naturally, we were all relieved and delighted. We asked him, did he have any suggestions? 'Ah yes, just one,' said Fellini. 'I have decided our hero is not going to be a writer. He's going to be a *director!*'"

Chodorov shrugged. "Absolutely," he said, "That's how it is with all great directors. They're smart enough to let you do your best, and when you're done, they take over. Because, in the last analysis, dammit, it *is* a director's medium."

Another brilliant screenwriter-producer, the late Nunnally Johnson, once recalled a discussion he'd had with his friend Walter Kerr, the New York theatre critic. "Kerr said to me once, very sadly, 'You film guys are so damn lucky. Those of us who work around the theatre—when that curtain comes down and the show closes on Saturday night, it's all over. The whole thing vanishes into limbo. All that's left are the programs people took home as souvenirs. But your history will last and last. Those films you made, with the stars giving their performances of the scripts you guys wrote ... they'll run and run and run..."'

That prediction was made long before the appearance of American Movie Classics and Turner Classic Movies, twenty-four hours a day, on our TV screens.

"Absolutely," said Chodorov. "You know something? I can go anywhere in the world today where, if I turn on the TV, I'll probably see a picture of mine. But of course," he added, sardonically, "do you think I get a nickel of residuals on anything that was made before 1948? Nope. That's the deal we made with the producers; can you believe how short-sighted we were? So if and when I ever get a residual check, it's usually for about sixty-eight bucks, on one of my last ones."

He grinned. "But I *do* get royalties from all my plays. The ones I was smart enough to get out of Hollywood and go back to New York and write!"

We'd talked most of an afternoon away, and we'd covered four decades of film history.

What would be the summation of his long and successful career?

He sat back in an arm chair and stared thoughtfully at the ceiling. Finally he said, "What the hell ... I guess I can tell you one thing. Even if you're a brilliantly talented craftsman, if you know the thing inside out, if you know the whole racket, if you know all the mistakes you must avoid ... *and* you like the material you're doing, you're crazy about it, you want to do it ... Still," he sighed, "the odds are greatly against you ... against doing something that will be first class. Because," he concluded, "that is the nature of the art."

Thank you, Mr. Chodorov. Your words should be printed in large letters, and posted on the walls of every film school.

And also in every executive office where cadres of studio people gather to offer writers their notes, in the process which is known as Development Hell.

EDWARD CHODOROV'S CREDITS

FILMS:

Convention City, 1933

The World Changes, 1933

Captured!, 1933

The Mayor of Hell, 1933

Gentlemen Are Born, 1934

Madame DuBarry, 1934

Kind Lady, 1935

The Story of Louis Pasteur, 1935

Barbary Coast, 1935

Living on Velvet, 1935

Snowed Under, 1936

The League of Frightened Men, 1937

Woman Chases Man, 1937

The Devil's Playground, 1937

Yellow Jack, 1938

Spring Madness, 1938

Woman against Woman, 1938

Tell No Tales, 1939

Rage in Heaven, 1941

Those Endearing Young Charms, 1945

Undercurrent, 1946

Devotion, 1946

The Hucksters, 1947

Road House, 1948

Kind Lady, 1951

Macao, 1952

Oh, Men! Oh, Women!, 1957

PLAYS:

Oh Men! Oh Women!

Listen to the Mocking Bird

Those Endearing Young Charms

Kind Lady

Cue for Passion

Wonder Boy

Decision

Common Ground

Senor Chicago

The Spa

M. Lautrec

RAYMOND CHANDLER on DIRECTORS

THE FEW (THERE ARE PROBABLY NOT MORE THAN A SCORE) REALLY GOOD directors make very few pictures. The average Hollywood director is just about competent enough to direct traffic on a quiet Monday afternoon in Pomona. But even the best directors often disfigure the creative integrity of screenplays in favor of what they choose to call showmanship.

There is an innate, permanent, and probably necessary struggle between what the director wants to do with his camera and his actors, and what the writer wants to do with his words and his ideas. When this struggle is reconciled, you may get a great picture. When it is eliminated by having both functions performed by the same man, you are much more apt to get the highest common factor of both talents. I know there are some exceptions to this, some famous ones in fact. They have, so far as I know, resulted from economic conditions which cannot be obtained in Hollywood.

…There are plenty of artistic people about. The point is in Hollywood they have to use their talents to bring in two or three million dollars.

— RAYMOND CHANDLER, *The Screen Writer*, July 1947

WRITERS and DARRYL ZANUCK

ONE DAY, THERE WAS A LONG AND ARGUMENTATIVE STORY CONFERENCE IN Zanuck's office, where Darryl and a pair of writers were struggling with a climactic moment in a love story. The sequence under discussion involved a wife, her husband, and her lover; the end result would be the death of one of these three. After endless wrangling, Zanuck stood up and rapped on the desk with his polo mallet for silence. "This is how it goes!" he ordered. "The wife is in bed; her husband comes in suddenly, and surprises her and the boyfriend. The wife reaches under her pillow, takes out a gun, and shoots him! There—now go and write it!"

One of the writers nodded and stood up. "Can I ask you one question? How did the gun get under her pillow?"

Said Zanuck, "*I* put it there!"

—LELAND HAYWARD, 1970

"HE WAS WONDERFUL TO WORK WITH," REMEMBERED WINSTON MILLER. "He didn't say 'I'm the boss, do what I say.' You knew if there was an argument, he was going to win it. But every writer loved to work with Zanuck because he respected writers, and you could talk to him, writer to writer. He ignored producers generally in conferences, he talked to the writer, which was unusual at studios. You could argue and he never threw his weight around. You'd go in and he knew your script cold. He would know every minor character, you didn't have to refresh him on anything."

—WINSTON MILLER, *The Screen Writer*

6. GLIMPSES of BEN HECHT

September, 2000

Ben Hecht by Frank Modell

THE TIME: THE MID-1970S. THE PLACE: THE SPACIOUS AUDITORIUM OF THE British Film Institute. The occasion? A long overdue tribute to the career of the legendary film director, William (Wild Bill) Wellman.

The past six days and nights had been occupied with the screenings of that veteran filmmaker's various films, beginning, of course, with his remarkable World War I classic, the silent *Wings*.

Those spectacular aerial dogfights over the battlefields of France were so close to Wellman's heart; hadn't he himself been a young veteran of those days in the battlefield skies above no man's land? And hadn't he kept on working, working steadily through all the decades he'd continued directing films, on through to his last tribute to his departed buddies, *Lafayette Escadrille*?

Those London audiences had been fortunate to witness a nonstop parade of Wellman's work, the complete oeuvre of this remarkably gifted director, one for whom such a tribute was long overdue.

Now, on this final afternoon, here in front of a packed house, here came Wellman himself, ramrod-straight, grey haired, walking out slowly onto the stage, waving and grinning as he received an ovation from these assembled film lovers, who knew that standing in front of them was a true example of Hollywood history.

"I don't make speeches, never could, unless somebody wrote me one," he announced. "But I'll try to answer your questions."

And when he sat down in a convenient armchair, there came the questions from his audience of enthusiastic British film lovers, most of them steeped in the current legend of the auteur—and if Wellman wasn't one, who was?—the French theory which posits that most films are the work of a director's vision. The final result only appears when and if the director makes it happen—with, of course, a certain amount of assistance from, say, his cast, also technical help from his faithful crew, and perhaps, that elementary road map provided by some unsung wretches, the writers.

Might Mr. Wellman explain how he managed to turn out as many as six films in one year, all stamped with his name, in those early days when he'd been under contract to Warner Bros.? "Well," said Wellman, "it went like this. You'd work on a picture for five or six weeks—six days a week … sometimes nights…We usually got Sundays off. Then I'd stagger home and go to sleep. Middle of the night, some guy on a studio motorcycle would come up the driveway to our house, pitch a manila envelope onto our porch, and buzz away. In the morning I'd open it up, and in that envelope would be my next assignment. Some script with a note from Darryl …that's Zanuck, he was running the studio then for J.L.…that's Jack Warner. And his note would say something like, "Bill, this one starts next Wednesday. You've got Lyle Talbot for your lead, and somebody like Patricia Ellis for the girl…Okay?'"

Wellman shrugged. "And that's how I got to do six pictures a year."

"Nonstop?" asked another member of his audience.

"Oh, I could maybe squeeze a couple of weeks vacation," Wellman conceded. "*Off* salary, of course."

"Excuse me, Mr. Wellman," asked another, "but didn't you have anything to do with the actual writing of those scripts?"

"Hell, no!" said Wellman, "I was too damn busy getting the pages onto film every day and not going over schedule. That kept the guys off my ass. Jack hated it when we cost him money, believe me."

"Well, who might be responsible for a script of, say, your film *Wild Boys of the Road?*" asked one dedicated film student, citing one of Wellman's early classics. "Was doing that *your* idea?"

"Hell, no, it was the writers," said Wellman. "Somebody in the story department came up with the idea, the guys sat with Darryl and wrote a script, and then, when Darryl okayed it... then it was my job—if Darryl handed it over to me—to make the best damn picture I could!"

He neglected to treat his audience to the classic Warner legend, one which involved an argument Wellman had had with his feisty boss, young Zanuck, who wasn't pleased with the pace and style with which the equally feisty Wellman was turning out scenes on some long-forgotten epic. Zanuck had been bombarding Wellman with daily memos, complaining about certain sequences, and how they appeared in the daily rushes. And Wellman had been pointedly ignoring Zanuck's complaints.

Matters came to a boil when Wellman was out on location at the Warner ranch, in Calabasas. A studio limousine pulled up, and Zanuck strode out onto Wellman's set to call a face-to-face meeting. Without hesitation, Wellman gave his cast and crew a break; the shooting stopped. Wellman then sat down in his campchair.

"What the hell is going on here?" demanded Zanuck.

"*Nothing*—until you get off my damn set!" replied Wellman.

Moments later, Darryl departed. And Wellman resumed shooting.

The questions continued. "Mr. Wellman, didn't you have *anything* to do with the selection of material?" asked yet another cineaste, trying to reinstate Wellman as an auteur. "What about a picture such as, say, *Public Enemy*? Wasn't that your idea?"

"Hell, no," said Wellman. "See, a couple of guys came in with an idea for a gangster picture, Tasker and Bright, I think, they were the ones. Zanuck snapped it up, and they turned out a helluva good script... and that's when I got into it... I *was* responsible for one thing, though; after the first couple of days, I looked at Jimmy Cagney in the rushes and I knew something was wrong—see, he was playing the leading man's pal— but Cagney was coming across stronger than the other guy! So I showed the stuff to Darryl and told him what I thought, and by God, he agreed with me... So we switched the two guys... and gave Cagney the lead— and whammo, when the picture went out, Warner had himself another star!" Wellman grinned. "Just a lucky break, I guess."

The audience was momentarily silent as the students of cinema history and the assorted film fans who'd gathered to pay obeisance to a bona fide auteur, and were now being treated to a set of pragmatic meat-and-potatoes style lessons in filmmaking, were attempting to digest crusty old Wild Bill's tutelage.

One of them tried again. "Excuse me, sir," he asked, "but you made so many different kinds of pictures, Mr. Wellman. How were you able to juggle all the styles — melodramas, and action pictures, and even romances? Wasn't it difficult to change pace?"

"No," said Wellman. "Not if the scripts were good. And believe me, they kept tossing good scripts onto my porch ... and damn it, they were a pleasure to shoot. See, back then, Warners was a good place to work; they had this story department in New York, used to dig us up wonderful material for pictures..." He grinned. "That's half the battle, guys. You get good material, it makes it twice as easy to turn out a good picture."

Once again, silence. One might even have said it was stunned. For this assemblage of 1970s film lovers to be told by this gruff old plainspoken veteran that over the years his role had been nothing much more than that of an efficient mechanic, one who'd functioned efficiently on a factory assembly line, day after day, turning out hits — not of his own vision, but based primarily on the talents of others — why, it bordered on pure heresy, did it not? So what would the French say when they heard this?

There came one more question.

"Mr. Wellman," asked another youngster, "can I ask you why it is that you made so few comedies?"

Wellman shrugged. "I guess it was because nobody ever brought me a good comedy script," he suggested.

"Ah, but you did make *one*," said the questioner. "An absolutely super comedy, in point of fact. *Nothing Sacred.*"

"Oh well, sure, I almost forgot," grinned Wellman. "I'm getting old and forgetful. See, Ben Hecht, he was the writer, he had that one all written, and he and Selznick brought it to me. David loved it, I loved it, so we cast Carole Lombard and Frederic March in it, and I guess it turned out to be a helluva funny picture, you're right about that."

There ensued a round of approving applause.

"But then," asked the persistent questioner, "Why didn't you and Ben Hecht do *another* one?"

"Good question," conceded Wellman. "Damn, I certainly wish we had! I kept waiting, but Ben never brought me another comedy...I guess old Ben was just too damn busy."

Which was certainly the truth. Ben Hecht had been busy writing for the screen, in one way or another, since 1927, the silent days—when he received that first clarion call from his old New York newspaper buddy, Herman J. Mankiewicz. "Mank" had been lured from his job in *The New York Times* drama department to come out and try his hand at writing film titles for Paramount, that thriving factory that turned out some fifty-odd pictures each year, all of which would promptly earn profits in the many theatres of the Paramount Publix chain.

The telegram Mank sent to his friend Ben Hecht, truly a symphony in pure cynicism, will long remain preserved in film history:

> Will you accept three hundred per week to work for Paramount Pictures? All expenses paid. The three hundred is peanuts. Millions are to be grabbed out here and your only competition is idiots. Don't let this get around.

Hecht, a seasoned newspaperman in Chicago, where he'd written a daily column as well as novels, and who would later be teamed with Charles MacArthur to write such major Broadway hits as *The Front Page* and *Twentieth Century*, promptly responded to Mankiewicz's siren song. And from those very early days, he began to earn considerable sums out West, either by selling stories or writing scripts beneath the sheltering Hollywood palms.

Hecht loved writing, and he loved even more being paid handsomely for his writing. From 1927 on, he would turn the film studios into his personal Sutter-type gold mine.

Mankiewicz would also provide Hecht with a brief lecture on successful screenwriting: "I want to point out to you," he instructed, "that in a novel, a hero can lay ten girls and marry a virgin for a finish. In a movie, this is not allowed. The hero, as well as the heroine, has to be a virgin. The villain can lay anybody he wants, have as much fun as he wants, by cheating and stealing, getting rich, and whipping the servants. But you have to shoot him in the end. When he falls with a bullet in his forehead, it is advisable that he clutch at the Gobelin tapestry on the library wall and bring it down over his head like a symbolic shroud. Also, covered by such a tapestry, the actor does not have to hold his breath while he is being photographed as a dead man."

"An idea came to me," wrote Hecht, years later, in his memoirs. "The thing to do was to skip the heroes and the heroines, to write a movie containing only villains and bawds. I would then not have to tell any lies."

Following his own instincts, Hecht did precisely that. His first effort in 1927, at Paramount, was *Underworld*, a story starring George Bancroft as a gangster named Bull Weed. It would be directed by the equally legendary Josef von Sternberg, and it was a major success. Hecht was off and running.

For years to come, his output for the stage and the screen would feature a constantly moving cast of raffish non-heroes and fast-talking con men, jovial villains, despotic city editors, desperadoes, their bawds, and innocent corruptible ladies — and a vast panoply of corruptors and their corruptees, always wise-cracking, customarily cynical, and constantly entertaining.

He would also keep busy peddling original stories, new and old, to producers all over town. First National bought his *The Big Noise*, while MGM grabbed *The Unholy Night*, which came from Hecht's trunk. In 1930, Paramount took *Roadhouse Nights*, and he would also sell *The Great Gabbo*, which starred Eric von Stroheim. And then in 1931, he and his partner, MacArthur, sold the film rights to United Artists for their smash Broadway success, a classic comedy of madness in a newspaper office, *The Front Page*.

Even in the midst of the Depression, Hecht thrived; he had become a very busy writer, able to commute between his home turf of Manhattan and points West. He had also acquired a young aspiring agent-to-be, Leland Hayward, who was out prospecting for clients in California.

Years later Hayward remembered those times. "I'd heard Ben could turn out a first draft at top speed. I was just a kid, scratching around Hollywood, trying to get started … hustling all over the place every day, and then, I finally came across something I hoped could work."

"There was this young oil millionaire in town, name of Howard Hughes, trying to make a name for himself as a producer. Nobody took him very seriously, even while he was finishing his first big picture, *Hell's Angels*, which was part silent, part sound.

"Anyway, I conned my way into Howard's office, and I found out he was looking for a writer to turn out a good gangster script for his next picture. He had a story of sorts, written by some guy named Armitage Trail; nobody ever heard from the guy again. So I jumped in and suggested he get Ben to do the script. I told him what a terrific writer Ben was, a big Broadway guy, how he'd been a newspaperman in Chicago, where he'd known all those various hoodlums from Capone on down personally — who could possibly be a better choice to write him his gangster picture?

"Hughes figured that Hecht might be a good idea, so I hustled back to Ben and pitched the whole deal to him. Ben wasn't impressed. He was doing pretty well on various deals — Ben always had something going — why should he take time out to work for this unknown Texas guy who wanted to be a big shot in the movies?

"But I was hungry," said Hayward. "And I wouldn't quit nagging Ben. Remember, this was in 1931, a very tough time. I was broke, and needed a client who would pay me a commission ... It was ugly; men were out of work everywhere; the only place where there was any hard cash was in the studios ... and some of them were on their way to bankruptcy ... But I told Ben this guy Hughes had real dough! Why pass it up? And I finally persuaded him by asking him how much he'd take to write this guy a script.

"Ben wanted a thousand bucks a day. 'Paid to me in cash, at 5 PM, and brought to me here at the house!'

"So I went back to Hughes, and told him I'd been able to persuade Hecht to do his script; I told him Ben's terms, and Howard didn't blink an eye. He nodded, and said 'Okay — it's a deal. But you tell Hecht I want a real tough shoot-'em-up script that'll knock the audience out of its seats, okay?'"

Such was the origin of what would become a classic gangster saga, titled *Scarface*.

"So Ben went to work," continued Hayward. "He was a hell of a fast writer — sometimes too fast. I didn't even know how fast he could go ... At the end of the first day, I went over to General Service Studios where Hughes had a dinky little set of offices; they sent me down to the

MAX WILK

paymaster's office and I signed a receipt, and the guy paid me—ten one hundred dollar bills! In those days, a load of cash, believe me."

"I carried the money back to Ben's house. There he was, typing away. I laid the ten hundreds on his desk; he handed me one for my commission, and kept right on typing away! I said 'Ben—please—*slow down.*'"

The process continued for the next few days; Hayward delivering his new client the daily greenbacks—while watching the accumulated pages of Hecht's script growing higher and higher. "I couldn't slow the guy down!" sighed Hayward. "I guess Ben had no faith that this script would ever be actually made into a picture; he figured he might as well grab as much of Hughes' dough as he could—and then run—so he could go on to other, more substantial projects!

"I came by his house next day with the cash. 'I've got an idea. I'm going to finish this damn thing tomorrow,' Ben told me. '*Ben*—for God's sake!' I said. 'Can't you slow down a little? Hughes isn't interested in you setting some sort of a speed record for writing!'"

But it was as if young Hayward had set out to flag down an army tank. Nothing stopped Hecht. On the night of the ninth day, Hayward arrived with his daily infusion of cash to find his client lounging in a chair, enjoying a highball.

Hecht waved at his stack of manuscript. "Done," he announced. "Finished the damn thing." And he handed Hayward his final payment.

"Nine thousand dollars—for the screenplay of *Scarface?*" sighed Hayward, wincing at the memory, years later. "Hughes was tickled with Ben's script; he showed it to Howard Hawks, Hawks loved it, and then they picked up this wonderful young actor from New York, Paul Muni, to play the lead. Then the picture went out and cleaned up—made a bundle for Hughes...And if old Ben really outsmarted himself on that one...he didn't care. He was on to something else. Ben was always on to something else.

"And as for getting it down in such a rush...well, that was always Ben's pattern," said Hayward. "He could turn out a first draft at top speed. Sometimes they were terrific, sometimes they weren't quite. I guess it was all those years of newspaper writing he'd done, all that racing against deadlines...Whatever it was, whoever was Ben's producer could insist that Ben

92

go back and do a rewrite, and Ben would argue about it—he hated rewriting. So he'd race through the second draft, and turn that in ... And then, if the boss remained unsatisfied, whether it was Sam Goldwyn or David Selznick, and they'd keep after Ben for another rewrite, he'd kick like a steer ... but he'd finally give in, and deliver...

"And that *third* draft," sighed Leland, "that was when Ben would usually come up with pure gold."

Fast forward, to Wellman's lone comedy success, Hecht's *Nothing Sacred*. According to Hecht's own reminiscences, his original comedy script had been turned out "in two weeks, on trains between New York and Hollywood!"

"True," agreed Hayward. "But David Selznick hated the ending."

Did Hecht come up with a rewrite?

No. His story, a typical Hechtian satire, dealt with a young lady, Hazel Flagg, who is diagnosed as having a fatal ailment which could kill her in a matter of months. Her cause is picked up by a newspaper, and her impending death becomes a national event. She is a doomed heroine, and everyone loves Hazel Flagg.

Then, it is discovered that her doctor has made a mistake. Hazel is not going to die, at least, not yet.

"Hecht's ending was that a birth of sextuplets drives her story out of the papers, and so everybody forgets about her," recalled Ring Lardner, Jr., many years later. "I was working for Selznick, along with young Budd Schulberg. Budd was out of town, and Hecht was unavailable, so David enlisted me to work on the ending with a writer, George Oppenheimer, who was then at Metro. And at the same time, he sent Ben's script to George S. Kaufman, to Moss Hart, and to Robert E. Sherwood, to see if *they* could think of an ending for Ben's script!"

The all-star talents approached by Selznick came up with nothing satisfactory.

"But luckily, *we* came up with the ending," said Lardner. "The one where Carole Lombard is on a ship ... after the newspaper has faked her funeral. Somebody comes up to her and recognizes her as Hazel Flagg, and she says 'I'm getting sick and tired of people mistaking me for that *fake!*' And it worked!"

Did Lardner receive credit? Certainly not—he was on salary, and such chores were part of his job. And did Hecht take bows for his sardonic comedy success? Certainly!

Years later, Hecht summed up his attitude towards screen writing in the biography he wrote of his constant collaborator, Charles MacArthur: "The honors Hollywood has for the writer are as dubious as tissue paper cufflinks."

Nevertheless, Hecht thoroughly enjoyed being part of that life.

"I saw Richelieu and Pocahantas and streets full of pirates," he wrote, years later, in *A Guide for the Bedeviled.* "Enamel-faced beauties in red and purple evening gowns; carpenters and wizards and Russian Dukes, poets and mud-caked jungle explorers, moguls, geniuses, pharaohs, and the Lady of Shalott—all pouring out of a cornucopia and hurling themselves into the manufacture of the world's greatest toy—the movies…

"Here in this city engaged in making a toy that was already sweeping the world clean of mah-jong sets, yo-yo sticks, and lonely evenings, was everything and everybody…Great thinkers, mighty swindlers, phantasts astride dreams as spavined as Rosinante, artists falling down stairs, poets screaming for help (I saw one catch fire in a fireplace seven feet high), millionaires who had not yet had time for a shave; here was a new-born aristocracy that had leaped seemingly out of nowhere—and over it all a promise of fame and riches unparalleled in the history of *belles-lettres.*

"…I am older and Hollywood is older, but I never enter it—even with a touch of lumbago—but that I hear again its calliopes playing and see behind its now conventionalized facades all the happy skulduggeries and zany glamour of our mutual youth. It is the only place on earth where an artist can play pirates and Indians, where an artist can sell his soul (nobody will buy it anyplace else for a plugged nickel!), where an idiot can make a fortune and a genius lose his shirt in a twinkling, where the travails and insanities of the world run always second. If God sent another flood," commented Hecht, "I promise you that Hollywood would photograph it, dub it for sound, and market it at great profit as a work of art. And rewrite it also a little, and put a happy finish on it so that it would get by at the box office."

Has anyone else ever summed up the madness of daily life in Hollywood with more accuracy—and vitriol?

But, like so many of his talented confreres who'd migrated West to sit in studio offices and take home a weekly paycheck, Hecht would soon become an expert in biting the hands that fed him, not only in Hollywood, but also in the East, which was where he and his collaborator MacArthur were presented with one of the most remarkable opportunities ever conceived of by a desperate group of production executives.

It was in the midst of the Depression when Walter Wanger, the head of production at Paramount's Astoria studios, persuaded his executive bosses to underwrite Hecht and MacArthur as the producer-writers of four productions.

It was an offer the talented pair couldn't possibly refuse; they would be their own bosses, in a business where most screenwriters arrived each morning to work on a studio assembly line.

"What a fantastic opportunity," commented Leland Hayward. "Here they were, the two wonder boys of Broadway, sophisticated, witty, talented. They could make whatever movie they wanted, write it, cast it with whomever they wanted... Can you believe anybody getting such a deal? *I* couldn't!"

It was as if the two writers had been turned into a pair of youngsters and let loose on the main floor of F.A.O. Schwartz with charge cards in hand.

But no studio, before or since, has ever been conducted precisely in such a fashion as Hecht and MacArthur ran theirs.

"When I arrived in Astoria," recalled George Antheil, the composer, "I had never scored a motion picture... My introduction to the movie business was significant and symbolic... Ben talked to me in his office, but when the subject of how much I was to get came up, he said, 'Let me introduce you to our president. He and he alone decides all matters of this kind.'

"So he took me to the room next door, which was marked PRESIDENT: HECHT-MACARTHUR PICTURES, INC., and told me to go in. I advanced to the desk where a little pinheaded gentleman in a high-wing collar was writing. He did not even look up. I advanced further, right to the desk. He still did not look up. I looked at what he was writing. He was *doodling!*

"Then he looked up and jumped right over the desk at me! He was a pinhead engaged from the local circus and took his job seriously. He always jumped right over the desk at all visitors, jabbering incoherently.

"Ben and Charlie employed him to divert peoples' minds from unpleasant questions…In their own office they had four doors with four great big photographs of nudes, blown up and placed upon these exits… On the walls of their office were huge signs, presumably to assist them in the writing of their scenarios. 'Is the public in on our secret?' said one, and 'Cut to the chase' was another. Admirable advice to any writer."

Arthur Mayer, who was handling publicity at Paramount in those demented days, reported other signs: "If it's good enough for Zukor [the head of Paramount], it isn't good enough for us!" And "We're going to make a picture a year if it takes us four years!"

"These," Mayer remarked, "were calculated to distract the attention of worried Paramount sales executives, solicitous to know when they would get their next picture, and of even more worried downtown bankers, solicitous to know when they would get their money back. The delays in production were not entirely explicable as the eminent producers Hecht and MacArthur preferred a few laughs a day to a few feet of finished film, and there was much goosing of cameramen, showgirls, and dignified visitors."

However, when the madcap pair of devil-may-care producers finally got around to turning out their first film, it proved to be very good, indeed. On a budget of $150,000, miniscule by Paramount standards even then, one of Hecht's short stories was adapted into *Crime without Passion*, which starred young Claude Rains as a criminal lawyer who mistakenly believes he has murdered his ex-mistress, played by the even younger actress, Margo.

In 1934, the picture did well in New York; the critics were impressed. But in the hinterlands (*Variety* referred to such bookings as "Stix"), it did less business.

Today, it is considered a minor classic. But not so for the next Hecht-MacArthur production.

"My first assignment for Ben and Charlie was a picture that was later advertised by a desperate Boston theatre owner as 'The Worst Picture in the World,'" recalled Antheil. "Very possibly it was that, for, try as I would, I couldn't understand the plot. Perhaps that was because Ben and Charlie changed it so often in mid-stream. Perhaps, too, it was because

Once in a Blue Moon, which was this disaster's title, had a cast of only one or two Americans; the boys had made the mistake of casting their Russian locale picture with mainly Russian-born actors!"

The film starred a Broadway comic, Jimmy Savo, whose work was mostly in pantomime; he may have been a Broadway star, but in this film, which ended up costing $350,000 or so of Paramount's cash, he proved to be no box office draw whatsoever.

Then in 1935, Hecht and MacArthur produced *The Scoundrel*, which starred Noël Coward. He played the part of a publisher based, it is said, on the publisher Horace Liveright, a true New York character. In the film, Hecht and MacArthur went into fantasy; their leading character returns to earth after his death, there to find one living person who will weep for his loss so that he may not suffer eternal damnation.

The picture got good reviews and even an Oscar for Best Original Story. More importantly, it also made a small profit. Very small.

But the fourth and final film to emerge from Astoria was a true disaster. *Soak the Rich* was released in 1936; it was a satire on communism: a rich girl falls in love with a college radical. It was nowhere near as funny as it must have seemed to Hecht and MacArthur, and it marked the finale of what had begun as a golden opportunity for the two playwrights.

Final score: two decent films, two disasters.

"I'll never know what perversity it was that caused Ben and Charlie to piss away such a golden opportunity," mused Hayward, years afterward. "Imagine being essentially your own boss. Able to do any damn thing you like, to hire anybody you want...and not be harassed by any executive who's butting into your work with notes on your ideas and your execution of them...Good Lord, that just doesn't happen in this business!...And here were these two brilliant guys we all expected so much from..." Hayward sighed. "It seemed to me, most of the effort they put in was dedicated to having themselves a good time."

Whatever it was within Hecht that drove him to be such a hedonist would also permeate his personal life. Married to an extremely bright lady named Rose, née Caylor, with whom he shared a large, rambling home in Nyack, New York, Hecht would also find time in Manhattan to amuse himself with certain other available females.

These were the post-Prohibition days, when there was a strike going on at Jack and Charlie's 21 on 52nd Street; all the waiters were out in the street, picketing the establishment.

"Ben was fond of entertaining a certain new lady friend," remembered Hayward, "and every day he'd bring her in and the two of them would occupy a front table.

"I got hold of Ben one day, and I said, 'Jesus, Ben, don't you think it's a little reckless of you, bringing that girl in and sitting her there in front of everybody? Just suppose your Rose were to come in from Nyack and catch the two of you there?'

"And Ben looked at me and said, 'Ah, come *on*, Leland, you know Rose would never cross a picket line!'"

Later, there would come a time when Hecht decided to disappear from Manhattan with a lady friend. It is not certain whether she was his companion from 21, but Hecht and his lady vanished from the scene for a considerable length of time. But not before Hecht made a prior arrangement to ensure secrecy—one that might have been one of his own plots.

Hayward's faithful and efficient secretary Kathleen Malley, one of Hecht's loyal fans, was appointed by Hecht to become his one and only contact. For the following few months she, and only she, knew where Hecht and his inamorata had vanished to; this circumstance put her in charge of any and all communications with him.

"Where the hell *is* he?" Hayward would demand, emerging from his office. "I've got to speak directly to Ben—I've got an offer he has to decide on!"

"I will let him know what you want, Mr. Hayward," Miss Malley would reply. "And as soon as he gives me his answer, I'll tell you."

And thus is how matters remained for all those months in which Hecht was gone. Until the pair returned to Manhattan, no one, save Miss Malley, had any idea where they were.

"I couldn't budge her!" sighed Hayward. "Can you imagine—my own secretary protecting my own client from *me*?"

Where had Hecht been? He would reveal it to his public with his customary bravado, when he wrote a play about his recent departure and titled it *To Quito and Back*. The play opened at the Playhouse Theatre in 1937, starring Franchot Tone and Frances Farmer.

It dealt with a fortyish writer who runs off to Quito, Ecuador, with a younger girl named Lola Hobbs. In Hecht's autobiographical work, he is confronted by the girl who asks, "Do you want to go back to her?" (meaning his wife whom he has left). "No," says the Hechtian character. "I want never to have left her."

And he did return.

He may have been received with enthusiasm by his wife, but he didn't manage to induce any from the New York theatre critics.

"We were playing across the street, at the Cort," remembers Haila Stoddard, who was then starring in *Yes, My Darling Daughter.* "We knew they'd posted the closing notice at the Playhouse. That Saturday, before the last matinee of their show, I had a visitor in my dressing room. It was Ben and he was leading a beautiful black standard French poodle, one of the most handsome, well-behaved dogs I've ever seen."

"Haila," said Hecht, "would you kindly befriend this wonderful creature? His name is Mugs, and he is most unique. He happens to be the only dog who's ever had his own membership card from Actors Equity!"

Mugs had been very much a part of the cast of *To Quito and Back,* so much so that the cast had petitioned Equity to honor him with his own card.

"I simply cannot set him adrift in New York without a play to go to, eight performances a week," said Hecht. "He badly needs the daily company of professionals. Would your cast consider taking him on, here at your theatre?"

"Well, I was enchanted by Mugs—and as always, enraptured by Ben —so I immediately agreed," remembers Miss Stoddard. "I kept him myself—who could turn down such a charmer as Ben, especially with that marvelous animal sitting there, staring into my eyes! We closed the deal on the spot—and from that day on, Mugs was a member of our company— and my life! Perfectly well behaved, always quiet backstage during the performance, and then, when we let him loose during the intermission to exercise, he'd go up and down the alley, racing away and always returning to the stage door in time for the next act!"

"Stayed with me until he died," she says. "…A constant reminder of what a thoughtful, caring person Ben could be."

"When in a writing mood, his output was enormous," recalled Herbert

Mayes, the editor of *Cosmopolitan* and *McCall's* magazine, among others. "He could spin off short stories, novels, plays, and scripts for films that proved to be spectacular successes. I think that 'The sonofabitch stole my watch!' the last line of *The Front Page*, which he wrote with MacArthur, is still the best last line I ever heard in a play...

"I had been trying to persuade him to speak to my weekly class at Columbia University. 'What could I say that your gang would want to hear?' he asked, and I said a description of his writing. 'If I told the truth, your kids would swear never to try writing. It's a terrible business!' It was not the writing itself that was so awful, he went on, but what happened when he got through. 'I'm alive and well when the typewriter is going fast,' he explained, 'but when the final paragraph or scene is done, I hate myself. I'm sure I've got a disaster.'"

No matter how he felt, in this remarkable confession, Hecht continued to turn them out, plays, scripts, short stories, newspaper columns — day after day.

"Ben didn't even bother to open his mail unless a check was enclosed," observed Mayes, "which he could determine by holding the envelopes up to the light. The story is told that a friend who had had no reply to several letters did once enclose a check, but it was a blank check. Hecht returned the blank check, but made no reply.

"I remember Herman Mankiewicz telling me about Orson Welles," said Nunnally Johnson. "Orson looked over the credits for *Citizen Kane*, and even though Mank had written the script and brought it to Welles, Welles couldn't stand having Mank's name on it. So he offered Herman $10,000 if he'd take his name off the picture. And it was tough for Herman, because he always needed dough so badly. Anyway, he anguished over it for a while, and then he went to his old pal Ben Hecht ... and asked Ben what to do about Welles' offer. Well, Ben was a realist, as always, and he said 'Herman, take his money and screw him!' Ben knew what he was doing — because later on, the Writers Guild stepped in and upheld Herman's screen credit anyway!"

Hecht's screen credits are somewhat difficult to pin down; he worked on so many films in which he was uncredited, and he also kept a stable of writers — dubbed the Hecht Factory — down in Oceanside, California, with whom he collaborated on various assignments. By Hecht's own confession, years later, he was involved in seventy movies.

An impressive list exists in the volume published in 1970 by Hecht's own Writers Guild, where there is a list of his official credits.

Sample but a few of the most outstanding, alone or in collaboration: *Gunga Din, His Girl Friday, Wuthering Heights, Angels Over Broadway, Comrade X, Tales of Manhattan, Where the Sidewalk Ends, Kiss of Death, Monkey Business, The Shop Around the Corner, Ride the Pink Horse, The Paradine Case....*

In 1952, Hecht wrote and produced—from two original stories of his own, *Actors and Sin.*

In the second story, his script based on *Concerning a Woman of Sin,* he created the character of an agent, Orlando Higgins, whom all of Hecht's friends and acquaintances could immediately recognize as his old friend and agent, Leland Hayward. Did Hayward mind being a character in one of Hecht's satiric comedies?

"Not as long as my character got top billing," said the masterful agent.

And whom did Hecht persuade to write the musical score for his film? None other than his old friend, the talented George Antheil.

"During the late '30s," Antheil recalled, "Ben and Charlie organized their own chamber music society, known as the Ben Hecht Symphonietta. I played piano, Ben played first violin, MacArthur essayed the 'Clarinet in B Flat Major,' and the other musicians included Charlie Lederer, one of Ben's best friends and often his collaborator, plus the gifted harpist, Harpo Marx.

"Our first rehearsal took place in a small room on the second floor of the house Hecht had rented. The personnel gathered and began to play. In the mist of the music, the door was suddenly opened and Groucho Marx yelled 'Quiet, please!'

"'Groucho is jealous,' said Harpo. 'He's jealous because we wouldn't let him join our group.'

"'But he only plays the mandolin,' remarked one of the other musicians. 'How do you fit a mandolin into chamber music?'

"The mystery remained a mystery until the door was opened again, and Groucho again yelled 'Quiet! You lousy amateurs!' He left the door open and stamped his angry way downstairs.... After a moment, there came a sound that raised Hecht's rented rafters — the 'Tannhauser Overture,' played by a full symphony orchestral. We rushed out to look, and there was Groucho directing, with great, batlike gestures, the Los Angeles Symphony Orchestra! At least one hundred men had been squeezed into the Hecht living room!

"...Ben finally had to capitulate; Groucho became a member of the Symphonietta!"

Sum up Ben Hecht? He spent most of a lifetime defying such analyses.

Curmudgeon? ("Los Angeles is Bridgeport with palms.") Cynic? ("In Hollywood, a 'starlet' is the name for any woman under thirty who is not actively employed in a brothel.") Idealist. ("I have written many stories about Hollywood and made much fun of its clap-trap splendors. I have criticized its whirligig castrations of the arts, its triumphs over sanity, and its coronation of buncombe. But in nearly all I have written there has been a lie of omission. I neglected to say that all these things I loved. How can you help doting on a town so daft, so dizzy, so sizzling; a town tumbling with the alarms and delights of a fairy-tale book?")

We shall, alas, not see Hecht's like again, which, although most movie-goers of today will not be aware, is our loss.

One may have to seek out some of Hecht's brilliance in, say, *Hallelujah, I'm a Bum*, with its lovely Rodgers and Hart score, sung by Al Jolson, and satirizing New York in 1933; or his fascinating thriller, *Notorious*, with Ingrid Bergman and Gary Grant, directed by Hitchcock; the rowdy epic biography, *Viva Villa*, with Wallace Beery; and of course, the battle royal between John Barrymore and Carole Lombard in *Twentieth Century* ("Lily Garland, I knew you when you were Mildred Platka!").

There are many more examples of Hecht's gifts, some of which are credited, some which he ghosted, and others done with whomever he was collaborating with down in that house in Oceanside.

It seems only proper to allow Hecht to give us his own closer. He summed it up toward the end (when he was unsuccessfully attempting to interest any of the studios in making a film written by him and based on the life of the famous California gangster Mickey Cohen):

"The mania that kept the first and second flowering of moviemakers working till they dropped; that turned every dinner party, drinking bout and love hegira into a story conference; that gave no hoot for politics, patriotism, global disturbances or anything else on earth except the making of a knockout movie; the mania that believed in movies as if God had sent them; that put the movies unblushingly beside Shakespeare, Shaw, Dostoevsky and Euripides; that regarded New York, Paris, and London as bourgeois suburbs of Hollywood; the mania that buttonholed a million of the earth's inhabitants and held them spellbound with the zaniest, goriest and most swivel-headed swarm of humpty-dumpty fables ever loosed on mankind—that mania is almost gone out of today's moviemakers.

"I'll not go on into what has taken its place."

Take a bow, Mr. Hecht.

Ben Hecht's Credits

ACADEMY AWARDS:

Underworld, 1927

The Scoundrel, 1935

ACADEMY AWARD NOMINATIONS:

Viva Villa!, 1934

Wuthering Heights, 1939

Angels over Broadway, 1940

Notorious, 1946

FILMS:

The New Klondike, 1926

American Beauty, 1927

The Big Noise, 1928

The Unholy Night, 1929

The Great Gabbo, 1929

Street of Chance, 1930

Roadhouse Nights, 1930

The Unholy Garden, 1931

The Sin of Madelon Claudet, 1931

Monkey Business, 1931

Homicide Squad, 1931

Quick Millions, 1931

The Front Page, 1931

Rasputin and the Empress, 1932

Back Street, 1932

Million Dollar Legs, 1932

Scarface, 1932

The Beast of the City, 1932

Queen Christina, 1933

Design for Living, 1933

Turn Back the Clock, 1933

Topaze, 1933

Hallelujah, I'm a Bum, 1933

The President Vanishes, 1934

Crime Without Passion, 1934

Shoot the Works, 1934

Twentieth Century, 1934

Upperworld, 1934

Riptide, 1934

Barbary Coast, 1935

Spring Tonic, 1935

Once in a Blue Moon, 1935

The Florentine Dagger, 1935

Soak the Rich, 1936

Nothing Sacred, 1937

The Hurricane, 1937

The Prisoner of Zenda, 1937

Woman Chases Man, 1937

King of Gamblers, 1937

A Star Is Born, 1937

Angels with Dirty Faces, 1938

The Goldwyn Follies, 1938

Gone with the Wind, 1939

At the Circus, 1939

Lady of the Tropics, 1939

It's a Wonderful World, 1939

Some Like It Hot, 1939

Let Freedom Ring, 1939

Stagecoach, 1939

Gunga Din, 1939

Comrade X, 1940

Second Chorus, 1940

Foreign Correspondent, 1940

I Take This Woman, 1940

The Shop Around the Corner, 1940

His Girl Friday, 1940

Lydia, 1941

The Mad Doctor, 1941

The Black Swan, 1942

China Girl, 1942

Journey into Fear, 1942

Tales of Manhattan, 1942

Ten Gentlemen from West Point, 1942

Roxie Hart, 1942

The Outlaw, 1943

Lifeboat, 1944

Cornered, 1945

Spellbound, 1945

Watchtower Over Tomorrow, 1945

Duel in the Sun, 1946

Specter of the Rose, 1946

Gilda, 1946

The Paradine Case, 1947

Her Husband's Affairs, 1947

Ride the Pink Horse, 1947

Kiss of Death, 1947

Dishonored Lady, 1947

Portrait of Jennie, 1948

Cry of the City, 1948

Rope, 1948

The Miracle of the Bells, 1948

The Inspector General, 1949

Whirlpool, 1949

Roseanna McCoy, 1949

Big Jack, 1949

September Affair, 1950

Edge of Doom, 1950

Where the Sidewalk Ends, 1950

Perfect Strangers, 1950

Love Happy, 1950

The Iron Petticoat, 1956

Legend of the Lost, 1957

A Farewell to Arms, 1957

The Gun Runners, 1958

Queen of Outer Space, 1958

The Fiend Who Walked the West, 1958

John Paul Jones, 1959

North to Alaska, 1960

Billy Rose's Jumbo, 1962

Mutiny on the Bounty, 1962

Walk on the Wild Side, 1962

Cleopatra, 1963

Circus World, 1964

Seven Faces of Dr. Lao, 1964

Casino Royale, 1967

Gaily, Gaily, 1969

The Front Page, 1974

Switching Channels, 1988

Kiss of Death, 1995

NUNNALLY JOHNSON on RESPECT for WRITERS

SOMEONE HAS SAID THAT AFTER YOU'VE FILTERED A STORY THROUGH producers, directors, and actors, you've nothing left that is suitable for any one over twelve to look at. But that isn't what we try for. Every picture produced means not stage money, or talked-about money, but real money—money taken out of a bank—and anyone who thinks we don't try to get the worth of that money is nuts.

Writers for the movies suffer a great deal because there are still geniuses in high places who, though they are unable to write anything or even spell, are continually becoming inspired. They'll yell "Somebody sharpen me a pencil!" and then they'll slit hell out of a script that a competent writer has worked on for weeks. But most of these guys are leftovers from the old silent days, and they are gradually moving on. The "idea men," most of them phonies, don't get the attention they once had. The idea man used to come busting into an office with some such remark as "San Francisco! Make a picture about the earthquake! Put a word man on it!" and for that they'd be paid a lot of dough. But dough isn't so easy to get any more.

Respect for trained writers is increasing. I think that pictures are a whole lot better as a result. The reason there are so many bad movies is because there aren't enough good writers to go around. After all, with three hundred pictures made each year, you can't find good men for all of them, and when we find them, we ask for the best they've got. Because, in general, it is the best pictures that pay off. And, like everybody else, we all want our names on stuff we are not ashamed of.

—NUNNALLY JOHNSON, *Writers on Writing*,
interview by Robert Van Gelder, 1946

7. HERE COME the BRITISH:
R. C. SHERRIFF and BENN W. LEVY

London, 1972

Poster for *The Invisible Man*, screenplay by R. C. Sherriff

IN THOSE DAYS, HOLLYWOOD HAD AN EVIL REPUTATION FOR THE WAY IT treated writers. With money galore, the heads of studios went about things in a big way, and enticed distinguished playwrights and novelists from all over Europe to come to Hollywood, but it was a dismal failure. Hollywood expected them to do what they were told, but eminent writers weren't used to that sort of thing. They were dominant in their own fields, and they expected to dominate if they turned their hands to screenplays. That wasn't any good for Hollywood, where the producers had always been bosses. It was necessary to work out a balanced schedule of pictures to meet demands for months ahead, and the producers had to decide upon the subjects. The writers were given stories that they thought were rubbish and told to make screenplays out of them. "They give you a bottle of ginger beer," one said to me, "and expect you to turn it into a bottle of champagne."

Most of them went home disillusioned and disgusted. A few stayed on because they wanted the money, but if they were given their heads, the results were too long-winded and out of shape for the screen, and they resented having their work vetted and pulled to pieces by men

111

they'd never heard of. They had their point, because when all was said and done, the Hollywood producers had no more idea how to write the script for a talking film than the writers had. They were all men groping in the dark.

Still wedded to the old technique of the silent film, Hollywood began by taking the structures that had served so well in the past and plastering them over with talk. They were like the men who made the first motor cars by fitting petrol engines to hansom cabs. All that came out of this costly first start was Hollywood's conviction that writers distinguished in other fields were no good for the talkies; they were an expensive nuisance, too arrogant and self-opinionated to fit into an industry that depended on team work.

A playwright just returned from Hollywood said "It's awful out there. They tear you to pieces, suck you dry, and throw you away like a worn-out shirt."

—R. C. SHERRIFF, *No Leading Lady,* 1968

CIRCA 1930 — SEVENTY YEARS LATER, HAS IT CHANGED ALL THAT MUCH?

"Was I induced to go out there to Hollywood?" asked Benn Levy. He chuckled. "Hardly."

He sat in a comfortable armchair in the snug drawing room of his Chelsea townhouse, forty years later, puffing on his fragrant Cuban, after-lunch cigar, an amiable middle-aged man who'd already warned me his memory was beginning to fail, a warning which proved to be patently untrue.

"The 'inducement,' as you put it," he assured me, "was totally unnecessary, because any young writer who had a normal interest in sex and money was only too ready to go to Hollywood. It was, believe you me, a happy hunting ground for both."

"…Why, thank you so much," remarked his strikingly attractive wife, Constance. She'd joined the conversation with more than a spectatorial interest; as Constance Cummings, a young film star, she'd first met Levy in California, on one of his forays; as his wife, she'd returned to London with him. And now, in the early 1970s, she had long since established herself as a major leading lady of the British stage. "…So I was merely your prey, eh?" she asked.

"From the moment I laid eyes on you, my dear," smiled Levy. "And ever since."

"Well, the feeling has always been quite mutual," she conceded.

Levy, now in late middle age, had combined a very successful career as a playwright (*Springtime for Henry, Mrs. Moonlight,* and *Evergreen* were three of his major successes) with an active career as a film writer. Later, after World War II, he'd also turned to politics and served as a member of Parliament.

Obviously, then, after all those years as a regular commuter between gray and gloomy London and far-off, sun-drenched California, he bore no resentment toward the manner in which he'd been treated as a salaried Los Angeles screenwriter?

"Lord, no!" he chuckled. "Quite the opposite, in point of fact. You see, most of us went there with a certain amount of skepticism, and that, of course, was justified. Skepticism in the sense that we didn't think we were going there to produce great art. We went out as journeymen, people who knew our jobs to a certain extent ... But rarely thinking we were going to make masterpieces ... My own view was, and still is, that until perhaps very recently, the possibility, even let alone the actuality, of a masterpiece?" He shook his head. "Never there.

"Not that it was the fault of those Hollywood moguls," he quickly added. "They weren't the offenders; they very modestly described their jobs as that of an industrialist. They were never pretentious enough to talk about it as an art."

Then who was it who did?

"Nowadays, it's the critics," said Levy. "Those chaps here and in France who're trying to find a justification for democratic theories of art. They've seized upon filmmaking as the great popular art. And they've got all their various idols ... Hitchcock and Truffaut, and so on." He shrugged. "But as for me, the only ones who were entitled to be taken seriously on any artistic level out there, at least then, were the comics. In particular, Chaplin and Keaton.

"And I believe this is partly because, although there was certainly a good deal of committee work behind their comedies, I'm sure, in the last resort, their films were the product of one man, one man's imagination, and so on. They didn't come off the usual studio assembly line ...

"Everyone who was familiar with the Hollywood set-up knew it was filled with people who thought they knew how the trick was turned." He smiled, "And some of them definitely did: people like Irving Thalberg and David Selznick, who had a remarkable run of successful filmmaking. They didn't make great pictures, that is—as I said—this was not their claim. They used the phrase 'great pictures,' but they didn't mean immortal masterpieces. They didn't think they were doing the *Last Supper* of Leonardo, or anything of the kind. They thought they were making tremendous moneymakers, and if they weren't tremendous money makers, they didn't think they were great pictures."

A picture that didn't make money was considered a bomb?

"Correct."

And a picture which made a lot of money was great—no matter how bad it was?

"Yes, absolutely!" said Levy. "And there were quite a few of those, believe me."

How could he explain the influx of foreign writers?

"In those early '30s," said Levy, "anyone who'd put pen to paper and had gained the slightest reputation as a writer, whether he was highbrow or lowbrow, was corralled and brought to Horror—" he grinned "— *Holly*wood. The competition for such people was so intense, and it brought about strange combinations of talent. Can you believe someone like Edgar Wallace, say, a great detective story writer, sitting in an office at RKO, working on the screenplay for *King Kong*?

"...There were all sorts of distinguished writers working on screenplays, no doubt about that. Aldous Huxley, Hugh Walpole, Christopher Isherwood, Wodehouse, of course, Noel Langley, Leslie Charteris, oh, and of course John Balderston, Frederick Lonsdale—he came over to do a script for his *Last of Mrs. Cheyney* very early on. Not that their work may have ever reached the screen," Levy added, wryly.

Can one explain that?

"Oh, yes," he said. "Because I suppose ninety-nine times out of a hundred, there were always previous or subsequent writers, as well!"

Wasn't that a dreadful situation for such creative types?

"I don't think so," Levy insisted. "If you're in an industry, and safeguarding your product, it is a perfectly reasonable thing to do. Certainly, it's not the way in which you can do, say, a great Bernini sculpture...by putting a group of different sculptors on it, one after the other, each one with instructions to improve a bit here, or there...But if you're making a car, or in this case, a movie, you can do precisely that sort of work. Look here, nobody knows what Aldous Huxley wrote in films, but everybody knows what novels he wrote, wouldn't you agree?"

Certainly true, except for perhaps a few cineastes who specialize in pursuing early Hollywood history.

"Such as yourself," smiled Levy.

Seen from the vantage point of a few decades later, the true irony of Levy's observation emerges; for his work in films he has little, if any status today, but as a playwright, he certainly does.

He proceeded to explore his own experiences in la la land.

"I don't think I ever did a movie as the sole author. I very often was the first. I think I may have been once or twice the last...Yes, now that I think of it, quite a few times. But you see, the final product had nothing to do with what I'd written, really very little."

Discouraging for one's ego, perhaps?

"I think it would have been," he conceded, "if I hadn't been led to expect it. You see, we went out there knowing how the process operated, and we got what we expected. One's self protection was that one did as good a job as one could, to satisfy one's own conscience...And if the producers didn't want to use our best, you could then tell yourself, well, you know, that is not my fault."

He sighed, and thought for a moment. "Of course, you came away at the end, you asked yourself, 'Why have they ever engaged me again?' Which they did, year after year. And I believe the reason must have been I was always leaving. After three months—always. I used to do three months' solid work, and then whatever offers my agent would bring to me, I'd say, 'No, I do not want to come back until later.' It wasn't really a tactic, you see. I was afraid of being sucked in and then becoming a little tool on some other man's big machine. That could be rather damaging."

In what way?

"Well, it was damaging to certain writers, who stayed there too long and too continuously," he remarked. "It didn't help them in their own work, not at all."

Wasn't it a constant tactic of someone like L. B. Mayer who, if he wanted to keep one of his newly arrived talents under his long-term control, would persuade the newcomer, be he an actor, or a writer, to go find himself a large Beverly Hills home, with the paternal blessing of Mayer, who would help the newcomer find a large mortgage? Once the mortgage was in place, the new owner would not only be working for Mayer, but also to pay down that long-term mortgage.

"Oh yes, absolutely," nodded Levy. "A rather insidious ploy. But then, one mustn't forget what a very luxurious lotus-eating life it was we all led there. You know, there were the pools, and the tennis, and the easy hours, and all those parties..."

"As well as the beautiful girls," his wife reminded him.

Levy smiled amiably. "Only until I met you, dear."

Had he first journeyed to California when sound films came in?

"Oh no, after," said Levy. "When they were becoming literate out there, and they needed dialogue from we British writers...or so they thought. No, for my very first film project I worked here in England, where I did the 'sound.'"

Sound? Would that be a euphemism for "dialogue"?

"Yes, I have lapsed into 1930-ism, I'm afraid," he apologized. "I did the 'sound' for Alfred Hitchcock's first talkie over here in London...A film called *Blackmail.* Then I went over to New York, where I had one or two plays open on Broadway, one of which was a success, *Mrs. Moonlight*— and after that, I could spend my winters out in California."

In those early days when there weren't the constant traffic jams, when the Hollywood hills were not crowded with developments, and one's life moved along at a far, far slower pace. The rest of the country may have been suffering from the Depression, but there were weekly paychecks available in the studios.

"Having a hit play in New York didn't hurt," he said. "They did pay me a lot of money."

At any particular studio?

"Well, I was at Universal, Paramount, Metro...Was I ever at RKO?" he mused. "I'm not certain I was."

"Yes, you were dear," said Mrs. Levy. "That was where I first met you."

"Ah yes," said her husband. "I remember I found you at RKO ... But was I working there, or merely following you?"

"I think, in between following me, you were making a film there," she replied.

"I don't remember ever having an office there..." he mused. "No, I must have just been following you, my dear."

"That's a very strange angle, my dear," said Mrs. Levy. "I've always remembered that I was following *you*."

"Lucky for me," said Levy.

"Doesn't he write wonderful dialogue?" observed his wife, affectionately.

Why were so many British writers attracted to Universal in the early '30s? Or was it vice versa?

"Oh, that had to be because of James Whale," said Levy. "He had been brought out to do the film of *Journey's End*, R. C. Sherriff's play ... and then I came out to do one with him, *Waterloo Bridge*, and after that I did a mystery film called *The Old Dark House*, which was based on a novel by J. B. Priestley."

A film which still stands out as one of the creepiest horror films ever turned out at Universal, a studio which was famous for that genre.

"Well, that of course is because of Charles Laughton," said Levy. "He gave such a frightening performance ... Charles had been in a play of mine in England. Of course, in those days, he was always given to overacting a bit, wasn't he?" Certainly an understatement.

And then, on to MGM. Which unit did Levy work for there, Thalberg's or Selznick's?

"I did a script of *Prisoner of Zenda* for David," said Levy. "But I don't think I ended up with the final credit ... that went to Donald Ogden Stewart."

What was it like, working for Selznick as a writer?

"Well, with any picture, remember this, in the final stages somebody has to say 'Make it.' And it certainly was never the writer, nor was it the director, because the ultimate hiring and firing of him — or them — lay with the producer. And although there was an awful lot of committee work ... which I always thought of as confabulation ... Much more confabulation than is healthy, believe me. Because one does not create a masterpiece by committee ... It's never been possible. Nevertheless, in the last resort, there was always a final author, a final director ... but theirs was *not* the final word. That was *always* the producer's.

"And," Levy said, "if he were somebody like David, or a Thalberg—although I never worked for him, but I imagine it was exactly the same—they were the men who took their own responsibilities. They had plenty of courage, and boundless energy ... and they were willing to gamble, to sit there in judgment, in complete self confidence ... They had to."

Would the same apply to someone like Zanuck?

"Absolutely," said Levy. "Although I never worked for him, either. But you see, in each instance, for these men, it was an all or nothing roll of the dice. And they were doing it all the time, every night and every day. They never thought of anything else."

But indeed, if they produced a real disaster, wasn't there always the fallback position, the insurance against loss? At MGM, Fox, Warners, or Paramount, weren't their own chains of theatres waiting to play off the stinkers, and to bail the studios out?

"Of course, but after the government moved in and forced the studios to dissolve their ties with their theatres, that changed everything," observed Levy. "If you make a bad film today, you can lose everything, eh?"

(In 1972, when we spoke, perhaps. But since that time, the studios have developed all manner of ways in which to recoup losses from bad first runs in theatres, such as video sales and rentals, cable and foreign sales, and who knows what other form of technology will follow after DVDs, which can now be played on PCs and laptops.)

"There are other changes since those days in the '30s and '40s," said Levy. "I think nowadays there are many more films that can be taken seriously. Very often they're just made on a shoestring by little fringe groups, and so on ... Sometimes they're as big as *A Clockwork Orange* [the Stanley Kubrick film then running in England] ... which I must say could never have been made under the sort of discretion we operated in, during my years in Hollywood."

That period when Levy functioned as a screenwriter will obviously go down in history as the most inhibited era of filmmaking ever known.

He sighed, remembering years back when the Hays office, later the Breen office, rigorously censored the content of every film emerging from the studios. "All day long we dealt with it—the constant inhibition— 'Jesus, you can't do that—what'll the folks in Oshkosh say?'

"…Most scripts were written with fear and trepidation.…Every line, every page, scrutinized; every motivation questioned. All those arbitrary rules, you know: the villain has to get his just deserts, a wayward girl must pay for her sins…Sex was never even hinted at, even by married couples." He shook his head sadly. "It was a set of values which were truly uncanny. You know, in retrospect, the simple fact that one was able to steer one's story through all these waters, and still manage to reach the opposite shore with a completed script…It still astonishes me."

How *did* one do it?

"Well, you see, it was a game," said Levy, smiling. "One really had to treat it as such."

A "game"?

Of course. Was it not Zanuck who'd developed his own sly technique for skirting around the Hays office censors? He would consciously have his writers add ten or twelve "blue" lines—double meanings which he knew would be considered offensive…And then the script would be sent to the Hays office, where it would be read, and Zanuck would get back a detailed letter ordering him to remove all the blue lines. At which point he would negotiate; fight for four or five of the offensive lines, and trade with the Hays people. "Well, I'll take *that* one out if you'll let me keep *this* one in…" went his game.

"Of course!" agreed Levy. "And then he would end up with the four or five lines that he'd wanted to keep in from the beginning!

"Yes, it was his version of the game," he said. "I thought of it more as croquet, playing on a field, going all through the various hoops, in and out, avoiding being tripped up…It was a game you played as well as you could. Otherwise, no game is worth playing, is it?"

Screenwriting as a highly skilled game, then?

"And not worth playing, if you fool around…But then, of course, they didn't expect your best. If you gave them your best, they didn't use it. What they wanted was your skill…" He waggled a finger. "Remember, your skill is only a tiny part of your real contribution as a writer. Skill is something far less easily defined; it's made up of your flair, your reactions to humanity…not even your knowledge, because it's something more important than mere knowledge, I think…and," he added, "if you're any good, you've got things that are indefinable, and which are only a source of embarrassment to a film magnate. But they *did* want your skill, and they wanted to use it."

Would that apply to such a perfectionist as, say, David Selznick?

"Oh, absolutely," said Levy. "He wanted to use one like a pen. And he was very good at it, you know."

A pen?

"Oh, yes, indeed," said Levy. "He had a whole collection of different colored pens on his desk, you see. One of them marked Vincent Lawrence, one of them marked Donald Ogden Stewart, one of them marked Benn Levy…and so on."

Would one of the pens be marked Ben Hecht?

"Oh absolutely! And then he'd go to work, assembling the different bits and pieces, colors, going from pen to pen…putting them together…and eventually, he'd then come out with a very saleable product."

Levy's analysis of Selznick's method would also explain the endless stream of daily Selznick interoffice memos to his writers, directors, and all the other technicians involved in his productions.

In one of said interoffice memos, one discovers Selznick's encounter with the British novelist, Hugh Walpole (as earlier reported by Sidney Buchman). Walpole had delivered script pages for an adaptation of Dickens' *David Copperfield*, and when Selznick had read them, he complained that most of what Walpole had provided him wasn't really Dickens. He accused Walpole of interpolating his own style of writing with that of Dickens! And according to one of the recent Selznick biographies, in a memo which he sent his British import, he kept on insisting, "Just use Dickens, you know, take the lines out of Dickens, they're good enough, we don't need to improve on Dickens!"

Levy shook his head sadly. "Wrong color pen, you see. How poor Walpole must have suffered in such a situation."

True enough, but when Walpole departed from California to return to the welcoming shores of Great Britain, he took away a considerable amount of money for his troubles, didn't he?

"And, one hopes, went back to being his own man," conceded Levy. "But he certainly wasn't as fortunate as I was. Mine was the classic happy ending. I not only came home with the money, but I also won the girl..."

Both he and his wife smiled fondly at each other.

"Are you *sure* I worked at RKO?" he asked her.

Benn Levy's Credits

FILMS:

The Informer, 1929

Blackmail, 1929

Kitty, 1929

The Temporary Widow, 1930

The Gay Diplomat, 1931

Waterloo Bridge, 1931

Transgression, 1931

Lord Camber's Ladies, 1932

The Old Dark House, 1932

Devil and the Deep, 1932

Unfinished Symphony, 1933

Topaze, 1933

Evergreen, 1934

Springtime for Henry, 1934

Melody in Spring, 1934

The Dictator, 1935

Desire, 1936

R. C. Sherriff's Credits

ACADEMY AWARD NOMINATIONS:

Goodbye, Mr. Chips, 1939

FILMS:

The Toilers, 1919

Journey's End, 1930

The Old Dark House, 1932

The Invisible Man, 1933

Badger's Green, 1934

One More River, 1934

Windfall, 1935

Dracula's Daughter, 1936

The Road Back, 1937

The Four Feathers, 1939

That Hamilton Woman, 1941

This above All, 1942

Stand by for Action, 1943

Forever and a Day, 1943

Odd Man Out, 1947

Badger's Green, 1948

Quartet, 1949

Trio, 1950

No Highway, 1951

Home at Seven, 1952

The Dam Busters, 1954

Storm Over the Nile, 1955

The Night My Number Came Up, 1955

Aces High, 1976

ANITA LOOS on ALDOUS HUXLEY

OF COURSE, WHEN MGM WAS GOING STRONG, IT HAD PRACTICALLY EVERY English writer in the world. I remember walking into the studio one day with Aldous Huxley, and we looked up at the directory of offices, and Aldous said, "Look at that directory. Every great writer from England and America is on there. How can we make the pictures so bad?"

...Actually, the pictures weren't bad. But we thought they were.

—ANITA LOOS, *People Will Talk*, interview by John Kobal, 1985

8. THANK YOU, HEPBURN and BOGART:
JOHN COLLIER

London, 1972

John Collier by Arnold Roth

"Author John Collier is crazy as a hoot owl. But perched on the gnarled limb of satire, he blinks down with dry wisdom at a world much crazier than he," said a *Time* reviewer.

The works of John Collier are entertainingly wild and wonderful.

They are not an acquired taste. Collier acquires *you*, and rest assured, once he has, you will remain his faithful reader. Go, seek out *The Touch of Nutmeg*, or *His Monkey Wife*, *Defy the Foul Fiend*, *Presenting Moonshine*, and his ultimate collection of short stories, *Fancies and Goodnights*. And let yourself be acquired. If your library does not have him reposing on a shelf, go directly to your nearest book store and begin with anything you can locate which bears his name.

You will never regret so doing.

Another reviewer characterized Collier as "collector of demons, connoisseur of jinn, and an old acquaintance of the devil himself."

It is extremely difficult to equate the same John Collier who induces such reviews, whose works are easily as witty as say, Saki, as ironic as anything by O. Henry, and certainly as fanciful as any flight of fancy by Roald Dahl, with the same John Collier who served out a decade or so of travail, earning his living by screenwriting in Hollywood and London, during the '40s and '50s.

But he was most definitely there, doing time at RKO, and working for Alexander Korda in London, Irving Thalberg at Metro, and tilting with Jack Warner out at Burbank. He even wrote a film for Sam Goldwyn (which he admits he and Goldwyn agreed upon; it was not very good).

We met in 1973, in his comfortable London cottage; shall we call it his digs? And he began to recall what it was like, back in those days when he was merely another one of that coterie of transplanted Brits, authors, playwrights, and lyricists who served their time out in sunny California, trying to master the art of writing for the American screen.

It was the usual London late spring afternoon. Grayish blue sky, clouds obscuring the sun. We sat in the cozy living room … and then, without warning, a fitful beam of sunlight came through one of the windows, its beam brightening up the carpet.

"Good heavens," said Collier. "That must be the sun. It's not due for several months. Pay it no heed; it will go away shortly."

"Not a bit like the California sun, is it?" I observed.

"I think I prefer the London one … whenever it appears," said Collier.

"Any particular reason?"

Collier shrugged. "The California sun is a Lorelei," he said. "It lures you out there … and then you're lost."

Was it because so many writers came out to L.A. thinking "I'll take a little money, I'll survive; and then I'll use that money to write something of my own"?

"Ah, yes," said Collier. "That is definitely part of it."

And then most of them just ended up on the beach?

Collier smiled. "But I ended up there too. However, it was a different beach. It was in Cassis, in France, and I went there in order to buy a boat. This would be back in the '30s … I saw a fishing boat I rather liked, and I wanted to buy it. They wanted 7,000 francs. And I wondered where on earth I could find that much money. And would you believe, right then, some little girl came riding up on a bicycle to hand me a telegram…. It was my London agent wanting to know, would I go to Hollywood to work for eight weeks, at $500 per week? And how could one possibly say no to that? In 1935, that was a huge amount of money."

So he accepted and bought the boat?

"No, I told the Frenchman I'd be back, and I wanted him to wait for me...And I went out to California, and they were waiting for me. Delightful experience. A picture called *Sylvia Scarlett*, at RKO. George Cukor was the director.

"I'd scarcely seen a motion picture in my life; I didn't know a thing about screenwriting. In point of fact, it was something of a mistake. Hugh Walpole had told George I'd be right for the job. George thought Hugh was talking about Evelyn Waugh...He was very surprised when I showed up, and I *wasn't* Waugh!

"But Cukor put up with it as well as he could, and he was very pleasant about my working for him...and a rather amateurish film emerged... Hepburn and young Cary Grant...But it did have bits that weren't bad. Luckily, they put me together with a collaborator, Mortimer Offner, who was a very witty and good writer. He helped me struggle through the structure...For I didn't know what made a film good at all...Believe me," Collier said, shaking his head, "there was never anyone in Hollywood at that time who knew less about writing motion pictures!"

Years later, in a history of RKO, *Sylvia Scarlett* is listed as "one of the most bizarre films ever produced by a Hollywood studio. Hepburn masquerading as a boy; her wooing by men and women was supposed to be funny, but didn't play that way. Producer Pandro S. Berman, who was the head of RKO at that time, was so horrified by the audience's violent antipathy when the film was first screened, that he told Hepburn and Cukor he never wanted to see either of them again! He later calmed down, even though at the box office the film was a complete disaster, losing $363,000—a very tidy sum in those dark Depression-era days."

Nowadays, six decades later, more sophisticated audiences enjoy *Sylvia Scarlett*. It enjoys a cult following among cinema buffs. A current review lists it as "off-beat, charming, comedy-drama." In its day, however, the word around Hollywood was that it was the worst "A" picture ever released by RKO.

"So I left, and went back to England," says Collier.

Didn't anyone ever ask him for an original story? "Not at all. At the time, except for a very few people, nobody knew who the hell I was...I mean, I'd had a few short stories published in *The New Yorker*...those people knew me, but out in California, there were very few who'd even heard of my work. Besides," he added, smiling, "after reviews such as RKO got, who would want to investigate my work?

"So I left and went back to England, and then I did another year's work on *Elephant Boy*, for Korda."

And what about that French boat he fancied at Cassis?

"It was there, but I still couldn't afford it. Anyway, Korda took me into a projection room, and we sat there watching hours of film that had been shot in Burma...without the advantage of any script! Just a director with his crew, shooting film of elephants. So we saw elephants coming this way, going that way, charging, retreating...Endless elephants!

"...And there were some shots of a little boy, about three feet tall, a charming little creature. That would be Sabu. Very small at the time. Later grew to become five foot ten or so, and very fat...

"Korda and I saw all this huge amount of film...and after about three hours of it, he began to utter hideous cries! What could he possibly do with all this goddamned film?

"So, very tremblingly, I said—after all, he was Korda, the legendary producer—that I thought it might be possible to intercut little scenes between the elephants, so that we might get a story line. It really wouldn't be that difficult to do...and although it made for a very primitive story line, it nevertheless did end up making Korda a coherent motion picture! One which, I may add, made a certain amount of money for him...and a star out of that little boy, Sabu."

Then Collier returned to California. "This time I went to work for Irving Thalberg, at Metro. I had a wonderful time with him. I'm certain he realized how completely ignorant I was, and he took that for innocence rather than ignorance, and he was always pleasant with me, and very patient."

Which film was Thalberg working on?

"Oh, this would be an original story. It seems he had Charles Laughton for it; he wanted to do a film about a London policeman, a 'bobby.' Laughton had just been the star of *Mutiny on the Bounty*, and he'd made a huge success, and as a result, he could call his own tune for anything... and this is what he wanted to do. So I was hired...and they put me up in a huge rented house in Palos Verdes Estates...and at last, I did get my boat!... Not in Cassis, but down in Santa Monica... And everything was going along swimmingly. One day Thalberg said, 'Well, this story is all right... Why don't you take this story and go across to England and see Laughton? How much shall we pay you? What would you like?'

"Well, I told him 'I can't take any money,' because I had done nothing. The story was just hastily worked out, in the intervals of enjoying myself by sailing up and down the California coast. I told Thalberg, 'I can't take any more of your money on this thing. I could go and see my old father in England, and I would also talk to Laughton.' And so I went, and *did* talk to Laughton... Believe me, that's when I earned the money!"

Laughton was difficult?

Collier nodded. "Considerably. Alas, while I was in England, Thalberg died. Very hard luck for me, because the moment the emperor died, all his slaves were stabbed... They went through the studio getting rid of all of Thalberg's people. I was a relatively minor part of the bloodletting. remember it was Sam Marx, the head of the story department, who informed me there would be no further need of my services at Culver City."

Collier did return to Metro, but not until 1942.

"George Cukor wanted me to work on another picture, one that was based on an old French play, thirty or forty years old; it had been done before, and they wanted to remake it, this time with Norma Shearer—she was, of course, Thalberg's widow, and it would be her final film. It was such a typically French play, it didn't adapt well for America, and I should have seen that. I'm quite sure I must have known it when I took the job, but working with Cukor was such a good experience, I never did anything but listen to him, and learn."

So a bad picture was, in fact, a learning period?

"Absolutely," said Collier. "Cukor was a wonderful director for writers because one would be writing for him. There may have been a producer, in fact there was, but he didn't appear during the preparation process..." He sighed.

"I still wish I'd had enough sense to let Cukor teach me more. But at that time, I was too ignorant, and I suppose, too obstinate to take advantage of such a wonderful opportunity to learn about filmmaking. Cukor was a man of great talent and wonderful expressiveness. He would be the person from whom one could acquire a great deal of pragmatic knowedge

... especially about actors and acting. Which, for a writer, was enormously helpful.

"And then, of course," he sighed, "when the job with him ended, and it was a foolish, bad film, there came the period of recrimination."

Self-incrimination?

"Oh yes, indeed," said Collier, sadly.

But it was a factory town, and one had to take the next job which came down the assembly line, correct?

"Oh yes," he agreed. "Because there was always money dangling in front of writers, not only me, but all the other Brits who'd been summoned out to California. The first wave of 'cricket players,' such as R. C. Sherriff, and Frederick Lonsdale, and don't forget James Hilton, with his *Lost Horizon*, and later on John Van Druten, and Christopher Isherwood."

And wasn't Ivor Novello, the playwright, summoned to Metro and put to work on *Tarzan* pictures?

"That was the corrupting influence of Hollywood," he said. "The fact that most people there, however high their salaries, were rather in need of another job. And it was sufficient pressure on them to make them take on the things they never should have taken on ... which they didn't do well, and ultimately harmed themselves and everybody else."

Which happened to Collier?

"Oh yes," he said, fervently. "Oh yes!"

He shook his head sadly. "Horrendous experiences, not because of what any other people did, but because I knew I was trying to do something I couldn't do!" Then Collier smiled sadly. "It was a question of making a sow's ear, not out of a purse, but out of the wrong sow's ear.

"Think of it," he remarked. "Someone like Aldous Huxley, for example. Can you imagine Huxley being called in by a major producer to work on a script about Lou Gehrig, the baseball player?"

No. It did somewhat boggle the mind, even the mind of someone who has heard dozens of lunatic Hollywood anecdotes.

"Oh yes, it was Sam Goldwyn," said Collier. "He'd evidently had so many writers working on his picture *The Pride of the Yankees* for Gary Cooper, and he wasn't happy with the work they'd done, so he decided that perhaps it was because American writers knew too much about baseball to write about it effectively ... If you can follow that logic."

It seemed somewhat complex.

Collier nodded. "So Goldwyn called Huxley's agent and insisted that he arrange a meeting for him with the noted author. He instructed the bewildered agent, 'Tell Huxley I need a new slant on it!'"

Collier shook his head in wonder. "Huxley was British and knew absolutely nothing about baseball. He was so nearsighted that he could not even follow a yacht race. He was completely averse to violent exercise, even as a spectator ... and he should consider working on the life of Lou Gehrig?"

And did Huxley come to the meeting with Goldwyn?

"As I heard it, he did," said Collier. "He came, he listened, and he left."

During all his years out there, what about Collier's own work?

"I think," he mused, "that I did write one story while I was there. In those days, and I don't exactly know why, I did various other things but somehow story writing got switched off."

Would it possibly be the pressure of being in a factory town, where everything which an author might write was customarily written with an eye for what the author's agent, or some producer who'd read it, might think?

"I'm not sure," said Collier. "It wasn't exactly the pressure. I think I turned off my creative impulses myself... But later on, I realize now, there is that factor that if one were there, and one was going to write twelve words, and if one wrote those twelve words for a film, then one would get *x* thousands of dollars... and if one wrote them for anything else, be it stories, or novels, or articles... one would only get *x hundreds* of dollars."

He nodded. "And this operates even with people who are not in urgent need of those dollars."

Another author, Irving Wallace, had once suggested to me that very little, if any, creative writing could be done in Beverly Hills. Wallace lived in Westwood and insisted that an author must never go below that town. "If I cross that invisible line," he said, "I'll be in Hollywood, or available to go out to the Valley, and I won't do any writing of my own. Below Westwood, you could be trapped into writing a movie like *Sincerely Yours,* with a leading man like Liberace!"

Of course, nowadays, Westwood is far too close. In order to be safe, one must go farther out, to Montecito perhaps.

Did Collier work for Goldwyn?

"Yes, I did a picture for him called *Roseanna McCoy*, but I'm afraid neither of us liked it very much. Goldwyn was pleasant enough, but I didn't learn anything from doing that script."

And Jack Warner?

"I had a long period there, around 1946 or so; I worked for Henry Blanke, who was an excellent producer, whom Warner used to browbeat all the time. There was one picture I did called *Deception*, with Bette Davis and Claude Rains... That wasn't very good, either. But then a remarkable thing happened. They put me to work on a screenplay based on C. S. Forrester's *The African Queen*."

"Warner had some idea it might make a picture for Bette Davis, with someone like John Mills playing opposite her... A very English sort of story, which is why they gave it to me. I just took Forrester's excellent story and it became very simple to turn it into a screenplay.

"So I spent time working on the script, and finally I turned it in, and it went up to Warner, who read it, and said 'Three million budget for *two* people—in a *boat? No way!*' and he proceeded to fire me."

Another ugly experience?

Collier beamed happily. "Oh no, not at all, not at all! What then happened is, Warner would discover, to his horror, that Bette Davis had the right in her contract to preempt any script the studio had—which meant, of course, the studio would have to *make* it—with *her!* When Warner realized she might in fact do this, he had to get rid of the script immediately, and so he ended up selling an option on it to me!"

Why Collier?

"It seemed like a good idea at the time," said Collier. "Warner was willing. Fortunately, I didn't have enough money to buy it outright, but I did have the money to put down on the option... which would later save my life with the income tax people, because the whole thing became a capital gains tax... I had a very shrewd attorney, thank heaven."

So Collier was in control of his own script, and the rights to it?

"Yes, and I sold my option to Sam Spiegel... and then he made a deal with United Artists, and hired Katharine Hepburn and Humphrey Bogart, and John Huston to direct, and I proceeded to become rich, because not only did I have a very large sum paid to me up front, as they say, but I also had ten percent of the picture's gross, and for the last ten years I have made a great deal of money."

In the archives of the Harry Ransom Humanities Research Center, in the collection of the works of James Agee, who did the final adaptation of *The African Queen,* one can find a letter from John Collier addressed to his British publisher, Hamish Hamilton, dated October 9, 1951, in which Collier wrote:

> I have served a ten-year term in this deplorable place and am now extricating myself and retiring to Mexico, where I intend to devote my ill-gotten gains to learning how to write without the distraction of economic pressures.

"All true," said Collier. "And one supposes thanks are due in absentia to quite a few people, eh? Jack Warner, who used to bore us all with his reminiscences of his war experiences, and Bette Davis, who will never know how much I owe her... And we certainly mustn't forget good old C. S. Forrester, eh?"

So Mr. Sam Spiegel got a major success, Katharine Hepburn and Humphrey Bogart earned kudos for their performances, James Agee got an Academy nomination for his work on the the script he'd inherited from Collier,[2] John Huston, in between his hunting forays into the jungle, earned bravos for his direction. While we, his readers, are the fortunate recipients of a decade or so of Mr. Collier's excellent short stories, written while he had no further economic problems.

So, there is something to be said about the uses of the cliché Hollywood happy ending, isn't there? "Indeed," commented Mr Collier. "When it works, it works exceedingly well!"

IT SHOULD BE ADDED THAT COLLIER DID RETURN TO SCREENWRITING, once in 1955 when he wrote the script for *I Am a Camera,* based on

[2] In conversation with me in 1972, Peter Viertel said, "Agee got credit on *African Queen* but actually, I rewrote the script with John Huston. Agee never wrote much for the movies... You ask John Huston sometime. Agee was a wonderful writer but he wrote his own thing. He wasn't really a movie writer."

Christopher Isherwood's *Berlin Stories*, and then a decade later when he worked with Millard Kaufman on a film called *The War Lord*, which starred the future head of the National Rifle Association, Charlton Heston.

On those two, it could be said he batted .500.

John Collier's Credits:

FILMS:

Sylvia Scarlett, 1935

Elephant Boy, 1937

Her Cardboard Lover, 1942

Deception, 1946

Roseanna McCoy, 1949

The Story of Three Loves, 1953,
    segment "The Jealous Lover,"
    "Equilibrium," and
    "Mademoiselle"

I Am a Camera, 1955

The War Lord, 1965

Some Call It Loving, 1973

ON EVELYN WAUGH

In February 1947, Waugh traveled to Hollywood to discuss with MGM the possibility of producing a film of his novel *Brideshead Revisited*, published in 1945. The film died when censors refused to allow divorce to be depicted.

Meanwhile, Waugh did little to endear himself to Hollywood people. An employee of MGM, writing Waugh's agent in 1947, reported that only she and her husband found the Waughs charming and appreciative. To all others, she reported, "Evelyn has been so constantly arrogant and rude... as to have left a trail of bloody but unbowed heads behind him. Some of this, I gather, has been utter mischief on his part and some of it has been complete misunderstanding of his particular variety of humor and wit."

Waugh liked Hollywood as little as it liked him, and he next exercised his "particular variety of humor and wit" by turning his experiences at Forest Lawn cemetery into his novel *The Loved One* (1965).

Which, ironically enough, would be made into a film in 1965, with a screenplay by Christopher Isherwood and Terry Southern... by the somewhat masochistic MGM!

JOHN HUSTON and ALLEN RIVKIN: "THE MALTESE FALCON"

JOHN HUSTON AND I WERE OFFICE MATES AT WARNERS—SHARED A secretary between us. One day he came in, tossed a book on my desk, took a stance, pointed a finger at the book and said "Kid, Warner said if I could get a screenplay out of this Dash Hammett thing, he'll let me direct it."

"He's already made it once," I reminded John.

"Never used the book the first time. You and I—we'll do this screenplay, huh, kid? Read it?!" I did. John was right. The first *Maltese Falcon* hadn't touched the story Hammett had written. I went into John's office to give him my reaction. "Let's go," I said, eager for another assignment.

"Fine, kid, fine. But first, before we do that—let's get it broken down. You know, have the secretary recopy the book, only setting it up in shots, scenes, and dialogue. Then we'll know where we are. Okay, kid?"

"Fine with me," I said.

About a week later, John ambled into my office, looking very puzzled. "Goddamnest thing happened, kid," he said, giving each word a close-up. My eyes asked what. "Something maybe you didn't know," he said. "Everything these secretaries do, a copy's got to go to the department. This *Maltese* thing our secretary was doing, that went there, too."

"That's routine," I said.

"But the department has to send everything to Warner—and he reads it!" John said. The look on his face said that Warner was a Peeping Tom, invading our privacy. "He read this Hammett book we had broken down, and he just called me on the phone," John said.

Now I really got worried. "Are we closed out," I asked, "for getting this done without any okay from anybody?" "Closed out, hell!" he boomed. "Warner said he wants me to shoot it—and I start next Monday!"

—ALLEN RIVKIN AND LAURA KERR, *Hello Hollywood*

9. REFUGEES in RESIDENCE:
BILLY WILDER

Los Angeles, 1972

Billy Wilder by Robert Andrew Parker

SHOULD YOU WISH TO KNOW ABOUT HOLLYWOOD HISTORY FROM THE '40S
on, as told to you by a gentleman who was responsible for making a great
deal of it, you should sit and listen to Billy Wilder. And in between his
anecdotes and witticisms, which tumble out in a fascinating stream, you
will learn a lot.

It was in 1972 that I tracked the master down.

I was interested in finding out about all the various refugees, those
European directors, producers, musicians, and writers who found themselves in peaceful Southern California, safe from Hitler's brutal hordes, but
for the most part unable to cope with their sunny new surroundings.

Who else but Wilder, himself a refugee from Vienna, then Berlin, and
finally from Paris, who had adjusted to the American film industry with a
vengeance, would know from his firsthand experience about this long forgotten chapter on the arrival of such writers and authors and playwrights
in Hollywood?

His collaborator, I. A. L. Diamond, one of the most witty screenwriters
of those years, had promised me he'd open the door to Billy, and he was as
good as his word. Thus, when I made it to Los Angeles, I was summoned

143

to Wilder's office in one of the buildings at the old Samuel Goldwyn
Studios. It was far from lavish: a pair of small rooms in one of the old
buildings. Since there weren't too many others around, no phones ringing,
it was an ideal place to schmooze.

Since Wilder had already been briefed by Diamond as to my quest,
we turned on my tape recorder, and for the next hour or so, history,
wit, wisdom, and anecdotes poured out of Wilder like some sparkling
fountain.

Yes, wit. Even on such a relatively unfunny subject as the trials and
tribulations of all those fellow refugees he'd known, who'd been uprooted
from their homelands by S.S. bullies in black shirts, and who'd fled for
their lives, one step ahead of the Gestapo.

So we turned the clock back forty years or so, to the mid-1930s, as I
asked him the question: how did all those various talented people manage
to adjust to America?

"Well," he said, "the architects, like Breuer, or the Bauhaus genius,
Gropius, they came over here, and even though their language was very
poor, they could teach architecture or build. And the composers, whether
it was Erich Wolfgang Korngold, or Miklos Rozsa, Franz Waxman, Arnold
Schoenberg, they were musicians, and their gifts could be expressed
through their work. But for the writers? It was extraordinarily difficult . . .

"A lot of them didn't come here first; they went to more familiar
ground, Paris. I myself went there for a year. Like an idiot, in high school
in Vienna, that was the *gymnasium*, you see, you took one big language,
which was Latin, and then you had to choose, at the age of thirteen,
whether to take French or English. Well, in those days French was still
regarded as 'the' language. So I took French, and when I found myself first
coming over to Hollywood in 1934, I was completely unable to speak
English—except, of course, the few things I'd picked up from American
talkies! So it took me a year, maybe a year and a half, over here just to be
able to converse, to order a meal, or put down a story, or anything, even
in bad English..." He grinned. "For a man like me, a real difficulty.

"Before I forget it," said Wilder, "let me tell you a story about another
writer who came here—a man I worked with in Berlin, at Uhlstein, the
publishing house—in those days, the biggest one...

"They had a magazine, comparable to *Vogue*—it was called *Die Dame*

—and this guy, the editor, was Erich Maria Remarque. He and I used to eat lunch every day; he had a real cushy job. The magazine only came out once a month. I was working on *Die Tempe*, a daily; in the afternoons I was a reporter. So Remarque sort of befriended me. Then, one day, he told me he was going to quit his job. I was stunned. 'This job? Once a month, a slick paper magazine, it's a pushover! We're working our asses off on the daily, and you're gonna quit *this?*'

"'Yeah,' says Remarque. 'My subconscious urges me to write a novel...'

"So I tried to talk him out of it—well, the novel I was trying to talk him out of writing was *All Quiet on the Western Front*! Good thing Remarque didn't listen to me, eh?" Wilder said, grinning.

"Well anyway, he comes to America—remember now, he's not Jewish, he's gentile—but very anti-Nazi. He had a place in Switzerland, but he chose to live here in L.A., at the Beverly Wilshire Hotel...Never wrote screenplays, but he continued writing novels...He did a sequel to the first one—called it *The Road Back* and so forth...

"So now, it's 1939, and I'm here, but I'm now an American citizen. Not Remarque. He's still a German citizen, and since now there's a war on in Europe, he's become an enemy alien! Which means he has to be back in his hotel suite every night by 9 PM—that is the law here for aliens. Being German, Remarque of course obeyed the law. Sure, he could've probably gone out at night—maybe nobody would have really bothered him out on Wilshire Boulevard, but no—he's back inside every night!

"...Now, living in the Beverly Wilshire is another guy, an art dealer named Sam Saltz. Saltz is the guy who subsequently became the great dealer of French Impressionists, he was a great friend of Bonnard, a buddy of the dealer Bernheim Jeune; he's out here in L.A., trying to sell some of his paintings, but nobody's buying!

"So these two guys strike up a friendship, and every evening at nine when Remarque comes back to the Beverly Wilshire, Saltz is waiting for him—he's an alien too—and the two of them need each other for company, see? And now, Saltz finally starts to sell Remarque some stuff; Remarque buys them out of boredom at first, but then he starts listening to Saltz, and looking at these masterpieces, and finally he's hooked...And so, years later, when Mr. Remarque is back in Switzerland, after the war is over, and he dies in Villa Ascona, the Italian part of Switzerland, and he leaves behind this absolutely fantastic collection of paintings...that all started in the Beverly Wilshire Hotel, because of a 9 PM wartime alien curfew! Impressionists? He had about eighteen great Cezanne watercolors, for which he paid Sam Saltz maybe eight, nine hundred bucks apiece!"

Once begun, Wilder's reminiscences poured forth, in a fascinating monologue.

"You know," he said, "whenever I talk to doctors or to psychoanalysts, I always tell them an episode from my days back then when I was a newspaperman; I was just a kid then, and I start by saying 'Would you believe that I *knew* Freud?'

"'*You* knew Freud? How dare you!' they answer, 'This is some enormous fetish you got, Wilder!' And I say, 'Not only did I know Freud, but I shook hands with him—and then he threw me out of his house!'

"And so many of the people who are writing about Freud—they always come around and say, 'Repeat that episode to me, please?' So I tell them, it was when I was working on a paper in Vienna before I went to Berlin. It was 1925 or 1926, and for that paper, every Christmas we would do a little inquiry. Sort of a roving reporter thing; you took a subject that was pertinent at that time, and then you asked famous people for their opinions.

"I remember the subject very well...It was that year we asked, 'What do you think of this movement, Fascism, and its leader, Benito Mussolini?' So the editor gave me a list of people to go and query, people I had to see, and on that list, would you believe I queried the playwright Schnitzler, Dr. Sigmund Freud, Adler, and the composer, Richard Strauss. And can you believe, I did them all in *one* morning?

"...So I went out, and whereas Richard Strauss was a dumbbell and didn't have much to say, and Schnitzler was a very erudite guy, after all, he was a playwright, and Adler ran off at the mouth, totally unstoppable. Okay, now I have to go to see Freud. It was lunchtime by then, he lived at Bergassen, number 9.

"Now in Europe, certainly in Mittel Europe, the doctor's office is in his apartment, so that the living room, also the salon, is also his waiting room. So I came in, I had a visiting card, I gave it to the maid, and she led me to the salon, and I could see one door open.

"There was the doctor's private room and there was the couch. *The* couch! Tiniest little thing you ever saw, with a kind of a Turkish carpet thrown over it. And another door…which opened soon after. It was the door to the dining room, where Freud was having his lunch with his family. And he came out with a serviette around his neck, and he's holding my card in his hand. He says, 'Herr Wilder?' I say, 'Yes, mein Herr Doktor.' 'You're a newspaperman, a reporter?' 'Yes, yes, yes!' 'Leave!' he says. Goes to the door and throws me out!

"…Later, I found out he hated newspapermen," said Wilder, "But look, isn't it better to be thrown out by Sigmund Freud, you know, than to have a pleasant conversation with some clown like Charlie Bluhdorn?"

Bluhdorn was an excitable Dutch Corporate raider, who had bought his way into the position of the boss of Paramount.

And in retrospect, Wilder's observation was right on the mark. Three decades later, who remembers Bluhdorn?

WILDER MOVED ON TO BERLIN AND SET HIS SIGHTS ON WRITING screenplays for the busy German film studios. He enjoyed relating the hilarious circumstances of his first film sale, which took place where he was living, in an apartment at Victoria Luiseplatz 11.

Where, ironically, today, a plaque identifies the site to passers by as Wilder's early Berlin residence.

"And perhaps it should also say B.F.— *Before Fleeing*?" he commented.

"Anyway, next door to my lousy little room, where I could hear the damn toilet going all night long, there lived the housekeeper's daughter. Every night she had some guy in there; I could hear either the toilet flushing, or her and the guy making love…What a symphony!

"So, one night, there's a crisis! The sound of *schtupping* stops, the door to the room next door opens, and then, right into my *own* room, a guy comes tip-toeing in. He's holding his shoes in one hand and his pants in the other! Now, there's more knocking from next door, and the girl has just let another guy in — and I can hear him, screaming, 'Where *is he*—I'll *kill the guy!*' and all that stuff…And now, I've got this other guy in his underwear, scared as hell, he's standing in my room like we're in a French farce by Feydeau! So pretty soon I find out he's a guy named Galitzenstein, he's a big shot, the head of an outfit called Maxim Films and here he is in my room, in his underwear!"

147

After reassuring Galitzenstein of his safety, Wilder did what any other writer would have suggested; he offered the producer a quid pro quo. "For saving his ass, I asked him if he would kindly read one of my screenplays."

Galitzenstein wasn't too interested. "He says to me 'Bring it to my office tomorrow!' 'No, no, tomorrow you'll forget you ever met me,' I said. 'Read it *now*!'

"The guy says he hasn't got his glasses! 'So?' I tell him, 'I'll read it out loud to you!'

"Galitzenstein makes me a better offer. He'll buy the script from me for 500 marks! So we make a deal, right there, sight unseen, he buys my script! He gives me the money...Then he sneaks out of my room. And guess what, the bum had left my script behind!

"...So the next day, I met the tootsie who lived in the next bedroom. She's out in the hall, and I say to her, 'Thank you for sending me Herr Galitzenstein last night, but you know, he's not really such a big shot. Do you think, next time, you could arrange to send me Erich Pommer?'"

Pommer was then the head of the mighty German UFA studios; the German equivalent of, say, Louis B. Mayer.

"I got to know all sorts of talented people in Berlin," recalled Wilder. "...and not always in such midnight crises. Berlin was filled with cafes and *kaffeehauses*, where a young aspiring screenwriter could sit at a table and do his writing on a portable typewriter, while at the same time schmoozing with the likes of, say Bertold Brecht the playwright, or Mies Van der Rohe the architect, George Grosz the painter, or Fritz Lang the director, or even the mighty Thomas Mann...

"But the most interesting of all those guys for me, in that time," said Wilder, "was Carl Mayer, a screenwriter. What a talent he was! He was the guy who wrote *The Cabinet of Dr. Caligari*, *The Last Laugh* for Emil Jannings...and that great Murnau picture, *Sunrise*.

"Mayer was a guy who'd come out of nowhere and became a great film writer...which," he added, with a smile, "is a profession all in itself. Something very few people understand."

And did Mayer, unlike so many of his Berlin confreres, migrate from Germany?

"No," said Wilder. "He stayed. Not like the rest of us."

Wilder's own migration from Berlin came after he had established himself as a successful film writer. He, along with Robert Siodmak, Edgar Ulmer, and the photographer Eugene Schufftan, who had the youthful Fred Zinnemann as his camera assistant, had collaborated on the small, witty film *People on Sunday.*

Short of finances, the young men used their considerable talents to shoot scenes all over Berlin, and when the film was finished, Berliners were pleased with its witty, documentarian style. From then on, young Wilder's career would blossom.

But when Hitler became chancellor of Germany on January 30, 1933, Wilder was perceptive enough to realize he should prepare to leave. S.S. men in black uniforms, clubbing defenseless Jews on Berlin streets were vivid evidence of what the future would bring. The night after the Reichstag fire, Wilder and his current lady friend departed Berlin. Destination? Paris.

Might he have considered returning to his native Austria?

"A lot of my Berlin pals figured they should go somewhere where they could speak the language," he recalled. "So they decided to go to Vienna, or maybe Prague. Not such a good plan, believe me. Anybody with half a brain could tell that Hitler was going to grab Austria, and then go after the Sudeten."

So Wilder found himself in Paris, still holding his Austrian passport, and with enough American cash secreted in his hatband to enable himself and his lady friend to survive.

They ended up in a certain Hotel Ansonia, near the Arc de Triomphe, where an assortment of other refugees from Berlin was already in residence.

"Peter Lorre was there, also Freddy Hollander the composer—he's the guy who wrote most of Marlene Dietrich's songs, both in Berlin and later out here in California . . . Then Franz Waxman, who'd been a jazz musician in Berlin, showed up. He finally made it to Hollywood and ended up writing great music scores, some of the greatest . . . and there was a guy I'd written with before, Max Volpe."

Paris would soon be filled with other emigres. Fritz Lang, who refused Josef Goebbels' offer to become the head of the great German film studio,

UFA; Erich Pommer, who had seen the ugly handwriting on the Berlin walls and had vacated that job. Eventually Pommer would end up in California, working for a time at Fox.

Wilder was involved in various film projects in Paris, but his ticket to America eventually came about through his friendship with another German refugee, the director, Joe May. "He was a guy who'd also been at UFA, and he'd gotten noticed when he made a picture called *Asphalt*... Somebody in California saw the film, and May ended up with a contract at Columbia Studios. So now that he was a producer, I sent him a script idea, something I called *Pam Pam*. He liked it—it was a comedy about a bunch of counterfeiters working out of a deserted theatre, who end up producing a show with a girl—the same girl who's been passing their phony money!

"Believe it or not, Columbia liked it too, and they offered me a contract, $150 a week, and transportation to Hollywood!" In January, 1934, Wilder sailed for New York.

It must have been hell for all such refugees, who were fleeing Germany and Europe to find safety in foreign lands, trying to scratch out a career without even knowing the language.

"Absolute hell," agreed Wilder. "These film people couldn't function—they were completely helpless! The others, the novelists like Thomas Mann, or Lion Feuchtwanger, or Franz Werfel... wherever they ended up, they could sit down with a pen, or a typewriter, and continue to do their writing. Others could translate their work for them. But for us, who worked in a visual medium, we had to shift into a new language. Like children, we had to learn to speak... how to write the simplest dialogue."

And what about the refugee actors?

"Oh, they had a terrible time adapting. Lorre... S. Z. Sakall... There was a wonderful guy named Sig Rumann, he'd come much earlier and learned a new language... you can see him playing comedy all the time... But think of all those other guys who had to struggle... Alexander Granach, Felix Bressart..."

Was it true that the great German actor, Albert Bassermann, could never actually learn to speak and understand English, but had to study his lines on the set with the help of an assistant, who taught him by rote, to speak each one of them phonetically?

"Absolutely," said Wilder. "A wonderful man, Bassermann...Not Jewish, but gentile, who'd opposed Hitler from the beginning."

But there were many other refugees who came to Hollywood and would have an easier time adapting than the screenwriters. "Yes, sure," said Wilder. "Directors and producers...guys like Joe Pasternak and Henry Koster...William Dieterle and Fritz Lang...And when Waxman came here he went right to work. And Hollander, too...

"Whenever Marlene Dietrich needed songs, he wrote them—"Falling In Love Again," "See What The Boys In The Backroom Will Have." And don't forget Erich Wolfgang Korngold and all those wonderful musical scores... *Robin Hood*, and *Captain Blood*. Can I tell you a great Korngold story? Nothing to do with the subject of writers in Hollywood, but very funny."

And who would say no?

"Korngold, you have to understand, was one of the stingier men who ever lived. And he was very, very friendly with a Polish composer, who also worked here in Hollywood, the great Bronislau Kaper. He's the guy who did dozens of pictures... The two guys saw each other a lot. But then one day, Korngold, the stingy one, meets Kaper in a market. And he says, 'How come we never see you?' And Kaper says, 'Oh, come on, now, Erich, now you know you have been in our house for dinner now twelve times, and you never invite us. Now come on, you know damn well why we don't see each other!' So Korngold says, 'My God, I never thought of it—but you're right, it is ridiculous... Tell you what, you and your wife, why don't you come over on Tuesday? Tuesday evening?' Kaper says, 'That's fine, delighted.' Little pause, and then Korngold says, 'I'll tell you what. Why don't you and your wife come *after* dinner?' And Kaper says, 'All right.' Another little pause, and Korngold says, 'Why don't you come after coffee?'"

So now we return to the problems faced by all those refugees who settled here in a strange, far-off, constantly sunlit land.

"A lot of us were part of a group who'd come here to weather the storm," recalls Wilder. "The Manns, the Schoenbergs...Erich Remarque, and all the rest...they had their Sunday kaffeeklatsches at places like Salka Viertel's house each week, where they could reminisce and wait for the day when they might return to their homeland...But not us picture people.

Guys like me, who'd wanted to come to Hollywood ... Hitler or no Hitler! Because we were finally where we'd always wanted to be! This town was where it was at. *Mecca!*"

One of the least documented phases of this Hollywood era is that several of the movie bosses, specifically the Warners, L. B. Mayer, and Harry Cohn, took it upon themselves to find writing jobs for some of the refugee film writers ... was that not factual?

"Correct," said Wilder. "L. B. Mayer, who was terribly outspoken about the plight of the Jews, refused to close down the Metro-Goldwyn-Mayer film exchanges in Germany because he always said he felt an obligation toward his stockholders to keep them on ... Eventually, of course, he had no choice; the Nazis took them over. But he was very generous here in California, when he took on a slew of those European émigrés."

I mentioned to Wilder that I had been in touch with a well-known European literary agent, George Marton, who had also migrated to America during those '30s. According to Marton, he had approached Mayer to offer him a deal for a group of refugee writers who were already here in the U.S. and were in dire straits financially.

Marton's sales pitch to Mayer was quite dramatic and effective. He said, "Mr. Mayer, I will deliver to you *ten* writers of good standing for the price you pay one contract writer."

Marton was successful; Mayer accepted Marton's clients and brought them to Culver City. As did H. M. Warner, who saw to it that some of the others were taken on at his Burbank studio.

"But you have to understand," Wilder pointed out, "in those days there were literally dozens of writers working at Metro ... so what if Mayer took in another ten or so? He had at least a hundred different pictures in various stages of preparation ... of which ultimately Metro would make, let's say, fifty. And don't forget, in those days, the studios controlled their own theatres, so they could push those pictures, good, bad, or indifferent, through their chains ... It was an enormously successful and profitable enterprise. But even so, some of those writers they took on later, the guys they'd taken on from Marton, succeeded extremely well ... which justified the whole thing.

"Remember," he said, "it was not like you took some charity case into your studio and said 'All right, here's your office, sit here, every week, and on Friday, you'll be paid three hundred dollars.' No way! Mayer and the others, Warner and Cohn, they expected something in return. And a lot of guys tried very hard to deliver."

How had Wilder fared, when he arrived in Hollywood at the behest of director Joe May, to work at Columbia on his *Pam Pam* project?

"To put it mildly, not so good," he said, grinning. "When they found out I couldn't speak English very well, I ended up doing most of the work at home, with the help of a translator. Remember, I'm the guy who didn't take English for my second language back at the *gymnasium*; so here I was, stuck with my damn French!"

So eventually the Columbia assignment disappeared?

"Into the sunset," said Wilder.

Then came another problem, one that was truly ominous. Wilder had only a six-month visitor's visa, and by then it had almost expired. He would have to leave Hollywood, to go out of the U.S., down to Mexico, where he could then apply for a re-entry at the U.S. consulate.

This event is how he would acquire the background material for his story for *Hold Back the Dawn*, is it not?

"What are you, a cineaste?" demanded Wilder. "Yes, it certainly was. I've often told this story, about waiting in the consul's office in Mexico, hoping and praying the guy would show me some pity, and let me back into the U.S. The guy asked me for my papers—all I had was a passport and a birth certificate and some letters I'd gotten from Americans who vouched for the fact that I was honest... So I was truly at his mercy.

"...So this guy asks me, 'What do you do professionally?' And I tell him I write movies. He says, 'Is that so?' He gets up and paces up and down and then behind me, I guess he was measuring me, something like that. Comes back to his desk, picks up my passport, takes a rubber stamp, and he stamps it! Then he hands it back to me, and he says, 'Write some good ones.'"

Who could write a better scene than that episode?

"God bless the guy," said Wilder. "Never knew his name, he was just an assistant or something, but I've spent the rest of my career trying to write good ones for him."

For which those of us who've spent hours watching his works should also be grateful.

And so, what was it like when, after a series of scripts with other producers (*Music in the Air* at Fox, one of Erich Pommer's few films in Hollywood) Wilder was finally brought into the Paramount lot as a writer?

"Same as Metro," he remembers. "Huge. Can you believe they had 104 writers under contract? So many that the writers' building offices couldn't handle them all! They had to open up one annex, then another! And everybody sat there, you got yellow pages, and six days a week, in your office, you *wrote*...Saturdays, you worked until noon. The head of the studio was a guy named Y. Frank Freeman, and one day he told me, 'Look, if we ever stop working on Saturdays, that's the end of the industry.'

"Maybe he had something there," said Wilder, "but frankly, I think that giving up those Saturdays was only a small contributing factor!"

Wilder's career at Paramount lasted for sixteen years. Obviously, he had conquered the language barrier, unlike some of the other recent fellow exiles who were unable to adapt to their new surroundings.

"That reminds me of another story," he said. "I remember when Warner Bros. brought that great director Max Reinhardt out here, and they put him to work making a movie of *A Midsummer Night's Dream*, with everybody on the Warner contract list. So one night I went to a party, all the expatriates were there, even Ernst Lubitsch, the genius director of comedies...

"Reinhardt made a little speech. When he spoke, out of reverence to this great legendary talent, everybody was silent. And Reinhardt said, 'You know, I have been directing now, years and years, and I just started making *Midsummer Night's Dream*.'

"He spoke with a very broken accent, and he went on. 'I have done that play over and over again, but I would like to go on record, here and now, to say that Mickey Rooney is the best Puck I ever had in my life!'"

A very prestigious Warner Bros. production, indeed, which Reinhardt co-directed with another recent arrival from Germany, William Dieterle. It would be Reinhardt's first film—and also his last. "He couldn't survive here; he wasn't a film director," observed Wilder. "Dieterle, however, certainly was. As was Lubitsch. Now there was a wonderful talent. It took me a long while before we got to work together," he said. "Not at Paramount. You know, that's where they had him for a time as the head of production

...an idiotic occupation for such a talent, because he never fitted in to such an assembly-line sort of function."

Was it true that Lubitsch learned he was being replaced as the head of Paramount production early one morning, when the studio barber who was shaving him confided in him the bad news?

"It sounds right," said Wilder. "Typical studio politics. You see, Lubitsch was an extraordinarily sensitive and fair man; he'd been here in Hollywood since the early silent days, but he always made it a kind of point not to work with a refugee because he did not want anyone to think he was favoring a *landsman*...When it finally happened, for me to start working with Lubitsch, with Charlie Brackett, on *Ninotchka*, was not very easy, because I had to overcome that."

But before that, hadn't he worked with Brackett for Lubitsch, on *Bluebeard's Eighth Wife*?

"Again, you're the cineaste!" commented Wilder. "Listen, you must understand where that problem of Lubitsch's originally came from. When Lubitsch arrived in California back in the '20s, he came here with his assistant director, Henry Blanke. Blanke ended up a major producer at Warners.

"Do you know what happened to them? Paul Kohner the agent, told me. Lubitsch and Blanke were staying downtown at the Alexandria Hotel, and they heard the sound of screaming below. When they looked down, there on Hollywood Boulevard were maybe a couple of hundred American Legionaires all shouting '*Throw the Huns out!*' How ironic...They still hadn't forgotten World War I! Incredible, yes? So now, can you understand why Lubitsch was, after all these years, still sensitive to such prejudice?"

To return to the careers of such other European refugees out in California: Bertold Brecht, the playwright, say. Could he be considered to have adapted to his enforced California exile?

"I met him quite a few times," said Wilder. "Up at the house of Elizabeth Bergner, the actress, on Mulholland Drive. She was another one who had managed to get safely out of Germany, but she didn't have much of a career here in Hollywood...Brecht? He was truly kind of a touching genius-type...at the same time, a free-wheeling plagiarist."

How so?

155

"In total adoration of America, without ever having been here!" said Wilder. "I mean, look at his play called *Mahagonny*, which he wrote in Germany... and the whole thing is about Louisiana, where he'd never been! And he also did a gangster play—long before he came to America; it was called *Happy End*, remember? But in defense of Brecht, that passion for America, that romanticizing of the life here, it was so typical of pre-Hitler Germans... Did you ever hear of a writer called Karl May? He lived in a suburb of Dresden called Radeborn, and there he sat and wrote—guess what? Books about the American West! A whole series of books about a Western hero known as Old Shatterhand!... And he never was here!"

"Brecht was in that same tradition. He was an American-phile, just loved this country, loved everything about it, the American words he heard here must have sounded very exciting to him... erotic, even."

According to Mary Baker, who was Brecht's American agent in his California years, while Brecht was there, he may not have learned to speak English, but he did write plays.

"Didn't know that," said Wilder. "Which plays?"

Arturo Ui, for one, reported Baker. The rise and fall of Arturo Ui, that remarkable combination of a gangster melodrama, in which the major character is so obviously patterned after Hitler. Blending fascism with gang wars... Another example of Brecht's fascination with American mythology.

But as for Brecht's attempts to work as a screenwriter, Baker also reported how he had worked on a film that Fritz Lang directed, *Hangmen Also Die*.

"Maybe," said Wilder, "but I wonder how much actual writing did Brecht do?"

According to Baker, Lang would bring Brecht pages of a script in work, and they would sit and talk about it, and then Brecht would work on it. In German...

"Quite possible," said Wilder. "It's quite interesting, don't you agree? Here's a guy, thousands of miles from his homeland, in the country he's always wanted to be, and yet, he's here in exile."

Perhaps an interesting idea for a novel?

"Already been done," said Wilder, promptly. "Have you ever read Erich

Maria Remarque's novel *Arch of Triumph*, the one about the Paris hotel where all the refugees are living? Well, there's a character in there, a doctor, a German refugee, living in Paris, and in order to keep himself alive, he's performing abortions in dirty kitchens... You know who that doctor really was? Dr. Max Jacobson... the same guy who is now in New York!"

The notorious Doctor Feelgood?

"The one and the same Dr. Feelgood!" said Wilder. "I knew him extremely well — in Berlin, he was *my* doctor! Talk about writers in exile! Here's this doctor, in exile, he cannot get a diploma, so he performs abortions... You know how old this guy is today? He has to be in the early 70s! But what a difference from his days in Paris, eh? Whenever he comes out here to L.A., I see him. Or I meet him on planes, he is accompanying Mr. Cecil B. DeMille to Egypt, because Mr. DeMille is going to do a new version of *The Ten Commandments*, during which Mr. DeMille has himself a heart attack, but Dr. Feelgood pumps him full of his amphetamine magic shots, so Mr. DeMille can still climb ladders and shoot the scenes — with maybe 6,000 extras all standing around!"

And there is also a list of other famous show business and political people who were the patients of the same Dr. Max Jacobson, ranging from our late president Kennedy, with his bad back, to Alan Jay Lerner, and Tennessee Williams, to a raft of other such celebrities, all of them devotees of Dr. Feelgood's little satchel full of magic elixir shots.

"Well, there's one exile who certainly made good," commented Wilder.

But adapting one's medical talents is far different from, say, trying to sit in a Hollywood studio office and to write a decent screenplay, in a foreign language, wouldn't he agree?

"Listen, if the truth be told," said Wilder, "language barrier or not, refugees or not, very few people in general make it here, writing scripts. Whether you were born in Dresden or in Oklahoma — just look at the percentage of writers who have actually made it here as a screenwriter, against the percentage of those who've come out here and failed! Expert writers from the New York theatre, or even Budapest — don't forget all the guys from there who came here in the late '30s. Ladislaus Fodor, Molnar, Bus-Fekete, Lazlo Vadnay... what about all those English authors and playwrights who came, here, tried it, and left. Novelists — who wrote best sellers, like Fitzgerald, or John O'Hara! Guys who've had their stories published in magazines ... Very few of them ever made it. And I'm talking about top-drawer writers, who've reached a respectable level in their careers. They get here, and they're stymied by the process. How can they adjust?"

"Listen, they had Mr. Faulkner out here at Metro, and he was in an office for two years, and nothing much came out except that I remember when he left, ultimately Norman Krasna took over Faulkner's old office, and there on the desk was a yellow tablet, and on that tablet, written on three lines was the entire output of Mr. Faulkner's wisdom for his two years, and you know what it said? 'Boy ... Girl ... Policeman.'"

And didn't Mr. Faulkner also leave behind a desk calendar on which he had ticked off every Friday of each week he'd been there?

"Oh yes, indeed," said Wilder, "Pay day."

"...Listen to me," he said, and now there were no more anecdotes forthcoming, but a generous helping of wisdom. "Motion picture writing is a profession in itself. It is a very difficult medium; you cannot just sit down and write a screenplay."

"I mean, men can come down from Tennessee with a poem, or out of the slums with a novel ... Women can write detective stories, college kids can come up with comedy material ... But in order to write a successful screenplay, you have to have gone through some kind of an engineering school.

"Most of those people who've come out here, not only the refugees like me, but the guys from New York, or Chicago, or even the graduates of film schools, they were just writers. Okay, so you're a writer, but you're not a *motion picture* writer. Some of their contributions might be used — most of the time, it wasn't! Why? Maybe there was some marvelous stuff they came up with which was too far above the head of their producer, or the guy running the studio ... But remember, back then in the '20s and the '30s and the '40s, this was always a producer's town. What the producer said was absolute law."

And today?

"All those studio bosses are gone, nowadays it's become a director's town," he said, shrugging. "Hey, maybe some day, it'll even become a *writer's* town?"

"Hardly," I suggested.

Wilder nodded, and grinned. "Hardly," he echoed.

"You know what the big problem is?" he asked. He waggled a finger. "Everybody wants to be a screenwriter. They all sit and look at movies, and after they've seen so damn many of them, in the theatres, or on TV, or on videotape, and they think, 'This is easy—I can write a film!'

"This applies to your cook. Your dentist. Your garage mechanic—they all say, 'Hey, I've got a great idea for a picture,' and they come to me and they say, 'I've seen movies all my life, and how would this be, here's an idea. And I say, 'It would be bad, it would be corny, you've seen it up there on a screen before, it wouldn't work, *trust* me!' . . . But they don't.

"What causes such arrogance? Their lack of respect for the craft. People do not realize—writing a film is very difficult. They do not realize that you must serve your internship, that you must develop a feel for it. And, additionally, you have to learn the mechanics!" He shook his head. "It is a craft that *has* to be learned!"

We sat quietly for a moment, and then Wilder sighed. "And then, of course," he added, "it takes a very strong spine to withstand the onslaught of the kibitzers. Of the *besserwisser*. The onslaught of the superiors, and most often, the directors, who pick up the pages, read the work you've done, and just cross it out!"

He shook his head, brooding on remembered angst. "I am often there when that happens, because I work on screenplays and I also direct. So people ask me the question, 'Is it important for a director to know how to write?' And I tell them, 'Absolutely not. What *is* very helpful for the director is to *know how to read*.'

"You would be surprised to know how few directors do. I mean, they read the pages, but they don't comprehend what's *there*. And they're too proud to come and ask, 'What did you mean by that scene? Just let's sit down and tell me. Act it out for me . . . what is that little chess move in this scene here, is that of any importance?'" he sighed. "They just don't comprehend . . ."

There then follows the inevitable thought that the auteur theory may be the worst thing that has ever happened to the film business. That ridiculous notion that postulates how each director wakes up in the early morning and says, "Today, I am going to create a picture," and then he goes down to the set, and says to his cast and crew, "Here is what I figured out for the opening sequence, let's get started on our first shots, which I'm now going to describe to you. So here we go."

"Agreed," grinned Wilder. "As a matter of fact, I won't even participate in those discussions about auteurs, because it's such damn stupid stuff!"

We had been talking for more than an hour, time filled with anecdotes, rare Hollywood lore, and wisdom. In between the laughs, he had certainly illuminated facets of that fascinated long-gone era of the refugee years for me, and for future cinema enthusiasts.

"Not cineastes?" he asked, slyly.

"If they'll listen," I said.

"Okay, so don't you need a closing title?" he asked. "We didn't have one to open with — but all movies used to have great titles in the sound era, before sound came in."

Yes, indeed, the silent films and their witty titles. "Done, of course, by writers."

"Okay," said Wilder. "Let's go for the closer."

He stood up, this gent who had left Europe to migrate to America, bringing little else but his wit, and had proceeded to make some of the most memorable films that film audiences have ever enjoyed. As well as his classic delineation, his *homage* to old Hollywood … *Sunset Boulevard.*

"Say, how about this?" he asked. "My whole life was spent between two Adolfs: Adolf Hitler … and Adolph Zukor! How's that?"

And who would dare to suggest a rewrite for such a perfect closing title?

BILLY WILDER'S CREDITS:

JOE and HERMAN MANKIEWICZ

JOE MANKIEWICZ USED TO TELL THE STORY OF HOW, HE, AS A STUDENT, took a seminar at Columbia, a course that was conducted by John Erskine, a famous writer of the time. There were four other students besides Mankiewicz, and as they were about to graduate, Erskine called them all together, and said, "I just want to warn you guys as a friend...never go to Hollywood."

So Mankiewicz took off for Europe. When he got there, in the early '30s, he received a cable from his older Brother Herman...the famous "Mank," telling him there was a job waiting for him at Paramount. So Joe succumbed to Hollywood and went out to Hollywood on the train, and when he arrived, his brother said, "Oh, you're in luck tonight, there's a big party at Ben Schulberg's house." Schulberg was then the head of production at Paramount.

They drove out to his home, they went in the door to be met by a hundred different people, very upper echelon, at a typically lavish Hollywood party. They went through the crowd, the champagne corks popping, waiters passing caviar, the orchestra playing, everyone enjoying Schulberg's hospitality, and the first person Joe ran into was *John Erskine!*

He asked his former teacher, "...What are *you* doing here in Hollywood?" Erskine said, "I came out here because they asked me to work on a picture!"

—PETER VIERTEL

10.   THE LATE MR. HARRY KURNITZ

1972

Harry Kurnitz by Frank Modell

"EVERYBODY WHO KNEW HARRY KURNITZ LIKED HIM," SAID KEN Englund, a fellow screenwriter. "His humor was never vicious or spiteful —in fact, more often than not, it was turned on his own quirks.

"I remember there was a time when he signed a contract to function as a producer-writer at a very large salary. Weeks and weeks went by, with both H. M. and Jack Warner watching those paychecks go out each Friday, and both of them beginning to chafe over Kurnitz's delay in getting a picture in front of the cameras.

"At last, after a few months, Kurnitz got one started. On the first day of shooting, there sat Harry, chain-smoking, peering through his thick glasses, watching all the activity on the set, nodding as if he really knew what it was all about, and then one of the Warners came down to have a personal look at this miraculous scene.

"Harry spied Warner—it was old H. M. the most dignified and certainly the most humorless of the three brothers—and he waved a cheerful hand in welcome.

"'Well, Mr. Warner,' he crowed, 'I think I've finally gotten the hang of it!'"

Kurnitz came to work in Hollywood in the late '30s. Besides films, he was also a detective-story writer, having written such novels as *Fast Company* under the pseudonym of Marco Page. He had spent his early years working in bookstores and antique shops, and he turned that knowledge to good use as the background material for his thrillers. He was also a very serious art collector and from that avocation there later came his Broadway comedy *Reclining Figure*. Kurnitz was very musical and played the violin; his knowledge of and love for classical music he was later to weave into his comedy *Once More, with Feeling*.

"He was an insomniac and a compulsive writer," said George Axelrod, a fellow playwright (*The Seven Year Itch*) and screenwriter (*The Manchurian Candidate*, among many others). "Harry had this thing about doing a certain amount of writing, come hell or high water. Since he didn't sleep well, he'd get up before dawn and write. He told me that once, in Loel Guinness' country house on a weekend, he woke up at 5 AM and decided to work. Only trouble was, there was no writing paper in his bedroom! Harry was so driven to write that he actually pulled out the lining paper from three bureau drawers in the room, and wrote four or five scenes on them before breakfast!

"Harry always wrote without making carbons. One weekend he was cruising on somebody's yacht on the Mediterranean—he enjoyed high-class trips like that—and he was sitting out on the deck, working on the script, with all the pages on the table. There was a sudden gust of wind, and the script blew overboard into the Mediterranean!"

"Without a second's hesitation, Harry, fully dressed and wearing his glasses, leaped overboard after it.

"'It was in mid-air,' he told me, afterwards, 'that I remembered I could not swim!'

"They pulled Harry and his precious script aboard a few minutes later. I thought it was such a marvelous incident that I wrote it into my own picture, *Lord Love a Duck*."

"Kurnitz would use any possible excuse to avoid disciplinary pressures," continued Ken Englund. "He got a considerable amount of dough to do the screenplay of *One Touch of Venus*, the Ogden Nash–Kurt Weill–Sid Perelman Broadway musical Universal had bought. But Harry absolutely refused to go out to work at their studio. Firstly, he loathed studio offices, and secondly, Harry was already beginning to become something of a social snob. He considered it far beneath his dignity even to travel from Beverly Hills out to San Fernando Valley, much less to *work* there. So he did the script completely at home, and had it delivered by messenger!"

"Harry came from a very poor Philadelphia family," said Leland Hayward, who produced the Kurnitz adaptation of the French comedy, "A Shot In The Dark," a hit that spawned an entire series of film comedies starring Peter Sellers as Inspector Clouseau. "At one time, when Harry was struggling to make a living in New York, he lived in a furnished room in the Lower East Side, near Greenwich Village. Harry told me he was so poor he couldn't possibly afford even a pint of whiskey, so in order to get high, he'd save up a few cents each week and buy liquid marijuana from a corner druggist — in those days, it was legal — something like extract of cannabis — and then Harry would pour the stuff over a box of ten cigarettes, let them dry out, and then he'd smoke them and get a mild charge. 'It was all I could afford in the way of corruption,' he said, sadly.

"Of course, later on, when Harry was making a lot of money, he developed elegant tastes to go along with his income. I was at a dinner party with him in Palm Springs one night," said Hayward, "A very big spread at Frank Sinatra's, a couple of years back, and the first course was oysters."

"They'd been flown in from the East, and Harry gave us a short lecture on oysters. He was passionate about them, he had researched them, eaten them all over the world, knew all about the different varieties, the French, the Portuguese, the English Whitstables, where the best beds were, and so on. He reeled off all the varieties you could find up and down the East Coast, and then finally he began to eat his own dozen, with great gusto."

"I thought I'd tease him, and I asked, 'Harry, don't you feel just a bit strange, eating something that's still alive?'"

"He peered at me through his glasses and wanted to know since when oysters were still alive."

"Well, I explained to him that if oysters *aren't* alive, you simply cannot eat them, they're inedible and dangerous. With all Harry knew about oysters, he didn't know that, and he refused to believe it. So finally, I called over the headwaiter and asked him. 'Oh no, sir,' said he. 'We only serve *live* oysters — we would never take the risk of serving dead ones.'"

"Harry pushed away his oysters, and then he glared at me. 'I want to thank you, Leland,' he said, 'for destroying my one remaining passion.'"

"And he never, to my knowledge, ate oysters again."

In one of Kurnitz's early screenplay assignments, Kurnitz and Mark Hellinger, his producer, agreed that Kurnitz should play a bit part, a la Hitchcock. He was assigned the role of a candy-store owner on the Lower East Side. "Harry said that was a role in which he could feel comfortable making his dramatic debut," said George Axelrod. "After all, it was an area he was familiar with. In the brief scene, the director explained to Harry that as part of his characterization, he should take a couple of bites out of his own candy stock. They wanted him to munch on some halvah, which is a rich almond-paste confection."

"'I am sorry,' said Harry, 'but I will only eat halvah providing I get stunt-man's pay!'"

In the years when she was beginning a career as an actress, Pat Englund, Ken's daughter, was a steady companion of Kurnitz, both in Hollywood and in New York. "One night we went past the theatre where they were having a big Hollywood-type premiere, and I told Harry I'd love to go, so he went in, spoke to a middle-aged man in the lobby, and we were immediately ushered right into the V.I.P. section inside. I was enormously impressed," she recalled, "and I asked him, 'Harry, who *was* that man?'"

"'Oh,' said Harry, 'that's Harry Cohn's brother Jack. He's sometimes known as Harry Cohn Without Charm.'

"We went inside, to a preview of a musical film; a biography of Chopin, *A Song to Remember*, and while the picture was on, Harry leaned over and whispered, 'You know, they sent this script to Art Tatum (the celebrated blind jazz pianist) but he felt it, and then turned it down.'

"On another evening, I went with him to the Stork Club, and we were in the Cub Room when Elliott Roosevelt came in and joined us. It was very heady stuff for me—there we were, sitting with FDR's son, who had just returned from a trip to Russia on behalf of some magazine, and he'd been received by Stalin, Timoshenko, all the Russian powers. He told us how they'd all been very warm towards him, and full of reminiscences about his late father. Elliott paused for a moment, and Harry inquired, 'But Elliott, didn't *my* name come up?'"

"And then there was another time, just after I got the part of Ado Annie in *Oklahoma!* on Broadway. Of course, I wasn't the original—that was Celeste Holm. I was just another one of a procession of ingenues who got their training by playing the part...but believe me, at that time it was a big deal for me, a real breakthrough in my career. I was absolutely bursting with excitement, and Harry took me to Sardi's for a celebration.

"We were sitting there," she recalled, "and Oscar Hammerstein himself walked in. Harry waved at him, and he came over and sat down with us. Well, you can imagine how nervous I was by then. Harry introduced me to Mr. Hammerstein. 'You must meet Patsy,' he said. 'She's going to do the part of Ado Annie in your show, Oscar.'"

"Mr. Hammerstein was very nice. He beamed and said, 'Fine, fine,' I mean, *Oklahoma!* was playing all over the place, and he certainly couldn't keep track of all the girls who were playing Ado Annie, but he behaved as if I were the first who'd ever had the part. And then Harry said, 'Yes, but before she takes over the part, Oscar, Patsy says she's been looking over your book and lyrics, and she's got a few criticisms for you. Now, Oscar, you don't mind a little honest criticism, do you?'"

"I couldn't stand it," said Miss Englund. "It was Harry's idea of a funny thing to say—but I actually burst into tears!"

Later on, when Miss Englund married Barney Lefferts, a writer whose family origins were from north of Boston, Kurnitz came to dinner at the home of the newly married couple.

"Barney had a few drinks and he began to show it," Miss Englund recalls. "Harry sat there and listened to Barney, and watched him, and then he remarked, 'I suppose this is what you mean by a New England boiled dinner?'"

Larry Adler, the virtuoso harmonica player who lived for many years in London, remembered a time when he was visiting in Hollywood, and was asked by his friend Kurnitz to accompany him to a Warner Bros. studio function.

The two were seated in an audience that was then treated to one of Jack Warner's customary speeches, peppered, as usual, with Warner's quips and unfunny ad-libs.

"Halfway through Warner's interminable monologue, Harry turned to me," said Adler, "and he whispered, 'I hope Jack finishes up soon—I'm beginning to run out of loyalty laughs.'"

"A couple of nights later I remember going to Ciro's with Harry, up on Sunset Strip, where Duke Ellington and his orchestra were opening. As we entered the club, we were hit square in the face with one of Duke's piercing climactic chords—a blast of music played by the entire band—which absolutely shattered our ears! 'It's their new transcription of *Sheep May Safely Graze!*' Harry cried.

"Harry could drink a lot, but he never really got drunk at all," said Adler. "I gave a party for him one night in London, and as the evening progressed, Harry went on drinking. But instead of passing out, he merely stretched out—right on the living-room floor, directly in front of the door. I'd hired a very proper butler for the party, and he came out of the kitchen carrying a tray of drinks; he looked down and found his access completely blocked by Kurnitz on the floor. The butler looked down at Harry, and Harry looked up at the butler. He blinked, and asked 'Can't you leap?'"

During the mid-1940s, when the nightmarish blacklist period descended over the entire motion-picture industry, Kurnitz became one of the victims.

"Harry was about as much of a Communist as any of the Hollywood liberals were, which was not much of a Communist at all," remarked one of his friends. "He certainly wasn't political—in fact, he was a hell of a snob—but his instincts were all decent, he had loads of friends who were liberal, and he kept them, and he didn't give a damn what your politics were, as long as you had talent. But back in those rotten days, which were hysterical with fear, the reactionaries who drew up those damned blacklists never gave a damn for truth. They smeared everyone with their lousy innuendoes—and that's what happened to Harry."

"Harry called me up one day and told me he was leaving Hollywood," remembered Ken Englund. "Said he was going to travel and become a full-time gypsy, a nomad. He'd go wherever the assignments he'd get would take him. I knew Harry had put together a marvelous collection of books and modern paintings. 'What are you going to do with all that wonderful stuff?' I asked him.

"'I got rid of everything,' said Harry, 'It's the only way to live—completely unfettered.'

"'You *sold* all those books?' I said, and it hurt me, because I knew how many years he'd spent collecting them. '*I* could never do that,' I told him. 'I love my books too much.'

"'Sell 'em,' Harry told me, sharply. 'And if you want a book—go to the public library.'"

Kurnitz went into a global orbit, but it was to be always a first-cabin nomadic life. The following years took him to London and to posh English country houses, to the sixteenth arrondissement in Paris, for winter weeks in Klosters, and on yachting trips on the Mediterranean.

When the Paris edition of an American drugstore opened on the Champs Elysees, Harry visited it and reported that it could compare with Schwab's Drugstore, on Sunset Boulevard. "Here," he wrote, "they try to give you lunch Hollywood style—a hot dog and vintage Beaujolais."

Allan Rivkin and Laura Kerr, two of his close Hollywood friends, reported that in London Kurnitz was invited to a Thanksgiving dinner that producer Sam Spiegel was giving in his posh Grosvenor House apartment. When Kurnitz looked around the table, he noticed that all the other guests, like himself, were political exiles from Hollywood. He seized his glass and stood for a toast. "To Sam Spiegel," he said. "A very brave man. Little does he know there's a thousand dollars on each of your heads!"

"...Harry was very fond of telling the story of how he'd gone to see the movie *Genevieve*," said George Axelrod. "Harry had fallen madly in love —who hadn't?—with its leading lady, the late Kay Kendall. Harry claimed that he'd come into the lobby of the Connaught Hotel and spied Miss Kendall sitting at a table, having tea. Without hesitation, he came over and said, 'Miss Kendall, I am madly in love with you.' Harry said, 'She looked up at me, holding her teacup, and she said, "Move on, my good man, or I shall call the manager—unless, of course, you *are* the manager."

"Harry had this wonderful reverence for titled people," said Axelrod. "I guess it went all the way back to his early days when he was really poor, back in Philadelphia. When he came to Europe, and met them, they were more important to him than anyone else. I was once talking to him in London, and he told me he was going to have a golf date with the Duke of Windsor. I said, 'Harry, from all I can gather, the Duke is a nice guy, but he certainly isn't the world's most scintillating conversationalist. Why do you insist on playing golf with *him?*' Harry looked reprovingly at me. 'He was once the *king!*' he snapped.

Harry's good friend, John Huston, in company with Truman Capote and Humphrey Bogart, produced a suspense film called *Beat the Devil.* The many creative people involved in the production enjoyed themselves hugely during the filming, but when the finished picture was released, it proved nearly incomprehensible. Said Kurnitz, "No matter where you come in during the running, you seem to have missed at least half the picture."

And in a discussion about the late actress Natalie Wood, Kurnitz remarked, "She is built like a brick dollhouse."

He once had a transitory *affaire d'amour* with a young lady in the South of France. Later, one of his friends inquired as to her general capabilities. Kurnitz thought about it for a moment, and then he remarked, "I have been in Volkswagens smaller than she was."

A short time before he died, Kurnitz came back to Hollywood for a brief visit. He joined George Axelrod for the annual Writers Guild awards dinner. As they drove downtown to the scene of the banquet, Kurnitz mused, "And now, tonight, we go to meet all the brightest creative minds in Hollywood—and their wives, the girls who looked so good to them, twenty years ago on Pitkin Avenue."

HARRY KURNITZ'S CREDITS:

ACADEMY AWARD NOMINATION:

What Next, Corporal Hargrove?, 1945

FILMS:

Fast Company, 1938

Fast and Furious, 1939

Fast and Loose, 1939

I Love You Again, 1940

Shadow of the Thin Man, 1941

Pacific Rendezvous, 1942

Ship Ahoy, 1942

The Heavenly Body, 1943

They Got Me Covered, 1943

See Here, Private Hargrove, 1944

The Thin Man Goes Home, 1945

Something in the Wind, 1947

The Web, 1947

Adventures of Don Juan, 1948

One Touch of Venus, 1948

The Inspector General, 1949

My Dream Is Yours, 1949

A Kiss in the Dark, 1949

Pretty Baby, 1950

Of Men and Music, 1951

The Man Between, 1953

Melba, 1953

Tonight We Sing, 1953

The Love Lottery, 1954

Land of the Pharaohs, 1955

The Happy Road, 1957

Witness for the Prosecution, 1957

Surprise Package, 1960

Once More, with Feeling, 1960

Hatari!, 1962

Goodbye Charlie, 1964

A Shot in the Dark, 1964

How to Steal a Million, 1966

PLAYS:

A Shot in the Dark

Once More with Feeling

GARSON KANIN: A HARRY COHN STORY

BEN HECHT AND CHARLES MACARTHUR HAD WRITTEN A SCREENPLAY entitled *Gunga Din*. Their agent, Leland Hayward, was offering it for sale to various studios. The accepted method at that time was to submit a property to the head of the story department of each of the studios on the same day, then wait for the offers, if any. In this way, agencies could not be accused of favoritism.

The Hecht-MacArthur script of *Gunga Din* was delivered. They were excellent screenwriters, perhaps the best of their day, and *Gunga Din* was an impressive achievement. Rudyard Kipling's poem is only eighty-five lines long and has in it no story, no dramatic structure. It is, at most, a character sketch. But Hecht and MacArthur, realizing that the title itself had exploitation value, had invented a story and written an exciting adventure drama involving the British Army in India in the late nineteenth century.

It seemed strange to Hayward that every studio with the exception of Columbia had made an offer. Could there have been some mistake? Had the script been delivered to Columbia? He decided to investigate, and called on Harry Cohn. "I thought I ought to check out about *Gunga Din*," he said. "Why?" asked Cohn.

"Well," said Hayward, "just that every studio but you is interested."

"I can understand that," said Cohn. "They're interested because they don't own it. I don't need to buy it because I already own it."

"What do you mean you own it?" asked Hayward.

"I've owned it for seven years," said Cohn. Hayward was stunned. "Who did you buy it from?" he asked, "I bought it from Hecht and MacArthur," said Cohn, smugly. "That's impossible, Harry. Seven years? They only finished writing it three weeks ago."

"Under this title," said Cohn. "When I bought it from them, they called it *The Front Page*."

Hayward, relieved, began to laugh.

"What's so funny?" asked Cohn.

"*Gunga Din*," said Hayward patiently, "has absolutely nothing to do with *The Front Page*."

"Have you read it? " asked Cohn.

"Of course I've read it."

"And you don't see it's the same picture?"

"Harry," said Hayward, "thank you very much. You've given me a great Harry Cohn story. I'll be dining out on this for weeks."

"Go to it," said Cohn. "Just don't try to sell me what I already own." It took no more than three or four days for the story to be widely disseminated. The town was, once again, laughing at Harry Cohn.

Then I read the script of *Gunga Din* and stopped laughing. Cohn was absolutely right; Hecht and MacArthur had taken not only the story, but the characters of *The Front Page*, changed the period, the locale, and the occupations. It was daring and ingenious, but it did not fool Cohn.

The picture was eventually made by George Stevens for RKO. When the hidden *Front Page* structure went unnoticed by a majority of the critics and practically all of the public, I admired Harry Cohn's perception more than ever.

—GARSON KANIN, *Hollywood*, 1974

11. OH PRESTON, WHERE ART THOU?
PRESTON STURGES

with Earl Felton and Edmund Hartmann, 2001

Preston Sturges by Arnold Levin

IT WAS IN 1947, WHEN THE EDITOR OF "THE SCREEN WRITER," THE monthly magazine of the Guild, posed a question to the membership: "Can screen writers become film authors?"

Back came a response from Preston Sturges.

> The genuine author is distinguished by his lorgnon, his love of talk and his hatred of writing. He has dandruff on his collar and needs a shampoo.
>
> Not being a genuine author, but only a playwright, it is so difficult for me to write prose, spelling out each word, wrestling with the grammar and tripping over the syntax, that I rarely contribute to symposia. What little I know of my profession I got out of a book called *A Study of the Drama*, by Brander Matthews, which cost $1.50.
>
> In closing, here are two pieces of advice given by two good playwrights: Dumas the Younger, and Pierre Veber [sic]. The first said, 'To write a successful play is very easy; let the beginning be clear, the end be short, and let it all be interesting.' The second said, 'Never be afraid

of boring them. When they are bored, they think they are thinking...
This flatters them.'

Half a century later, this fragment of Sturges' attitude remains an exquisite example of his sardonic point of view, not only concerning his work, but towards the world he inhabited.

When he wrote it, he had compiled a remarkable list of memorable comedies, films such as *The Lady Eve, Hail, The Conquering Hero, The Miracle of Morgan's Creek, The Palm Beach Story, Sullivan's Travels, The Great McGinty*—works which will be run and rerun as long as there are audiences who wish to roar with laughter and relish Sturges' unique brand of satiric madness.

Who, actually was this brilliant, gifted gent?

Thirty years ago, I queried his good friend and collaborator on *The Beautiful Blonde from Bashful Bend*, Earl Felton. Would he try to give us some sort of insight into Sturges? Back came the following letter:

Dear Wilk:

...Preston is virtually a mystery here and abouts because he was such a goddamn snob nobody could get near enough to him to say more than "hello, sir," and humbly touch a forelock. By this, I don't mean he was a prick. Correction. He was that also, but a mighty charming one and greatly feared—at one time. It goes without saying, at that "one time" I didn't know him well myself, but I tried, feeling, wrongly, that we had a lot in common, if for no other reason than we were both writers on the same lot, Paramount, and both owned boats.

Christ, he sure corrected me on that issue! My boat was a mere 30-foot stinkpot. His was a magnificent 75-footer, designed by himself, replete with a sail far too small for her, a trick bar much too large, and insufficient power, together with a concrete ballast which came asunder, in a Honolulu race, bringing his craft, the *Destiny*, in at last place!... As I remember the boat was presumed lost for a damn long time, but since he was too elegant to stoop so low as to race it, he quite naturally was not aboard!

He had still another boat, this one power, which lay rusting over the years in the lee of his diesel engine factory at Wilmington (another one of Sturges' many enterprises, which like his opulent restaurant The Players failed miserably).

I suppose the utter worst error I made was to classify myself to him as a writer. This infuriated him so, that he bade me show him a view of my ass, in promptly leaving the environs of his table at the Paramount commissary!

But all that was before we became grudging pals, and by that time, we *did* have a few things in common — mostly, his increasing indebtedness with his accursed (and magnificent) cafe, The Players . . . and our individual girlfriends, not to forget my original story, *The Beautiful Blonde from Bashful Bend*, which he loused up into one of the worst pictures Fox ever made . . . a cinematic disaster that not only lost heavily, but wiped out forever the even-then glamorous figure that was Betty Grable!

By then, too, Preston not only owed most of the waiters in his cafe, having borrowed their life savings to keep the fool thing going, but was in danger of losing the *Destiny* for dock rentals that were seven years overdue! Finally, he gave the boat to me, which meant merely that I was able to talk a waterfront pal into having it towed away, to become a scummy fish barge, anchored off Huntington Beach!

. . . As for the girls, I recall one night at his home, when we sat together, staring down gloomily at the winking-twinkling lights of the town, alone because our broads had cheerfully deserted us after an earlier, mortifying drunken scene at his café . . . Preston sighed, managing a worldly smile, and said, "Old boy, shed no tears over them. Rather let us congratulate ourselves." I thought he was going to add something to the effect we were bloody well rid of them, but he continued, "Can't you see it, Earl? What absolutely giant fellows we must be to have won and lost two such ravishing bitches! A common chap could never even get to know them!"

I later married mine, and I must say, belatedly, Preston was completely right . . . If we had only stopped when he said we were ahead! . . . A worse broad I never knew, but at the time, Preston was correct.

. . . I fear, however, I may have given you the wrong impression of both the man and his creation, The Players. The man was much larger than I depict him. He was too large for this smelly resort, and the big

183

studies were scared to death of him. A man who was a triple threat (writing, directing, and producing!) kept them awake nights, and I'm positive they were all waiting for him to fall on his face so they could pounce on him and devour this terrible threat to their stingy talents ... In this, alas, I was right. They pounced, and they got him good. But Preston knew the great days, when he was turning out marvelous pictures ... those days when his can glowed like a port light from everyone kissing it!

...And he did love The Players. It was some place, absolutely a marvel, on Sunset, across from the Garden of Allah ... Matchless food, service, decor, etc. But with the serious drawback of Preston usually being present, turning his baleful eyes on any patron he did not know personally, so embarrassing that even those who knew him, and perhaps erred by calling him by his first name, were grateful to leave their meal untouched, and slink off!

He definitely regarded The Players as his private club, and when it began to fail on account of his own massive extravagances (an entire hydraulically propelled stage, rising in the midst of bewildered diners, with a live show going on, written by himself, of course!) he kept on pouring more good dough after bad...

And then, at one lucky stroke, very much like one of his own screenplays, he was able to sell his home above Franklin, near Vine Street, to the authorities who were building the new Freeway, for a huge sum. As well as the parking lot next door to his cafe, for a net of around a quarter of a million, at a time when practically nobody was giving The Players much support!

Because, by that time, The Players had gradually dwindled down from an "in" place, to one off-limits. But none of this slowed his runaway imagination to make it more lavish. It was his great white whale, and he'd become Captain Ahab ... He added a hamburger counter on the ground floor level ... Shortly, this latter extension became all that was left of the original grandeur, and Preston, ever the dramatist, used to take perverse delight in wearing his tattered dinner jacket nightly, as he served up the greasy hamburgers in person, making loud, drunken jokes about how the mighty had fallen!

You can easily understand it was a sort of sad, sardonic Sturges humor, the same as you can find in most of his pictures ... But Preston never wept, and he maintained his haughty, unbearable attitude towards the public, right up to the finish, when the whole masterpiece went under, folded ... Barbershop, escalating stage, triple kitchens ... the works.

He didn't bother to lock it up that bleak night. He didn't have to. The L.A. Sheriff's office had already padlocked it ... Inside, locked up with some of his treasures, were memories of all those many movie figures of the '40s, not to forget the faces of the personalities themselves ... the Bogarts and their hideous quarrels, the stars and starlets, the royalty of Hollywood, Howard Hughes, the people from across the street at the Garden of Allah, Bob Benchley and Dorothy Parker ... Marilyn Monroe ... well, you name 'em, they'd all been his customers. All of them treated exactly the same by Preston, with the immense aplomb and icy cool of a man so insulated from life that he was positively unaware of World War II except to deplore, frequently, that everything fine, good, and worth having, everything he stood for, was being ruined by "that man in the White House!"

About all Preston did for the war effort was to permit Roosevelt to buy the model of the H.M.S. *Bounty* from the ship model builder who had been working on the project for Preston for two years!

Ironically enough, it was Metro who had Preston on trial, later, to write a treatment of the *Bounty* story, for a remake. "Treatment?" He didn't even know what one was ... But he assumed I did ... and hoped I might explain it to him. But to no avail.

I'm afraid Preston was wrong, all the way, and if, as they say, a man is judged by his friends, he was both one of my best, and my worst.

...After he butchered my *The Beautiful Blonde from Bashful Bend,* he gave me an engraved solid gold watch, and the insignia on it read "For Earl, Who Forgives Me For Ruining A Lovely Thing."

And, even if Twentieth Century Fox did not, I *did.*

After Sturges died, Edmund Hartmann offered the following:

Chevalier Bard, Roland, Richard ... Preston Sturges was a man in armor, at a time and a place when armor was no longer any protection … certainly not in Hollywood.

He was born and passed away in the wrong century.

I can remember when his young wife presented him with a new baby. When she came home from the hospital, Preston had assembled his entire staff from the Paramount studio, plus a few of his closest friends. They assembled outside Preston's home, on a sunny California morning, quite a crowd. When the limo arrived, Preston opened the door and escorted her out of the back seat; the baby, now ensconced on a large pillow, was carefully carried out, and then the entire assemblage was treated to Preston and his new heir.

A fitting entrance for the new Sturges. Or so Preston believed.

Oh yes, I've heard all the tales of his contempt for his inferiors; his infuriating attitudes during his salad days, when he was the resident genius at Paramount. Perhaps most of the world's picturemakers gave us good, bad, or indifferent variations of the works of D. W. Griffith, or Eisenstein, or Chaplin and Keaton. But Preston added a good deal of his own startling flashes of insight into character.

…*Hail, the Conquering Hero.* An elderly woman looks at the painting of her husband, killed in his youth, in the First World War. She is envious … He will always be young. *The Great McGinty.* Brian Donlevy, now a powerful politico, recalls his years of poverty and child labor. He had to wrap candy, in a factory, hour after hour … He remembers it with pleasure … He *liked* wrapping candy.

… And *Sullivan's Travels.* A depressed Hollywood director who is determined to stop making comedy, in order to make a serious story, *Oh, Brother, Where Art Thou?* And by one of Sturges' tricks of fate, Sullivan ends up down South, in a chain gang … where once a week, a picture is shown to the assembled convicts, a cartoon comedy … and the convicts roar with laughter … They *laugh!* And Sullivan has discovered a truth … that what most people have in their lives is only the gift of comedy. Chained to his fellow convicts, he has learned.

And of course, he returns to Hollywood to make a comedy.

The night when The Players closed, and he'd lost it, along with his mansions and his yacht, and the millions he'd invested, Preston turned to his wife … his usual baronial, unperturbed self.

"Don't worry," he reassured her. "When the last dime is gone, I'll go sit on the curb outside there with a pencil and a ten-cent notebook and start the whole thing over again."

Alas, it was not to be.

There were no more ninth-reel rescues in Sturges' career.

In order to pay off Sturges' debts to him, the head of Paramount arranged for Sturges, the ex-fair-haired boy, to spend six weeks "consulting" on the set of another director. Thus Sturges' salary would recoup the debt.

How ignominious, day after day, for him to sit there behind another director, one who never called on Sturges for any opinion or advice, who totally ignored the late wunderkind of the Paramount lot.

He sweated it out.

He was a hell of a man, and he left his audiences then and now with a magnificent legacy.

In 2001 the Coen brothers paid him tribute by naming their new film *Oh Brother, Where Art Thou?*

Somewhere, Preston must be laughing.

PRESTON STURGES' CREDITS:

ACADEMY AWARD:

The Great McGinty, 1940

ACADEMY AWARD NOMINATIONS:

Hail the Conquering Hero, 1944

The Miracle of Morgan's Creek, 1944

FILMS:

Fast and Loose, 1930

The Big Pond, 1930

Strictly Dishonorable, 1931

The Invisible Man, 1933

The Power and the Glory, 1933

Child of Manhattan, 1933

They Just Had to Get Married, 1933

Imitation of Life, 1934

We Live Again, 1934

Thirty Day Princess, 1934

Twentieth Century, 1934

Diamond Jim, 1935

The Good Fairy, 1935

Love before Breakfast, 1936

Next Time We Love, 1936

Easy Living, 1937

Hotel Haywire, 1937

If I Were King, 1938

Port of Seven Seas, 1938

College Swing, 1938

Never Say Die, 1939

Christmas in July, 1940

Broadway Melody of 1940, 1940

Remember the Night, 1940

Sullivan's Travels, 1941

New York Town, 1941

The Lady Eve, 1941

The Palm Beach Story, 1942

Safeguarding Military Information, 1942

The Great Moment, 1944

The Sin of Harold Diddlebock, 1947

I'll Be Yours, 1947

Unfaithfully Yours, 1948

The Beautiful Blonde from Bashful Bend,
    1949

Vendetta, 1950

Strictly Dishonorable, 1951

The Birds and the Bees, 1956

Rock-a-Bye Baby, 1958

Unfaithfully Yours, 1984

SAMUEL HOFFENSTEIN: "NOTEBOOK of a SCHNOOK"

I write a scenario for moving pictures;
I let myself go without any strictures;
My mind works in bright ascensions;
The characters swell and get dimensions:
The heroine rises from Gimbel's basement
To what could be called a magic casement,
By sheer virtue and, call it pluck,
With maybe a reel and a half of luck;
She doesn't use posterior palsy
Or displace so much as a single falsie;
She scorns the usual oo-la-la
And never ruffles a modest bra,
(The censor's dream of the cinema).
She doesn't find pearls in common oysters;
She sips a little but never roisters.
The hero's gonads are under wraps,
He never clutches or cuffs or slaps —
In heat Vesuvian, or even Stygian
He acts Oxonian or Cantabrigian
With maybe a soupçon of the South —
Cotton wouldn't melt in his mouth.
The plot could harmlessly beguile
A William Wordsworth honey chile;
The Big Shot's hot and the little shotlets
Wake their wives with contagious hotlets.
So what happens? The usual factors —
The studio simply can't get actors,
Directors, cutters, stagehands, stages,
Or girls to type the extra pages:
The way it ends, to put it briefly,
Is what happens is nothing, chiefly.

— SAMUEL HOFFENSTEIN, *Pencil in the Air*, 1947

12. THE BLACKLIST:
DONALD OGDEN STEWART in EXILE

1972

Donald Ogden Stewart at work on a new play

WHEN PHILLIP BARRY'S "THE PHILADELPHIA STORY" WAS REVIVED ON Broadway as the musical *High Society*, the critics were polite and friendly, but they could not help wistfully comparing it to the 1940 film version which starred Katharine Hepburn and Cary Grant. Ironic, indeed. For years, Hollywood was accused of reducing solid-gold dramatic hits from New York and London to double feature assembly-line dross. Not so with Barry's clever play. That original MGM production, with its first-rate cast as directed by George Cukor, has, after all these years, proved to be one tough act to follow. But if so many other Broadway hits, even those guided by Cukor, floundered on film, how is it that Barry's comedy survived the transfer from Broadway to Culver City not only unscathed, but enhanced?

The answer is the screenwriter who turned that brilliant play into a sparkling film — the late Donald Ogden Stewart. But if you had asked Stewart himself how he came to win the Academy Award for Best Screenplay in 1940, he would say, "I didn't really do much with Phil's script. It was so good — I stood back and got out of the way of his characters." Possible, but not probable. Any writer Louis B. Mayer paid $5,250 a week had to be worth it, and that was Stewart's salary until he left

Hollywood at the age of fifty-seven—under something of a cloud—and took up permanent residence in London. Stewart gave Mayer full value during his two decades at MGM—all the way back to the early '30s, when he was Irving Thalberg's favorite crafter of comedy.

Stewart and his wife, Ella, settled in a London far less chic than now. They bought a remarkable pink house with a terraced garden, high on a steeply winding Hampstead street known as Frognal. There at 103, within the walls that had once belonged to Prime Minister James Ramsay MacDonald, the Stewarts kept open house, dispensing tea and sympathy, wine, wit, and hospitality to friends, visitors, and fellow expatriates—of whom in the '50s and '60s there were many, thanks to the infamous Hollywood blacklist.

Don—nobody ever called him anything more formal—was a jovial, lanky gentleman, blessed with modesty and a gentle wit. "Success was always easy for me," he said, adding, "maybe a little too easy, toots." He had flourished first as a practicing humorist during the '20s in Manhattan, where his cronies included F. Scott Fitzgerald, Robert Benchley, Dorothy Parker, Edmund Wilson, and Herman Mankiewicz. When Don's good pal Ernest Hemingway wrote *The Sun Also Rises*, a thinly disguised Don was immortalized as one of the characters.

He wrote several successful Broadway plays, and then he answered the siren call of Hollywood very early, even before the advent of the talkies. "Those were the days when you could have a lot of fun out there," he recalled, during a series of conversations we had in the early 1970s. "It was in 1926, and here I was, a Yale man—so of course the first thing they put me to work on was a screenplay called *Brown of Harvard*." There were journeys back and forth between Hollywood and New York. But then came the talking picture, and by 1931, Don had moved out to stay.

Decades later, Don, settled in London, was to find himself historic. No matter how much he had accomplished on his own, he had become a legend because of his friends. His phone rang steadily with requests for interviews. "All anybody wants to know is what really happened with Hem and me when we ran with the bulls at Pamplona!" Don would complain. "Or how come old Scott had such a terrible time trying to write screenplays at MGM, or was it true that Dotty Parker almost set fire to herself in a story conference with Hunt Stromberg—as if I knew that!"

Don and Ella attracted a constant parade of friends, as well as the historians. Charlie Chaplin and Oona, his wife (with or without children), Katharine Hepburn (who, during a strike of garbage men, made special trips to Frognal in her Rolls and picked up Don and Ella's garbage to have it disposed of at Claridge's!), S. J. Perelman (with whom Don had labored in the Culver City vineyards), painters, politicians, Third World diplomats, old political buddies—all filled the house with argument, gossip, and laughter.

Guests were surrounded by a jungle-like array of plants and Ella's amazingly eclectic collection of art: Klee drawings, Walker Evans photographs, Picasso and Grosz, African Bakota masks, Japanese netsuke, and Ming china. In drafty back rooms were Marini sculptures and rare Ernst pieces. Ella's treasures spilled out, helter-skelter, in all directions. Amidst all these treasures, browsers in cinema history, including myself, came to question Don about his own remarkable screenwriting career. "It wasn't much," he would complain. "Surely, you don't want to rehash all that stuff, do you?" Indeed, I did. Despite his own modest self-appraisal, Don's name is on the credits for such landmark films as *Dinner at Eight*, *The Prisoner of Zenda*, *The Barretts of Wimpole Street*, *Marie Antoinette*, *Kitty Foyle*, and *Love Affair*. And *Holiday*, which he and Sidney Buchman adapted from Phillip Barry's play.

Holiday was the first Hepburn vehicle Don worked on. He went on to do *Without Love* and *The Keeper of the Flame*. In the last, Hepburn starred as the widow of an American neo-fascist would-be dictator. "Now that one is the picture I'm proudest of having had anything to do with," he said. "It expressed the most about fascism which was possible at the time—at MGM, in 1942. I. A. R. Wylie had written this novel about the possibility of fascism taking over America, and I didn't change her story at all. When we were making it, we had to keep it all very quiet. After all, our boss L. B. Mayer was not exactly a liberal type, right?... L. B. went to see the picture at the Music Hall and got so sore at the political attitudes of the script, he got up and stamped right out!"

Don hadn't always been a liberal. Educated at Yale, part of the jazz-era New York '20s scene, he had enjoyed life along with all his sophisticated pals. But when the Depression settled in, Don's political consciousness flared into life. "I think the turning point for me came when things got really tough, in 1932, and L. B. Mayer, who was a big pal of President Hoover, called us in, one by one, into his office. There he was, sitting behind that huge desk, almost on a throne, and he began to cry. Old L. B. was a marvelous weeper. He said, 'Oh, this Depression, it's just terrible, isn't it?' I said, 'I guess it is, Mr. Mayer.' Then he said, 'Don, I'm going to have to ask you a terrific favor, personally. To help me stay in business, I want you to agree to take a cut in salary.' And so help me, he began to cry again! I said, 'Well, L. B., for heavens' sake, I'm only too glad to be of help.' What else could I say? Later on, of course, we found out everybody in the whole place had taken a cut—except L. B.!

"But after that, some of us out in the studios began to feel a certain amount of awareness. In 1935, we got together to organize the Hollywood Anti-Nazi League and started trying to alert people to the threat Hitler was. There was going to be a meeting at which we would do a reading of Irwin Shaw's new play, *Bury the Dead*. The day of the affair, Sam Marx, the Metro story editor, came into my office, shut the door, and said, 'Look, Don, Irving won't like it if you take part in this meeting.' I guess that was when I took a stand. Good Lord, I knew about Irving—he'd been a socialist himself. As a boy he'd made street-corner speeches in New York —and here he was, trying to keep me from exercising the right of free speech, just because he had me under contract!"

If the League and other organizations were Communist fronts and he and others involved were somehow duped, Don remained unashamed. "Oh sure, maybe they were," he said years afterwards, "but I don't have any excuses to make for what we were doing then. Far from it. If you'd been to any of our rallies and meetings and heard the speeches—my Lord, I even got Ernest Hemingway to come address the League of American Writers on the war in Spain, and Hem certainly was no dupe—you'd have recognized that what was being said was really good old honest American anti-fascism. We were trying to prepare America for an understanding of what was really going on in Hitler's Germany and in Italy… That's what we were worried about, toots. And we were damned right to worry, wouldn't you agree?"

Politics make strange bedfellows. The creation of classic hit movies makes even stranger ones. Producer-director Leo McCarey was one of

Hollywood's most fervent anti-Communists, but Don and Delmer Daves wrote the screenplay for McCarey's *Love Affair*. "Leo was great fun — as a person," Don recalled. "Sure, he was mixed up in that outfit dedicated to the preservation of American ideals — whatever that meant — along with John Wayne, Adolphe Menjou, Ward Bond, Sam Wood, and a whole bunch of others. Those guys really despised everything we were doing — politically — but when he wanted a good script, Leo could forget politics. Our relationship was strictly business. We talked story — never Spain."

And as for Stewart's other employers? "Well, Jack Warner and his brother Harry went along with the blacklisting, but when they needed a script for *Life with Father* it didn't seem to bother them much when they hired me, in 1947. And the year after that, L. B. Mayer assigned me to Sinclair Lewis's book, *Cass Timberlane*, for Spencer Tracy and Lana Turner."

So when did the guillotine blade finally descend? "It was right after I did *Edward, My Son* that I got knocked off," Don recounted. "That was in 1949, and they were beginning to close in on me. Ella and I came over here to London so I could see the play, and then I wrote the screenplay for Spencer, with George Cukor directing. There were some people who spread the story around that Metro had sent me out of the country so I couldn't be served with a subpoena by the House Un-American Activities Committee guys. But I did go back to Hollywood, and I never did get subpoenaed." Don shrugged. "Maybe they were looking for some other Don Stewart, just like in a plot for a Hitchcock picture, you know, and they chased that poor guy all over, thinking that he was me? Who knows? Anyway, I'd written a play — *The Kidders* — and an English producer wanted to put it on here, so we came back to London — and we've been here ever since.

"By that time, Metro had decided I was unemployable. But I had one of those wonderful contracts, negotiated by Leland Hayward, with iron-clad clauses — and since I hadn't done anything reprehensible — at least nothing in public!" Don beamed, "my lawyer negotiated a very lovely settlement... So, in a way, I was ahead of the game."

Not at all like some of the other unfortunate victims of the blacklist, who'd struggled to earn a living under pen names, for so many years.

Don shook his head sadly. "Please don't remind me," he sighed. "We stay in touch with as many of them as we can, over the years. It's something like a brotherhood of pain; we try to sustain each other."

While so many other talented playwrights and authors and writers had floundered in the Hollywood film factories, Don had kept at it from the silent days of the 1920s for almost half a century. Had he managed to develop some modus vivendi that had enabled him to stay on track? "Yes, I did come by some rules," Don admitted. "For whatever they're worth. First, you had to try and find out who the star of the picture you were writing was going to be. That's primary. It's very disconcerting to have written something for Joan Crawford, and then find out it's actually going to be Lana Turner...Secondly, never, never tackle a screenplay at the beginning. Let the producer and his writers do a couple of drafts and mess it up...Then, after they've made all the mistakes possible, and they're faced with a shooting date, you can come in and rewrite that mess, and be a big hero. And finally," Don said, softly, and unsmiling, "you had to learn not to let them break your heart."

Donald Ogden Stewart's Credit

Academy Award:

The Philadelphia Story, 1940

Academy Award Nomination:

Laughter, 1930

Films:

Brown of Harvard, 1926

Humorous Flights, 1929

Traffic Regulations, 1929

Rebound, 1931

Tarnished Lady, 1931

Finn and Hattie, 1931

Red Dust, 1932

Smilin' Through, 1932

Going Hollywood, 1933

Dinner at Eight, 1933

Another Language, 1933

The White Sister, 1933

The Barretts of Wimpole Street, 1934

No More Ladies, 1935

Reckless, 1935

The Prisoner of Zenda, 1937

Marie Antoinette, 1938

Holiday, 1938

The Night of Nights, 1939

The Women, 1939

Love Affair, 1939

Kitty Foyle: The Natural History of a Woman, 1940

Smilin' Through, 1941

A Woman's Face, 1941

That Uncertain Feeling, 1941

Keeper of the Flame, 1942

Tales of Manhattan, 1942

Forever and a Day, 1943

Without Love, 1945

Cass Timberlane, 1947

Life with Father, 1947

Edward, My Son, 1949

Europa '51, 1951

The Prisoner of Zenda, 1952

Escapade, 1955

Summertime, 1955

An Affair to Remember, 1957

Moment of Danger, 1960

Love and Death, 1975

Love Affair, 1994

BERTOLD BRECHT DEPARTS

"WHEN WE FIRST WENT TO SALKA VIERTEL'S HOUSE IN HOLLYWOOD," SAID Ella Winter, "we met Bertold Brecht, who was there with his wife, Helena Weigel, who was later to run the Berliner Ensemble."

"He was like a man you'd expect to be the gardener," said her husband, Donald Ogden Stewart. "If you didn't know who he was, you couldn't imagine what he was doing there at Salka's..."

"...and his wife was a typical hausfrau," added Ella.

When Brecht appeared in front of the House Un-American Activities Committee, he left Washington that night by plane for Paris.

The Stewarts were in Paris, at Les Invalides Station, and Ella reported she saw Brecht standing there, wearing a large hat, smoking a cigar. She went over, not believing it could be him, to make sure, and finally established that he was, in fact, Brecht. What was he doing in Paris, when they had just read the testimony he'd given, the day before, in Washington?

"I had a ticket booked on every airline out of Washington for every day. I waited, until they finally got to me, and I testified, and I left," said Brecht. "I know that when they start to accuse you of stealing the Empire State Building, it's time to get the hell out!"

HOWARD KOCH on AYN RAND

IN OUR STUDIO [WARNER BROS.], TWO OF THE LEADING ACTIVISTS IN social-political causes were Dalton Trumbo and John Howard Lawson. At the opposite political pole was Ayn Rand, employed by the studio for a brief time to write the screenplay based on her popular novel, *The Fountainhead*...In later years she founded the cult which she called objectivism—whose cornerstone is unbridled individualism, the God-given right of a power elite to impose its will on a less advantaged minority. Over the years she had gained a considerable following among people of her persuasion...

Needless to say, she did not have much of a following at Warners and kept herself pretty well isolated. My contact with her was a curious one. When Robert Rossen left for Columbia Pictures, his office opposite mine was assigned to Miss Rand. Between our rooms was the outer office occupied by our secretaries. Her secretary passed the word to mine that Miss Rand wished not to be disturbed...At times, when my door was opened, I caught her peeking in at me from her office as though I was some sort of alien creature she was studying from a discreet distance.

One winter day her scrupulous privacy broke down. It was pouring rain and when it rains in California, which is seldom, the heavens open up and the gutterless streets are quickly flooded. Apparently Miss Rand had no car and at the end of this particular day was unable to get a taxi. Her secretary whispered to my secretary, asking whether I would let her ride with me as far as Hollywood...So I crossed the forbidden threshold and said that of course, I would be willing to take her. This was my first close look at her. She was small, dark-haired, thin-faced, with watchful eyes.

In the car I started a casual conversation, at first briefly, then more volubly as we drove down Cahuenga Pass to Hollywood Boulevard, her destination. I stopped the car. Before she moved, she looked straight at me.

"I didn't know you were this way at all."

I was surprised. "What way? What do you mean?"

She didn't answer until she had climbed out of the car and faced me. Her tone was as accusing as though I had committed eight of the seven deadly sins. "You wrote *Mission to Moscow*."

Before I could make any response, she closed the door and hurried away. I don't know what sort of person Miss Rand expected to find seated beside her, possibly a commissar in the guise of a screenwriter.

—HOWARD KOCH, 1979

13. MARRIED ... with TALENT:
ALBERT and FRANCES HACKETT

New York, 1972

Albert and Frances Hackett

Chances are, if you're lucky, you can enjoy a good marriage. But a good collaboration with another writer, which is another form of marriage?

Much rarer.

Often, in the early days of screenwriting, a team would consist of two writers yoked together by chance or by choice (usually the producer's). One such partner would be the fount of ideas, always on his feet, throwing gag lines, tossing off old and new jokes, pitching plot suggestions as he paced back and forth. He would be "the talking writer." In story conferences with the producer, he would be the verbose babbler.

His partner, who sat at the typewriter, had the job of getting it all down in proper script form, line by line, scene by scene. His billing? "The writing writer."

Of such partnerships, dozens of assembly-line studio screenplays were spawned—some to die aborning, others to be filmed and to die at the box office.

What went on in those smoke-filled rooms, day after day, in the Writers Building? Ask any writer who served time in such a relationship, and you'll discover that the nitty gritty of collaboration means staying in that work space, hour after hour, arguing, suggesting, discussing, wrestling with unsolved plot problems, rewriting, cutting lines and (whether one feels up to it or not) turning in a daily ration of pages—while attempting to stay on a first-name basis with your collaborator.

Not an easy way to earn a living. Or a screen credit.

The major problem is ego. All writers, good or bad, come equipped with one. And that daily session in a small space with another such ego— it may produce a script, but it also breeds argument, angst, and hostility.

Being fifty percent of a two-person writing team is a bit like marriage, without the side benefits of sex.

There's a tale of two legendary screenwriters, circa the early '30s. Both of them were capable of writing alone, but somehow they'd been shackled by success to work with each other. At first, they managed well enough, but personalities intruded. Soon, each partner had grown to despise the other. Would that they could divorce—but alas, it was economically impossible. William Lipman and Horace McCoy, the two writers, were in demand with producers only as a team; it was not possible for their agent to sell them as individuals. (One can almost hear their agent paraphrasing the old backstage classic cliché: "They don't want you *alone*, baby ... they want the *team!*")

Eventually, Lipman and McCoy ended up working out a system whereby they might continue to secure assignments as a working team. It was during the Depression, remember, and jobs were scarce; desperation led to a system of avoidance.

One of them would spend the day, by himself, writing in their office. Finished by 5 PM, he'd depart. After supper, the other would appear, to read the pages left behind and then carry on writing. Late at night, he'd leave for home; the next morning, his partner would pick up where the other had left off!

This Cox and Boxian arrangement continued for some time, but eventually, ego triumphed, and their structure came apart. Each man went on his own way. What became of Lipman? More screen credits. Alone, McCoy would write a classic novel, *They Shoot Horses, Don't They?*

In extremely rare cases, collaborating teams have actually been married couples, capable of bringing home their labors from the studio office to the toaster bedroom suite and then back again the following day. Such teams provided new meaning to the old phrase "pillow talk." In the early silent days, Anita Loos and her husband John Emerson worked very successfully. Eventually, alas, personality problems caused a permanent rift. Think also of Garson Kanin and Ruth Gordon, who were able to merge their talents, he as a director and she as a leading lady, to produce both Broadway comedies and original Hollywood screenplays. *Adam's Rib*, *Born Yesterday*, *Pat and Mike*, to cite only a few.

Buy tickets to *Kiss Me Kate*, and you will enjoy the brilliant libretto provided to Cole Porter by Sam and Bella Spewack, a team who spent many profitable years traveling back and forth between Broadway and Hollywood writing films and plays. In fact, they would turn their studio experiences into a hilarious Broadway comedy, *Boy Meets Girl.*

Dorothy Parker and her husband, Alan Campbell, also managed to write in Hollywood, as did Sid Perelman and his wife Laura.

But one of the very earliest and longest-lived husband-and-wife teams to arrive in Hollywood, back in the early 1930s, was the skillful married couple known on both coasts as "the Hacketts."

Albert and Frances Hackett's list of screen credits is remarkable, both in length and in variety. Their first film, *Up Pops the Devil*, was based on a play they'd produced on Broadway. Over the ensuing decades, the team was responsible for such first-rate works as *The Thin Man*, *Naughty Marietta*, *Lady in the Dark*, *Easter Parade*, *Seven Brides for Seven Brothers*, *Father of the Bride*, *The Pirate*, and the enduring Christmas classic that arrives every year, *It's a Wonderful Life.*

Their play, *The Diary of Anne Frank*, which ran on Broadway in 1955, won them the Pulitzer Prize; they later adapted it into a highly successful film.

It was a sunny morning in 1972 when they sat down in their Central Park West living room and reviewed their early days in California. What was it like at Metro, in those frantic days when Manhattan playwrights were being shipped out by the trainload to supply "dialogue" for the new wave of "all-talking" pictures?

"Oh, it was amazing," said Albert Hackett. "To give you an idea of how confused things were, I remember once we were sent into a conference room. I don't remember how many writers there were, but they'd decided

that Frances and I were going to do the dialogue for this project … We had
no idea what it was. They'd figure out the story, and then give it to us.

"We listened to them all talking, and the idea they'd come up with
seemed to be 'Spend Money and Bring Back Prosperity.' Who knew what
they meant by that?"

"Not us," chuckled Frances. "But everybody thought, 'That's a wonderful idea! We've really got something there—right?' So we went to our
office, and there was another guy who was supposed to write the continuity for us … Sullivan or something. And he came to see us, very excited.
'I've got the opening sequence! It's a man, he's a very mysterious character,
and he comes downstairs, he's got a grip full of money … As he comes
down the stairs, see, this grip breaks open, and he has bills flying all over
the place—and he scoops it all up, stuffs it all back into the bag, and he
hurries out … And he's mysterious as hell! I don't know what he's mysterious about, I haven't got that yet!' Then he left.

"The next day," she recalled, "we went over to the main office and told
them we were wasting their money by putting us on this thing, because we
didn't have a clue as to what was going on … And they were all very dis-
heartened by that … But so were we"

Hackett shook his head sadly. "One day they came to us and sent us
to see a producer … He was in his office, laughing and laughing, and he
said, 'What do you think of a story with Clark Gable and Jean Harlow …
and the picture is called, *Nice Girls Don't Swear?*' And then he went into
gales of laughter, so we smiled and laughed, too. And he asked, 'Funny?'
And we said, 'Yes, very funny.' And then he said, 'Go ahead—write it.'

"So we went away bewildered, and we spent a couple of hours trying
to figure out something to go with that crazy title, and then we went to
have lunch, still bewildered at this thing … And while we're eating, Sam
Marx, the head of the story department came over and said, 'I just want
to tell you, *we* don't own that title!' So here we were, with *nothing!* And
after another night of wondering what to do, the next day we went into
the producer and told him we thought we were wasting his time … And
we got off that thing pronto."

"That's how it was in those days," said Mrs. Hackett. "Very frustrating
for all the writers who were around."

"…And there were so many out there, then," recalled her husband. "It was a remarkable time. Such an illustrious, incredible group of people, all working in Hollywood! Dottie Parker, Ogden Nash, Lillian Hellman ... Sid and Laura Perelman ... Dashiell Hammett. Every important playwright or author came out ... all over town! One time I sat down in the commissary, a man came in and sat down, you couldn't see him because his back was toward us, but later, I got a look at him ... he had the saddest, most tragic eyes. He sat there for a bit, fussed with his briefcase for a minute, and then got up, without having anything to eat ... It was Scott Fitzgerald. Just breaking in to picture writing, low in spirits ... lonely and disturbed ... trying to learn an entirely new medium. He was working on something for Hunt Stromberg, the producer, called *Infidelity*. Didn't work, I think..." He shook his head sadly. "We all know what a terrible time he had out there."

"What about Ogden Nash, that wonderful poet?" said Mrs. Hackett. "He came out to Metro and he really hated it. He and Sid Perelman were put on something called *How to Win Friends and Influence People!* which was a book by Dale Carnegie, of all people! And Ogden was miserable and he was sick, too. He used to run a fever every afternoon, around 4 PM ... But who could blame him? What are you supposed to do with a project like that? Carnegie's book was a how-to book; it had no story at all, nothing to do with movies. And here are these two guys, one a brilliant satirist from *The New Yorker* and the other a brilliant poet, and they're assigned to make something out of nothing? Impossible."

"Actually," mused her husband, "didn't Ogden actually work on something that we did? He did the adaptation of an Otto Harbach musical operetta, *Firefly*, for Jeanette MacDonald."

Which seems an unlikely assignment for Nash, the lyricist who would later write, with Kurt Weill, the classic "Speak Low" in his brilliant *One Touch of Venus*.

On which he collaborated with Sid Perelman. "Oh, that's another sad story," said Hackett. "Sid and his wife Laura had written a play called *All Good Americans*, and Hunt Stromberg, the producer we worked for there, gave it to us to read and said that Metro had bought it. We read it and we thought it was very funny. We thought we'd be working on it, but no, suddenly the play just disappeared. We didn't know what had happened, it just vanished.

"Well, years later, I found out they used the Perelman play for *screen tests!* All the kids, the contract youngsters who were at the studio, in the school, or being trained, or whatever, they were using scenes from this play in *tests!* We never knew what had happened...and of course, it was the kind of thing that drove writers crazy."

Is the legend of P. G. Wodehouse, the brilliant British writer who'd been brought out to Metro then, and who never wrote a line for two years while he was on weekly salary, a true story, or is it a myth?

"Not at all," said Mrs. Hackett. "What I heard was that they would call him at his home—he lived somewhere in Beverly Hills, and they'd say, 'Mr. Thalberg wants to see you now," and he would say, 'Oh, absolutely.' And then he would walk from Beverly Hills six or seven miles to Culver City...By the time he got over there, he was a bit tired, but he'd go in and say he was there for his appointment. They said, 'Oh, Mr. Thalberg has gone home.' So Wodehouse would rest a bit and then he'd walk back home."

"There's another story about some author who came out there...I can't remember who he was, it was so long ago, but he had a long beard, like George Bernard Shaw, and somebody told me the man kept trying to get into the studio and find out what he was supposed to do. And poor man, he was so lost, he couldn't get anybody to tell him where to get inside the studio, which gate...And then he finally found a gate where the extras came in...and the studio guard looked at him and said, 'Sorry...no beards today.'"

Those were the days of the Depression, and everywhere outside the Metro gates, there was dire economic poverty in the Culver City streets... while inside, enormous sums of money were being wasted.

"I'm not sure how much was being wasted on writers," observed Mrs. Hackett, dryly. "Mostly, it was on star salaries and bad pictures."

But eventually, what about that famous day when L. B. Mayer called everyone in the studio together to announce how dire things were and insisted everyone take a fifty percent cut in salaries?

Is it any wonder everybody in the studio began to organize? Secretaries, technical people...even us, the writers!" recalled Hackett

"We always said, Louis Mayer made more communists than Karl Marx," said his wife. "Actually, everybody took a cut except Wallace Beery.

212

But he was so tough. On every picture he did, the last scene would come, and Wally would look around the set at the furniture, and say, 'I'll take that,' and grab it, whatever he fancied and start home with it … And they'd say, 'Wally, look, we may have to do a retake on this scene.' And he'd say, 'Okay, if there's a retake, I'll lend it to you!'"

"Finally we got to do a picture," said Hackett, "and we had a crazy time on that. It was something called *A Lady*. It was an English play. The leading part was a girl who always wanted to be a lady, and it ends up, she's a prostitute in France, where she's got a house … And her illegitimate son is in the British army, and guess what, he comes to her house … Anyway, the final scene of this terrible play is that her son has killed somebody in the house in some involved brawl, and she says, 'I did it!' … And the boy gets off, free. And now she's mopping up the bar, weeping, and she says to somebody, 'That was my son, and I always wanted to be a lady.' And the guy behind the bar says, 'Well, he's a gentleman, your son is, because his mother was a lady.' … And that, believe it or not, was the final curtain!"

A typical mediocre melodrama of the '30s?

Hackett nodded. "The worst sort. And there we were, stuck with this terrible play, and we didn't know what the hell to do with it. Anyway, we started by making her into an American chorus girl who came over, so at least we knew what she'd be like, and then we started to try and write it …

"And then George Kelly came in to visit us … he'd drop by every few days—"

George Kelly, the playwright? Who had written *Craig's Wife*, *The Show-Off*, and *The Torch Bearers*?

"Oh yes, he'd come out to work in the pictures, too," said Hackett.

"And we were friends, old friends, because I'd been in *The Show-Off*, in New York," said his wife. "We used to talk about what we were doing, and he would come up with suggestions, and finally, one day, he told us he'd been put to work on a play which sounded very much like the one we were working on—and it *was!* They'd forgotten to tell us—and that's how we found out we'd been taken off."

"Poor George," says Hackett. "He had no idea what to do with this terrible play, but he tried, and sent in scenes—he usually worked off the lot. Finally Hunt Stromberg, the producer, gave it back to us … Oh, it was such a terrible job. We tried everything. We thought of making the leading

213

lady somebody like Sophie Tucker! Well, finally we finished it, and they actually made it."

REVIEW: THE SECRET OF MADAME BLANCHE, 1933: "Another dip into the 'Madame X—Sin of Madelon Claudet' corn bag. Irene Dunne and Douglas Walton played mother and son who didn't know who they were until he committed murder, whereupon she took the blame."

"It was truly a stinker," sighed Mrs Hackett. "I remember there was a trade paper called *Motion Picture Herald*, and they used to have a section in it from exhibitors all over the country who'd write in—it was called "What The Picture Did For Me." And when we read it, about our picture, one guy wrote in and said, 'Look out for this one, boys, it's a Stinkola!' And another one wrote, 'Pay for it—but *don't* play it.'"

"But in spite of that, we stayed with Hunt, and he was our boss for many years. He was a wonderful producer to work with...because when we were working with him, it was just like working in the theatre...We were in on everything, the casting, the rushes...the works," said Hackett. "We had this wonderful feeling of being part of it, with some responsibility for doing our best work."

Rare, indeed, in a studio structure where writers would finish a script and then have nothing to do with it from then on.

"Things were very tough for writers," sighed Hackett. "All those poor people, earning salaries and sitting in cubicles, trying to struggle with stories like *The Lady*—or being told, 'Here's a title, go make a picture out of this.'"

"Hunt was different from so many of the other producers," recalled his wife. "They were guys who'd get a script finished, and then they'd send it around to some other writer, and ask him to read it, and then say, 'What do you think?' And the writer would probably say, 'Well, it's a little... shaky, here and there.' And the producer would say, 'Well, why don't you brush it up a little?' And the writer would be sitting in his office, hanging on to his job, and tinkering with the script, brushing it up, changing lines here and there, so he could look like he was actually doing something, when he was really lousing up the script.

"It was always the producer's fault. Because nobody had the courage to say, 'This is all right, it works fine—I'll stand behind you. This is what we'll shoot.'" she said.

Could it possibly be that they didn't know?

"Oh well, they *didn't* know! Absolutely," said her husband. "So many of those Metro producers really didn't know anything."

And were afraid to say anything because their ignorance would show?

"Sure, and they would go on, look at some other picture there, one that had been successful, and try to make it conform to that pattern. Whatever had been a hit last week, that was what they wanted to do."

It has become very fashionable lately to refer to these times as the golden era of Hollywood, but when one looks over those so-called golden years, the ratio of really good films to bad ones is remarkably low. Mostly, what was being turned out on the studio assembly lines was truly terrible.

"Absolutely," said Mrs. Hackett. "There's no other word for it. Somehow, with Hunt it was different. But he was rare. At Metro, he was only accountable to Irving Thalberg ... And he'd have the guts to say to us, 'This is the way it is, this is how I see the picture, it's the way we'll go, and I trust you two to write it for me.'

"And he *listened*... Not many writers could have that going with a producer ... We could go off on a vacation and when we'd come back we'd say, 'We found a beautiful actor in New York,' and he'd say, 'Who, who?' and we'd say, 'He's a young guy named Jimmy Stewart,' and next thing you'd know, they'd signed him up, and he'd come out, and he ended up in one of our Thin Man pictures. Not the first one. Stromberg put him into *Rose Marie*, which we wrote ... and he played Jeanette MacDonald's brother."

It was also the era when writers were being categorized by their abilities. One writer might be good for dialogue, another for action sequences, a third for love scenes, and so forth.

Mrs. Hackett smiled, "Someone once told us, 'I've heard a wonderful thing about you two.' They said, 'The Hacketts can write a whole picture. They can do the beginning, the middle, *and* the end.'"

"There was another team like us there," her husband said. "Bella and Sam Spewack, they were awfully good, and also fast. Between us and the Spewacks, we used to turn out almost a quarter of the pictures each year!"

"We were known as the gentile Spewacks!" she added.

What were Dashiell Hammett's experiences at Metro?

"Well, at first, it was *The Thin Man*, and they bought the book, so he didn't have to do anything...But he came out anyway, and after the picture came out, which we'd written for Hunt, and it was such a big hit, Metro wanted to buy the two characters of Nick and Nora from him. But Dash wasn't stupid; he held out on that and wouldn't sell them. So they settled by asking him to write another story...and they got one from him, and we wrote it. And the third time, they wanted him to come up with another, and he suggested a story about dope..." recalled Mrs. Hackett.

"Which was absolutely out of the question, they wouldn't touch dope," said her husband. "And we were hung up...But Dash was a good friend, and a very generous guy, so he came in and gave us a plot idea for *Another Thin Man*, and we wrote it.

"But then he said, 'I am absolutely not going to do any more of these things,' and we knew we weren't going to either! And that was the end of that. And we were also beginning to get tired of writing for Jeanette MacDonald, with or without Nelson Eddy."

"We put in a long stretch at Metro..." said Mrs. Hackett. "But we were never glamour; we were just very busy writers."

And who *was* glamour?

"Oh, the way somebody like Don Stewart was...Or when someone like Hugh Walpole came over from London to do dialogue for *David Copperfield*. Or when they hired Frederick Lonsdale to come from London to work on a script of his play, *The Last of Mrs. Cheyney*."

"Do you remember there was a table in the middle dining room, where the high-priced writers ate?" said her husband. "We were never allowed there, we weren't earning a big enough salary to sit with them."

"Oh yes," said his wife. "I remember once there was a writers meeting, and you know who showed up? Aldous Huxley and H. G. Wells, among others. Amazing!

"And then, during the late '30s, then all those refugee writers would appear, Germans and Austrians...and they were all hoping to get jobs. It was so sad. We'd see them again and again at lunchtime, people like Franz Werfel and Lion Feuchtwanger...and other playwrights...They were waiting for somebody to use them...I'm not sure any of them actually did get work."

"But then, there were plenty of other people who had tough times," said Hackett. He shook his head. "So many years ago, a lot of it comes back to me just sitting here and talking about those days—horror stories, actually. I remember Jimmy Gleason, he was an actor who also wrote... Anyway, he took a job at Metro to write a version of a play... it was called *Turn to the Right*. They owned it. And so they sent him the scripts they'd already had written on it... It was something like eighteen scripts! Piled high on his desk, and they sat there, all those versions written by other writers."

And what happened to it?

"Who knows?" shrugs Hackett. "Did it get made? I doubt it."

"I know another horror story," said his wife. "A dreadful story. There was a writer, Wilbur Daniel Steele, a very fine writer in fact. Married to a woman, Norma Mitchell, she never thought of herself as a writer, but she was an actress. She and Russell Medcraft had written a play called *The Cradle Snatchers*. Some studio bought it, and so out they came, Norma and Wilbur; she was getting jobs all the time out there, but Wilbur? He couldn't get arrested. And finally, he got a job at Paramount. Now this was a man whose short stories were published, he'd won awards, and you've never seen anybody so proud, just to get a job in a studio...

"And finally he finds out they wanted him to work on a story of his *own*—one that they haven't even *bought*!... And then, they tell him, they want to change his story... which is why they brought him in. Well, he wouldn't do it... He told them, 'This is the way I wrote this originally, you know.' But they still didn't buy the story from him... They'd had everybody working on it, and they didn't even know they didn't own it, isn't that ridiculous? And what made it even worse was he was being paid *half* of what his wife Norma was getting.

"One night they came to our house for dinner, and he was out in the hall with me, telling me all this... and he began to cry. It was so humiliating for him, so horrible... He just could not adapt himself to what people who were so crude and stupid were doing to his own work—which they didn't even own.

"...Norma finally couldn't stand what it was doing to him, and they both went home; she couldn't let this happen to him any longer."

They broke quite a few hearts out there in sunny California, didn't they?

Mrs. Hackett nodded. "I just remembered another one... Don Marquis."

The author of *Archy and Mehitabel* came to Hollywood?

"Indeed he did. It was one of those *Skippy* things. He was very bitter... He'd write little snippets of scenes... Scribble them on little pieces of paper. And somebody would come into his office and take those things out of his wastebasket and say, 'Would you please sign a release on this?' Out of his wastebasket! He'd thrown it away, and they wanted a release because it was written on studio time."

The idea of bringing a writer of the status of Don Marquis to Hollywood to work on a picture like *Skippy* does indeed boggle the mind. Why would he come?

"He needed the money," explained Hackett. "He was a man who always needed it... Same reason Faulkner came...

"I remember once we had an office in the old Metro administration building... Turned out we were using Faulkner's old office—a curious kind of a little place. And there on the desk was a single yellow pad. He'd left it; on it he made a calendar... He had all the weekly paydays circled ... And then he'd written at the top, 'Boy Meets Girl'. That's all there was on the pad."

(Billy Wilder reported this differently—but then, that's the problem with legends, isn't it?)

"Oh, there were so many other writers out there during those years," said Mrs. Hackett. "We were always running into people like John O'Hara. He came out and worked on some very strange assignments... usually at Fox, I think it was."

Strange, indeed, for the author of *Butterfield 8* and *Appointment in Samarra* to be sitting in an office working on such assignments as *I Was an Adventuress* and *He Married His Wife* (on which he is one of *six* writers credited for the screenplay).

"He wasn't very happy out there," she recalls.

But O'Hara managed to get a novel out of his experiences in Southern California. His novel, *Hope of Heaven*, is a thinly disguised story of his love affair with a girl whom he encountered in a Beverly Hills bookstore. Along the way, he describes the difficulties of writing screenplays with considerable angst.

And what about the wittiest lady who occupied a regular seat at the Algonquin Round Table of the '20s? Dorothy Parker was out West, earning a living in the studios, wasn't she?

"It wasn't easy to get her to concentrate on work," said Hackett. "She obviously loathed what they assigned her to do, she and her husband, Alan Campbell. We had an office right next door to theirs, and the walls were thin, and we could hear Alan pushing, pushing her to write. That was his whole job ... Oh, Dottie was so brilliant; at night, when we played parlor games, she'd come up with those wonderful cracks.

"But when it came to writing screenplays, everybody knows how much she despised working on scripts," he said. "When Hunt Stromberg put Dottie and Alan to work on *Sweethearts*, which was an operetta for Jeanette MacDonald and Nelson Eddy, she hated it so, she wouldn't make any contribution at all ... Poor Alan, he had to sit at the typewriter and try to keep going on it all by himself. He'd sit there trying to get her to help him, and we could hear him saying, 'So and so says,' and then he says, 'and now, what does *she* say?... Dottie, *don't use that word!*' because all she was saying was 'Shit, shit, *shit!*' And his voice would get higher and higher, all through the day, and Dottie sat there with a piece of knitting in her lap, smoking, and occasionally saying 'Shit, *shit!*'

"...But we always had hopes for her, perhaps if she got onto something instead of *Sweethearts*, maybe things would get better..."

And quite often, they did. Miss Parker contributed lyrics to a lovely ballad with composer Ralph Rainger, "I Wished On The Moon." And later, she and Campbell were hired by David Selznick to write the screenplay for *A Star Is Born*. "And that turned out to be a beautiful job, didn't it?" said Mrs. Hackett.

"But we knew how she felt," said her husband, sadly. "Every so often, out there, you'd be given a story to do, and if we thought we were going to stink on it ... then we'd do our best to back away. Self-preservation, you know.

"But on a lot of them, we couldn't manage to do so ... We couldn't get off before we made the stink!"

There are very few *stinks* on the Hackett list of credits.

Obviously, in the midst of all the madness and the mayhem of studio production all those years, Mr. and Mrs. Hackett managed to do something right, most of the time.

Sit back and enjoy the fruits of their considerable labors each night or so, on AMC and TCM. And be grateful for their very successful marriage.

Frances and Albert Hackett's Credits:

Academy Award Nominations:

The Thin Man, 1934

After the Thin Man, 1936

Father of the Bride, 1950

Seven Brides for Seven Brothers, 1954

Films:

Up Pops the Devil, 1931

The Secret of Madame Blanche, 1933

Penthouse, 1933

Chained, 1934

Fugitive Lovers, 1934

Hide-Out, 1934

Ah, Wilderness!, 1935

Naughty Marietta, 1935

Rose-Marie, 1936

Small Town Girl, 1936

The Firefly, 1937

Thanks for the Memory, 1938

Another Thin Man, 1939

Society Lawyer, 1939

The Hitler Gang, 1944

Lady in the Dark, 1944

It's a Wonderful Life, 1946

The Virginian, 1946

The Pirate, 1948

Easter Parade, 1948

Summer Holiday, 1948

In the Good Old Summertime, 1949

Father's Little Dividend, 1951

Too Young to Kiss, 1951

Give a Girl a Break, 1953

The Long, Long Trailer, 1954

Gaby, 1956

A Certain Smile, 1958

The Diary of Anne Frank, 1959

Five Finger Exercise, 1962

It Happened One Christmas, 1977

Father of the Bride Part II, 1995

DOROTHY PARKER in a SERIOUS MODE

ONE NIGHT IN THE LATE 1930S, WHEN THE SCREEN WRITERS GUILD WAS being organized, one of the dissidents at the meeting (who did not approve of such an affiliation) said, "Screenwriting is a soft racket," and added, "I see no reason to rock the boat."

"Especially when the Mothership [MGM] objects," quipped Dorothy Parker.

And shortly afterwards, she wrote this acid rebuttal, titled "To Richard, With Love."

"...I do not feel I am participating in a soft racket (and what the hell, by the way, is a hard racket?) when I am writing for the screen. Nor do I want to be part of any racket, hard or soft. I want to earn my living, and naturally, I prefer it to be a good one...I have never in my life been paid so much, either—well, why am I here, and why are you, Mr. Schayer? But I can look my God and my producers—whom I do not, as do many, confuse with each other—in the face, and say I earned every cent of it...

"When I dwelt in the East...I had my opinion of writing for the screen. I regarded it—all right, sue me—with a sort of benevolent contempt, as one looks at the raggedy printing of a backward six-year-old. I thought it had just that much relationship to literature. (I still do—all right, take it to the Supreme Court!) I thought, 'Why I could do that with one hand tied behind me and the other on Irving Thalberg's pulse.' (Fooled you, that time, didn't I?) Well, I found out, and I found out hard, and I found out forever. Through the sweat and the tears I shed over my first script, I saw a great truth—one of those eternal, universal truths that serve to make you feel much worse than you did when you started. And that is, that no writer, whether he writes from love or for money, can condescend to what he writes...What makes it harder in screenwriting...is the money you get.

"You see, it brings out that uncomfortable little thing called conscience. You aren't writing for the love of it, or the art of it, or whatever; you are doing a chore assigned to you by your employer and whether or not he might fire you if you did it slackly makes no matter. You've got yourself to face, and you have to live with yourself. You don't—or at least, only in highly exceptional cases—have to live with your producer."

—DOROTHY PARKER, "To Richard With Love,"
Screenwriters Magazine, 1936

14. WAVES of LAUGHTER:
EDMUND HARTMANN

Santa Fe, August 2000

Edmund Hartmann on the backlot

THE ASSEMBLAGE OF SCREEN CREDITS AMASSED OVER FOUR DECADES BY THE prolific writer, Edmund Hartmann, began back in the mid-1930s, when the young emigré from St. Louis had his name on the screen for the first time, on an eminently forgettable B picture, *Don't Get Personal.* For the next few years, Hartmann would continue to earn a somewhat sporadic living working on other such "programmers" at various studios.

How to define those long-forgotten assembly line epics? They were modestly budgeted a two- or three-week shooting schedule and were customarily relegated to the bottom half of the double-feature bills which ran at one's local theatre during the '30s and the early '40s.

Major studio films, which played the top of the bill and earned high film rentals, were known as "A's." On the bottom half of the program, a slot was reserved for such "B's" as *Wanted, Jane Turner, The Man Who Found Himself, Law of the Underworld, The Last Express,* and *Big Town Czar,* one-hour masterpieces—all of which would keep Hartmann gainfully employed.

B pictures were shot quickly and written just as quickly. "I worked all over town," says Hartmann. "Universal, Fox, Warners — they all had B units, grinding out product. I even got called over to Republic once, out in the Valley, when things were slow. That was where a man named Nat Levine ran a real low budget factory. They expected you to turn out a script in one week, and by Friday, you were closed out, finished or not. Producers would come into the office where a writer was working, and as soon as he finished a page, the producer would grab it out of the typewriter and run down to the set, where they were waiting for the next scene!

"Somebody took me around on a tour of the studio; I remember going into the sound stages where they were turning out nine-, maybe ten-day pictures. Would you believe they were so cheap that the studio painters had orders never to paint the sets any higher than the tallest actor in the picture? Why waste paint on something that wouldn't be seen on the screen!

"Luckily, I was rescued from such a fate," he says. "I changed my career. I began to realize that you could get work writing comedy films with a hell of a lot more security than you could get by picking up week-to-week jobs, working on those mysteries and action/adventure B's. You see, back in those days, there were fewer comedy writers out in Hollywood, and every studio had its own cadre of comedians under contract.

"Paramount, for instance, had W. C. Fields, Burns and Allen, Bob Burns, Jack Oakie; Warners had Joe E. Brown and Hugh Herbert, Frank McHugh; RKO was home to Wheeler and Woolsey — remember them? And later, Joe Penner and Lucille Ball; Fox had the immortal Will Rogers, and later, the Ritz Brothers. MGM had Jimmy Durante or Bert Lahr, later Red Skelton...

"So guys who could create (or remember) gags, or figure out funny situations and farce plots — they worked much more steadily. Comedy was easier pickings ... so I decided to go back to my first love, which was providing performers with laughs."

Hartmann's first experience in comedy had begun earlier, in New York, when the young man arrived on 44th Street seeking his fame and fortune in the theatre. In those early '30s, during the very bottom of the Depression years, Broadway was struggling to keep the lights on in the Midtown legitimate houses. But very soon, he would find a job as the silent writing partner with songwriters Lew Brown and Ray Henderson working on a musical comedy, *Strike Me Pink*.

Six decades later, he shakes his head. "That was a very strange experience," he recalls. "Lew Brown had opened the show out of town and it didn't do well at all, and he decided to bring it into New York for repairs. But he had no money. In those days, nobody did. But somehow, Lew found a backer, a man named Waxey Gordon. Not exactly a businessman; actually, a very powerful New York gangster. Face it, in those days when apple sellers were out in Times Square selling apples for a nickel, who else would have any substantial cash but a gangster?

"Lew Brown was a very persuasive guy; he managed to talk Waxey into putting in a big chunk of cash as an investment in his show. Lew already had his leading lady, Lupe Velez—later she became a big movie star as "The Mexican Spitfire," remember? And he also had a charming singer named Hope Williams. But they all figured they needed a comedian; so they decided to get Jimmy Durante; he was a wonderful guy."

But Durante was in Hollywood, working at MGM. "Jimmy told Lew he'd love to come back to Broadway, but he couldn't do it now; he was scheduled to make a new picture…

"Lew reported this to Waxey," says Hartmann. "Waxey was not the kind of guy who'd take a 'no' from anybody. He picked up a phone—I was there when he did it—he reached Durante out in Culver City. 'Jimmy,' he said, 'we're going into rehearsal a week from this Monday, here in New York, at 11 AM. Be here.'

"And would you believe it, that Monday morning at 11 AM, when we went into rehearsal, Durante walked into the theatre."

Such was the power of a well-connected, big-time gangster in those roaring mid-'30s.

Strike Me Pink went into rehearsal. "Waxey and his 'boys' began to show up at rehearsals," says Hartmann. "Big goons, all of them in dark overcoats and snap-brim fedoras, sitting in rows there in the orchestra seats, smoking cigars and watching. Most of the time, they were there to watch the chorus line. Which, as I remember, was a bunch of some of the toughest looking girls I'd ever seen. Later, I found out why. They were all the girlfriends of Waxey's boys!"

Finally, after weeks of confusion and struggle, Lew Brown's retooled *Strike Me Pink* opened. The reviews were decent, but customers did not materialize to fill all those empty seats ... which in those dark days sold for a mere $2.20.

The empty seats remained empty.

Out of capital, Lew Brown had no alternative but to put up the closing notice and cut his losses.

"Then Lew had a visit from Waxey," says Hartmann. "He told Lew he'd heard the show was closing. 'Too bad,' he said. 'When do I get my money back?'

"'Sorry, Waxey,' said Lew. 'But we lost the money. All of it.'

"'I'm sorry too,' said Waxey. 'So when do I get mine back?'"

Brown attempted to explain the situation to his partner. "That's not the way we operate in the theatre, Waxey," he said. "If you put up the money for a show, and it flops, that's it. Goodbye money."

"Not my money," explained Waxey. "I don't give a damn how you guys operate in the theatre. I get *my* money back. So when do I get it?"

What transpired then?

"Lew Brown knew Waxey wasn't fooling around," recalls Hartmann. "He didn't have any money, and he didn't want to end up floating in the East River ... or sinking, with a pair of cement boots on his legs! Which is what happened to people who crossed Waxey. It didn't take him long to figure out what to do, which was to pack his bags and hop on the next train for California."

Gordon would send some of his boys out to locate his missing ex-partner. But as soon as Lew got to California, he holed up under an assumed name in a Hollywood apartment hotel.

"Pretty soon, he hooked up with another songwriter, Jay Gorney," says Hartmann. "Jay was working on a new musical picture at Fox, and they needed a lyricist for him. Jay got Lew the job, on condition that Lew wouldn't come into the studio. So every day Gorney showed up at the studio, and Lew stayed in his apartment out of sight. And by making a lot of phone calls back and forth, they finished writing the songs for the picture!

"Lew could never be sure somebody in L.A. wouldn't spot him and maybe tip off Waxey in New York. Or maybe Waxey had sent a couple of guys out to L.A. to find him … So he never budged out of his apartment."

But the saga of *Strike Me Pink* was not yet concluded. There remained another remarkable, third-act twist.

One evening, stir crazy and unable to remain holed up any longer, Brown agreed to go out of his apartment to a movie with Gorney. He put on dark glasses and a fedora hat to disguise himself.

When they arrived at the nearest Hollywood Boulevard theatre, they discovered that this night, a studio preview had been scheduled. It was the first showing of a "kiddie" two-reeler, starring some talented moppets. One of them, a blonde-haired little creature, was happily demonstrating her dance numbers in the theatre lobby, for anyone who was willing to watch her. So obviously talented was the little blonde that both Gorney and Brown became fascinated with her.

They found the girl's mother nearby and suggested she bring her little daughter out to Fox the following day.

When she appeared, Gorney escorted the child and her mother up to visit the office of Winfield Sheehan, the current head of Fox. Sheehan, who'd begun his career as a New York policeman, was now a power in the film business. He may not have had much previous experience in spotting talent, but even he could detect the little blonde girl's charm. On the spot, she was hired; she would get a small part in a forthcoming Fox musical.

Fox was teetering on the edge of bankruptcy, but the musical, *Stand Up and Cheer*, became a smash hit. Audiences loved that little blonde, who may have had fourth billing, but who stole the show. Which is how Shirley Temple rescued Fox.

But Waxey Gordon, back in New York, would never recoup his investment, nor would he know about Shirley Temple … Shortly afterwards, he was nabbed by police on a legal charge. He pleaded with the cops to shoot him; he knew that under a New York state law, were he to be convicted, he would go to jail for life. It would be his fourth conviction.

But the police would not oblige him … Later, another New York mob hitman did oblige Waxey, and Waxey died in an alley.

"Quite a story, eh?" remarks Hartmann all these decades after the fact. "Come to think of it, it could be the plot for a comedy musical, maybe

with Woody Allen as the naïve young Ed Hartmann in from St. Louis and
Peter Falk as Lew Brown... or maybe he'd be Waxey.

"But maybe we'd have to change the time frame," he muses. "Too far
back for today's audience. Say, that reminds me of one of the producers at
Universal, where I worked, a true studio genius... We had a lot of those,"
he remarks, sardonically.

"This particular guy called me in for a conference. He handed me a
script and asked me to take it home overnight and read it. 'It needs a fix,'
he said. 'You're a bright guy, Hartmann; read it and see if you can't come
up with some way to fix it, okay?'

"It was a very strange story," recalls Hartmann. "One that needed a
switch. So I thought about it, and next day I came back to the producer.
'I think I've figured out what's wrong; your story is fine, but it's set in the
wrong history period,' I told him. 'Seems to me you could take this whole
plot and set in another era. It could possibly work in, say 1840.'

"'1840?' the guy said. 'When was *that?*'"

HARTMANN WOULD SERVE AS A WRITER-PRODUCER OUT IN THE VALLEY AT
Universal for many years, and along with coping with the daily executive
stupidity, he would also encounter his share of bigotry, as well.

"I had to do a musical, and one night I went to a Sunset Strip club, and
I heard Nat King Cole, who was absolutely terrific. So I arranged with his
agent to hire Nat for a number in my project. When the front office heard
what I'd done, they were furious. Using a black singer in an all-white
musical? Didn't I understand that simply wasn't permitted? What the hell
difference did it make if Nat was the hottest attraction in town? Universal
sold pictures all over the South; exhibitors would raise hell with them. 'Do
you realize he'll be singing on the same level floor that *white* girls have
been dancing on?' yelled Cliff Work, who was the head of Universal. 'Fire
the guy—get somebody else!'

"Well, I wasn't about to give up on a talent like Nat," says Hartmann.
"So I figured out a way to get around my boss. I had them build a small
portable kitchen set with a stove and other equipment, one which could
be wheeled on. And there would be Nat and his trio wearing kitchen
clothes, as part of the staff. Now, that took Nat and his trio off the dance
floor, right? So, I went down to see Nat, and when I told him what I'd

figured out, with him and the others coming on as cooks, he looked at me, and he didn't say a word, but he knew exactly what I was suggesting…"

Did Cole refuse?

"Oh no, he knew the rules, too," says Hartmann, all these years later. "And he wanted to do the picture as much as I wanted him in it. And we both knew that was the way we could shut up Cliff Work…

"Oh, I could tell you lots of other such stories," he says. "And the stupidity wasn't only the private property of the executives. I was doing a picture with Abbott and Costello, and I hired a couple of black performers to be in a sequence, on a Southern riverboat. One day, the ingenue in the picture came into my office, and she said, 'I heard you've hired some black people for the picture. Do they have *lines?*' I assured her that they did. 'And they *remember* them?' she asked me. 'Oh, absolutely,' I told her. '…Isn't that wonderful?' she said, shaking her head.

"She simply couldn't believe blacks could handle acting scenes, along with whites.

"…But you must remember those were the days when black actresses played cooks and housemaids and very little else… 'Beulah, peel me a grape.' Remember? 'Oh, ma'am, you sure are funny. Yuk-yuk-yuk.' …And as for black actors, they were always used strictly as clowns, for comic relief. Stepin Fetchit, for one, he always played his role as lazy … and then there was Mantan Moreland, 'Mistuh Chan, Mistuh Chan, don't leave me alone in this haunted house!' And Willie Best, 'Who dere? Who said, "who dere?" when I say, "Who dere?"' … and the inevitable line … '*Feet, do your duty!*'"

OVER THE YEARS AS A TOP-RANK COMEDY PRODUCER-WRITER, HARTMANN was deeply involved in observing and coping with the daily habits of his contemporary legendary comedians. W. C. Fields, for example.

"I remember when Bill was making *My Little Chickadee* at Universal," he says. "There was never any love lost between him and his co-star, Mae West. Mae began hostilities by complaining about her billing. She demanded to know why she did not receive top billing. 'A lady is *always* first,' she insisted.

"'…And what about Mr. and Mrs.?' demanded Fields.

"There was another time when Eddie Cline, who was directing Bill in some comedy, told me that Fields had come in with a whole new scene he'd stayed up all night writing. Bill did a lot of his own comedy material, using pen names...Mahatma Kane Jeeves, Charles Bogle,...or Otis Cribblecoblis.

"This particular scene called for all the members of the cast to sit in a semi-circle facing Fields, who sat on a large chair in the center. Then, each of the actors was given a line to read—all of the lines relating to what a great man W. C. Fields was...

"'Did you shoot this thing?' I asked Cline. 'Oh, absolutely,' said Cline ...He knew on which side his bread was buttered. 'But, what are you ever going to do with it?' I asked him."

Eddie shrugged and changed the subject...

This unique piece of film may still be hidden somewhere deep in the Universal vaults, but alas, it has never yet been found.

But Fields' major problem did not revolve around his ego; as is legendary, it was his daily intake of alcohol. ("Water?" he says in one film. "I wouldn't drink water. Fish fuck in it!")

At Universal, no matter how carefully he was watched each shooting day, by noontime invariably the great man had imbibed enough to eliminate any possibility of coherent scenes being shot during the afternoon.

Where could his booze be coming from? Sharp-eyed Universal executives finally tracked down the source. Each morning, Fields would arrive on the set in a wheelchair with wicker arms; each armrest was deep enough to contain various needed items. In Fields' chair, those items were rubber hot water bottles.

In the morning, after each shot, the star would repair to his wheelchair, and while waiting for the next set-up, he would take a casual nip from one of his hot water bottles. Water? No indeed. The bottles were loaded with supplies of medicinal martinis.

And once that plot had been discovered, Fields resorted to another. Desperate times call for desperate measures. In a far corner of the soundstage stood a water cooler. Fields would approach it, muttering of thirst. Downing a paper cup or two, he would return to his wicker chair. By noon, he would be once again out of action.

The water cooler was discovered to contain several gallons of Gordon's gin.

"And in the middle of all this, sober or not, the man was able to complete several of the funniest comedies ever to come out of Hollywood," sighs Hartmann. "*The Bank Dick*, for one, and *Never Give a Sucker an Even Break* and *My Little Chickadee*... Today, all of them classics."

AND THEN, INTO HARTMANN'S UNIVERSAL REALM WOULD ARRIVE ANOTHER pair of comedic geniuses: Bud Abbott and Lou Costello.

Were it solely for their immortal rendering of the sketch "Who's On First?" the roly-poly Lou and his straight man, Bud, would certainly have earned their place in comic film history. But those two ex-burlesque comics would go on to become the most prolific and popular performers who've ever ranked number one on the list of box office draws, where they remained, for many years.

And their saga is almost as remarkable as any musical comedy plot... including the tale of *Strike Me Pink*.

"It was like Shirley Temple at Fox, years ago," says Hartmann. "Bud and Lou rescued Universal from going under. Hard to believe, even now. Here they'd come out from New York, on a three-picture contract, just a pair of small-time burlesque comics nobody had ever really heard of; they'd finished the first of three very low budget pictures, *Buck Privates*— nothing much, a typical Universal quickie musical. Then the executives assigned them to do more of their burlesque routines in two more low-budget pictures, bang bang, and out.

"...Nobody around Universal had the vaguest idea these guys could be a hit. Sure, they were rowdy and funny, but remember, there was a lot of funny stuff around Hollywood then... And Universal was in deep trouble, so much nobody would believe it. Most of the Universal producers weren't producers by trade, they were all old theatre-chain exhibitors, guys who'd been brought in to shore up the company. Right at this moment, they were so desperate for working capital that in order to raise some ready cash, these guys got on the phone to their exhibitor pals around the country. And they passed on the word that although *Buck Privates* was a low-budget B picture, one which ordinarily earns flat-deal rentals, could their buddies please, as a personal favor, play the picture as an A—thereby bringing in a percentage of the gross?... Which would be an infusion of desperately needed cash," he recalls.

We are on the edge of the abyss, and it's the eighth reel.

Can the studio be rescued from going over ... or ...?

"Now for the customary Hollywood-style twist," relates Hartmann. "*Buck Privates* goes out to the theatres, and it's an immediate hit! A smash! Audiences love the two of them, and these two guys, unknowns excepting for burlesque and a single Broadway show, *Streets of Paris*, are instantly transformed into major star attractions!"

And overnight, cash is pouring into the Universal bank accounts.

"Now here's the capper," says Hartmann. "Bud and Lou had completed their three-picture contract, and they're going back to New York, to pick up some bookings. And the Universal executives, who are jumping up and down on the box-office reports for *Buck Privates*, suddenly realize—they don't have the boys under contract any longer!

"So they rush a couple of executives over to the hotel where Bud and Lou are staying—the boys are packing their bags up in the hotel room—and suddenly the Universal guys come charging in, all smiles, and they're waving a *new* three-picture contract at Bud and Lou, with big raises written in for their salaries. 'You can't leave, guys—we love you!' and all that stuff ... 'We won't leave here until you sign with us—please.' ... And Bud and Lou looked at the numbers on the new contract, and they signed. Why not?"

Somehow, the entire episode seems straight out of a classic ninth reel finish.

"But one which always makes an audience happy," warns Hartmann. "Remember, clichés are clichés because they're based on truth!

"...So from then on, those two comics who'd been sneaked into a B picture, and became overnight stars, certainly began to take their new stardom seriously."

The Universal commissary, at lunchtime, was a daily stop at which the tourists, who were being shown around the studio, could stare at the various stars eating lunch. "They were looking for Turhan Bey, and Maria Montez, and Donald O'Connor—the usual names ... They'd wander past the tables staring," recalls Hartmann, "and they'd pass my table, and look and say, 'Oh, he's a *nobody*.'

"Anyway, when Bud and Lou were making their first pictures, in the early days, they used to enter the commissary very quietly and sit down to their lunch. But by the time they'd made their first big hits and then made it to that annual list of top box office draws, they'd revised their noontime entrance. Now that they were major stars, they'd hired a three-piece band, a drummer, a trumpeter, and an accordionist—*plus* a guy carrying the American flag! How's that for an entrance?"

Was it difficult to work with them?

"Not at first," says Hartmann. "They were extremely good at what they did. They had terrific timing, and they had a guy, John Grant, who worked with them all the time. He was quiet, wore a suit ... looked like a real estate salesman, but he knew all the bits—those burlesque sketches from the old days that Bud and Lou had done ... Not only 'Who's On First,' but also classic stuff like 'Floogle Street,' and 'Slowly I Turn,' and 'The Gun Isn't Loaded.' And Grant knew how to construct comedy routines for their solo spots, and we could integrate them into the script; they relied on him. It all worked very well.

"And as for Bud and Lou, they were a real team. Whenever Lou missed a line, Bud could whisper it to Lou under his breath ... You couldn't see it. Amazing ... They'd never miss a beat!"

But as time passed, with mounting success for the pair, their relationship did not remain amicable ... to say the least. "On the screen, Lou is the butt of all the jokes, the little guy who gets pushed around, who constantly makes mistakes and who has to suffer for them ... while Bud is the constant voice of authority, the one who keeps his partner in line, who berates him, the disapproving scold, who serves as a surrogate father figure...

"...But, if we rehearsed one of those routines long enough," remembers Hartmann, "somehow that funny little overgrown boy Lou played would begin to disappear, and a much meaner, older man would appear ...someone who was definitely *not* likeable."

And who continued to exist, even after the cameras stopped rolling.

"Lou began to make demands, constantly. He insisted he should get more money than Abbott. Somehow or other, Abbott finally caved in and agreed to a different salary split. But if that wasn't enough, when their weekly checks arrived, Lou ripped open the envelope and marched around the set, to show everyone how much more he was making!

"...Then it began to get ludicrous," sighs Hartmann. "I remember when they were loaned out to Metro for a picture. Something called *Lost in a Harem*, and of course, while they were at Metro, which was a far more classy studio than Universal, the boys were treated with much more respect.

"So when they finished the Metro thing, they came back to us at Universal, and Lou called a meeting to give us a list of demands for their future. He told us, 'From now on, there will be no more retakes. We will shoot scenes once—and *only* once. Got it?' ...How about that for an ego-trip?

"That was only the beginning. He told us, 'If we decide to play a game of cards on the set, the shooting will be suspended until we *finish* the game. Understood?' ...And finally, Lou told us, 'I will have my private dressing room here on the set from now on, and when my door is closed, nobody will disturb me until I come out...nobody—and you know damn well why! Is that understood?'"

So what does one say to a pair of stars whose pictures are keeping a studio solvent?

"Very little, except yes," replied Hartmann. "Because they'd learned what they were worth and they were on a real ego trip. And in typical Hollywood fashion, their ego problems became harder and harder to deal with.

"Every once in a while, Lou would see a prop of some kind on the set, or a new piece of furniture he decided he liked, and at the end of the day's shooting, he'd pick it up and take it home...

"If I chided him for doing that, he said to me, 'Listen, as long as I'm making a lot of money for these bums at Universal, I can do whatever I want, see? When I stop making money for them, they'll kick me right out.'"

Out of the mouths of comedians...

"Then, after a while, the relationship between the two men deteriorated into true hostility," sighs Hartmann. "It got so bad that offstage, they never spoke to each other. When they finished a shot, they'd both walk off and disappear into their dressing rooms. They'd both become truly paranoid.

"If we were doing a scene, and Lou might ad-lib a word or two, or made a slight change in the dialogue, he immediately considered himself as the man who'd created the whole thing!... But that, of course, is typical behavior when you're dealing with comedians... It's not enough for them to be stars—they cannot acknowledge anyone else had a part in making them successful... and if they're obnoxious, so be it. *They're* the ones who're out there, getting the laughs, aren't they? Without them, you're nothing, right?

"I remember, some years later, towards the end of their careers, when Lou announced to one and all that he was going to go into business for himself. 'From now on,' he told me, 'I am going to produce my own films!' He made the basic mistake—the one that always brings them down —of *financing* his own pictures... That brings them ultimate control.

"Lou said, 'I'm going to tell you one important thing I've learned. On any picture I'm going to make on my own, I can tell you— *there will be no inserts!*'

"...I couldn't figure out what the hell he meant!" sighs Hartmann. "Inserts are short pieces of film, shots which are usually a close-up of a calendar, a telephone ringing... or perhaps a newspaper headline... or rain on a window, or train wheels on a track... You make an insert shot purely to make a story bridge or to indicate the passage of time... that sort of thing.

"And here was Lou, after all these years in Hollywood, making dozens of pictures, telling me how he's learned this magic lesson, the one which guaranteed him success as a film producer, using his own money!"

And the end result?

"Lou's picture was a total flop," says Hartmann. "As if I needed to tell you. Lost all his money."

But while the team were reigning stars, their audiences remained loyal and ardent fans. "I remember one night we took out a new picture to preview, one I'd put together for them, the last one, actually, they did for Universal... *Abbott and Costello in Society.*

"It had been a very difficult one to make, actually, because both of them wanted to finish it and get the hell out of the studio. They gave me a deadline; they told me they'd be leaving California by such and such a time on next Friday, whether we were finished or not. No retakes, no changes, they actually rarely showed up as a team, so I had to shoot each one's scenes *separately*—which was a tough way to make a picture, believe me...

"Anyway, we finished the damned thing, by hook or crook, and put it together, and took it out to the preview theatre. And would you believe, that night, the minute their names came up on the screen—Lou's ahead of Bud's—of course the preview audience began cheering! Then, after the titles, we showed a shot of a faucet dripping—in the picture, they played plumbers—and the audience immediately started laughing! Bud and Lou meant comedy—even after all these years! And they were still stars...

"Later on," says Hartmann, "I did another picture with a team of comedians, Olsen and Johnson. Big stars in New York, who'd done *Hellzapoppin*, and *Sons of Fun*...major hits. So Universal figured they might become another Abbott and Costello team...So we brought them out and shot a picture, took it downtown again to preview it.

"We went to the theatre, where they'd hung out a big banner that read PREVIEW TONIGHT: UNIVERSAL COMEDY STARS!...In came the audience— the place was packed—they obviously figured this had to be another Abbott and Costello picture. So on the screen comes the Universal logo and then the two names 'Olsen and Johnson.'...Would you believe the audience stood up and started to walk out? After all these years, they'd come to see Bud and Lou, and nobody else!"

It's decades later, and after all this time, in reruns on AMC and TCM, in the bins at Blockbuster, and in foreign theatres, the knockabout pair are still entertaining audiences with their misadventures, with "Who's On First?" and "Slowly I Turn," "Floogle Street," and dozens of other classic bits done with exquisite timing.

"And with no inserts," comments Hartmann, dryly.

And what happened to the team, after all their years of top-drawing stardom in the theatres?

"Oh, that was sad," says Hartmann. "They'd both earned huge amounts of money for all those pictures they'd made...and lost it all. Their agent, it seemed, had stolen them blind...and of course, when Lou finished his ego-trip as his own producer, he'd been cleaned out, completely. So Bud and Lou ended up broke. What a shame."

Another classic film ending: the comedian whose career ends in disaster. Ever since the silent years—Arbuckle, Keaton, Charles Ray.

Usually ending up in a Fellini film.

HARTMANN LEFT UNIVERSAL TO MOVE HIS TYPEWRITER AND HIS WIT TO Paramount, where he soon was at work creating comedy scripts for Bob Hope.

"We had a terrific relationship," he says. "I wrote seven Bob Hope pictures. We did *Fancy Pants, Casanova's Big Night, My Favorite Spy, The Lemon Drop Kid, Sorrowful Jones, Paleface,* and *Here Come the Girls.* It was very steady employment, believe me."

Was Hope, as most comedians are, difficult about the screenplays that were offered to him?

"I never found him so," says Hartmann, "but remember, I was a very lucky guy there. I could be teamed with such brilliant comedy writers as Hal Kanter or Frank Tashlin... or producers like Bob Welch. Guys who really made it a pleasure to go to work at Paramount every day.

"We had a very efficient modus operandi," says Hartmann. "The producer and I, or my collaborators, would sit down and come up with a plot line. Then we'd create comedy sequences for Bob and whoever they had in mind for his co-star, usually somebody like Hedy Lamarr, Jane Russell or Dorothy Lamour. Then we'd finish a script... When it was done, it went up to the front office. If they okayed it, then there was a regular procedure involved in getting Bob to agree to do it."

Hope spent a good deal of spare time golfing in Palm Springs. "We'd make a date to go down there, and when Bob came in from his golf game, we'd be waiting to present the script to him.

"He would never read it. We'd be ushered into his living room, the producer and I... and Bob would be lying down on his couch. He'd wave us to a couple of chairs, and it was, 'Okay, fellas, let's get started.'

"...So off we went, reading him the new script. Meanwhile, remember, there's a phone by Bob's couch, and it kept ringing. He'd take the calls, we'd wait, and then when he finished, on we'd go with the reading... He got calls from everywhere—I can remember once, he had a call from President Eisenhower in Washington! We listened to Bob chatting with him, and then we'd pick up where we left off! We went on and on, jug-gling the script with the phone calls and watching Bob's reaction to the script...and then finally, we'd get to the end.

"At that point, Bob would look up from his couch and either he said, 'Okay, I'll do it,' or he'd tell us, 'No, forget it.' No was a definite no, and everyone at Paramount knew better than to argue with Bob Hope. Why force their star into a picture he'd been unhappy to do? It would show all over the screen. Remember one thing; in a comedy, it's important to keep your star happy...

"So the rejected script went back to Marathon Street and was filed away on some story department shelf. As for me, I must have been very lucky. I can only remember one script that Bob turned down. All the others got a yes."

After Hope agreed to do a picture, there was another regular procedure; he would turn the script over to his cadre of writers.

"Bob kept a very bright bunch of guys under contract; they worked for him every week providing gags for his radio show. They were also on call whenever Bob needed material for his endless personal appearances or functions where he'd do stand-up material—and later, when he went out to tour for the USO all over the world.

"I remember hearing how Bob would pay his writers, each week," says Hartmann. "He'd get them out to his Toluca Lake mansion, and they'd wait downstairs in the main hall. Bob would be upstairs, on the second floor, and he'd pick up all their checks; he'd stand up there, he'd flip all the checks into the air, and when they landed, all his guys would have to scramble for them!... There was also a legend about one of the guys, a new writer who found his check somewhere on the carpet, picked it up, tore it in half and walked out... How's that for an exit gag?

"...So Hope's writers would each go over our script, and then they'd turn in all sorts of one-liners for Bob, to help punch up his part... Unfortunately, that rarely worked out. We could be doing a picture like *Paleface*, which took place out West on the frontier during the 19th century, and we'd get rafts of one-liners from Bob's writers, all sorts of topical jokes about the 1940s! Useless.

"The guys also hung around Bob on the set, usually when he and Bing Crosby were making their *Road* pictures, and on movies like that their one-liners made much more sense. Especially because Bob and Bing had a wonderful little guy always working with them, Barney Dean. Barney was very helpful; he could not only pitch jokes, but he also had an impeccable sense of timing. He knew when a joke wasn't right for a particular scene or situation. So he became their official 'no man.' One of the writers might come up with some kind of a flip one-liner, Bob would listen,… then Barney would shake his head and say, 'No, Bob, not *here*… Some other place, but not *here*.' So Bob and Bing always listened to him; they respected his critical judgment.

"Matter of fact," muses Hartmann, "Hope was pretty damned sharp about judging comedy material. That may be why he stayed a star for so long.

"I remember once, when we were making *Fancy Pants*—which was a re-make of that wonderful old Charles Laughton comedy by Harry Leon Wilson, *Ruggles of Red Gap*—in the middle of shooting, I came up with an idea for a comedy monologue Hope could do. It was based on the idea of an American commenting on British customs… I stayed up most of the night writing it, sharpening the jokes, and getting it right. It would take place in the scene we were shooting the next day, while Hope is watching a cricket match for the first time.

"I brought it in in the morning and I showed it to our director, an old pro, George Marshall. I told him I'd already showed it to Bob Welch, our producer, and he'd loved it. So Marshall scanned it and shook his head. 'Forget this junk,' he said. 'I've written a few comedy notes here on the script page, and I'm going to shoot the scenes *my* way…'"

Was that a typical example of an auteur at work?

"No," says Hartmann, dryly. "It was an example of a studio director throwing his weight around.

"…So about eleven in the morning, we took a break, and Bob sat down at a table, while Marshall and his crew were setting up for the next shot. Now, on that table were the pages I'd shown to Bob Welch and George Marshall, the ones he'd just tossed aside. Bob picked up my pages and began to read them… started laughing. Believe me, Bob knew good material when he read it. So he brought it over to Marshall. 'This is great! When are we going to shoot this?' He waved the pages at him. 'Isn't this terrific, George? I can't wait to do it!'

"...So Marshall glanced at the pages, and without missing a beat, he said, 'Oh yeah, Bob, I'm glad you like it as much as I do...I figure we could get to shoot that monologue right after you finish your next shot, okay?'"

After all his years in Hollywood, Marshall was an expert hand in playing the old Hollywood game, COA—"Covering One's Ass."

And what of other comedians, such as Jerry Lewis, for whom Hartmann labored on *The Caddy*?

"That wasn't a difficult job at all," he says. "Not with a wonderful writer such as Frank Tashlin collaborating with me. Tashlin had started as a cartoonist, and so he usually thought in visual joke concepts. Which made him absolutely perfect for a performer like Jerry, who did so much physical comedy.

"We'd sit in the office working on the script, and every day Jerry would come in and sit with us, tossing ideas at us or coming up with ad-libs. A lot of his stuff was good, and so we'd put it into the script. Which made Jerry feel good; he loved being a contributor...and as we all know, he ended up becoming his own director...and producer."

Did Dean Martin ever contribute?

"Never showed up; not once. He'd be out golfing or whatever. But Jerry assured us, 'I'm only here to protect Dean's character...This is going to be the best picture Dean's ever made, believe me!' ...So every day, Jerry would suggest cuts, here and there, on the pages which Frank and I had written while he wasn't there. And after a while a pattern emerged, Tashlin and I noticed; most of Jerry's cuts were in the scenes where Dean had the lines!

"You know how everyone who writes about him is constantly harping on the point of how difficult Groucho Marx was? Well, I never found him so," says Hartmann. "I wrote Groucho a sketch for the annual Writers Guild Awards Show; that has to be the toughest audience any comedian could possibly perform for, right? Well, Groucho got big laughs with what I'd written, and later, when he ran into Y. Frank Freeman, who was then the head of Paramount where I worked, he made a special point of telling Freeman, my boss, what a good comedy writer I was. Now, how difficult would you say that was?

"Oh, Groucho was brilliant. I remember one night I was downtown at a ballgame; Groucho and I had adjoining boxes at the stadium where the Hollywood Stars, the home team, played.

"It wasn't a good night for the Stars; they were playing badly, and the local fans began to boo them. Groucho leaned over to me, took out his cigar, and said, 'He jests at Stars, who never felt a wound.'

"Not bad for an ad-lib, eh? I've never forgotten it...

"I've been very lucky with most of the comedians I've worked for," Hartmann said. "When I think of all the various talents I met, all those years. Harry Ritz, of the Ritz Brothers... they're forgotten now, but in their time they were big stars. Jack Oakie, Ben Blue, oh, and Judy Canova. Do you remember her? She was a very droll lady who specialized in hillbilly comedy. Specialized in singing comedy songs...

"I remember once, we were making a Judy Canova picture, and her whole family came out to visit, so she brought them out to the studio. They were from Arkansas—they'd never been out West before... probably never out of Arkansas, either. Anyway, she brought them up to the head of the studio, and he welcomed them to Hollywood, and he was trying to be nice, so while they were all standing around, he asked, 'Hey, folks, is there anything special you want to see while you're out here in sunny California?' And one of Judy's relatives said, 'Matter of fact, there sure is. We'd like to see us a Jew!'"

"YOU LOOK AS IF YOU'RE HOPING TO END THIS INTERVIEW SOON," REMARKED Hartmann. "That makes two of us. But we'd better find a big laugh for the finish. Another ad-lib?

"How about the one about my friend, Les White, who was one of Bob Hope's gag men for many years. Les was sick, and in a room at UCLA hospital, and while he was lying there, the door opened, and a very large nurse peered in, and she asked, 'Mr. White, is there anything I can do for you?'

"And Les looked up, and he said, 'Yes. *Don't sing!*'"

Definitely a sock finish, Mr. Hartmann.

Edmund Hartmann's Credits:

Films:

Wanted: Jane Turner, 1936

Without Orders, 1936

The Big Noise, 1936

Don't Get Personal, 1936

Hideaway, 1937

Behind the Headlines, 1937

The Man Who Found Himself, 1937

China Passage, 1937

The Last Express, 1938

Law of the Underworld, 1938

Two Bright Boys, 1939

Ex-Champ, 1939

Big Town Czar, 1939

Beauty for the Asking, 1939

The Last Warning, 1939

Diamond Frontier, 1940

South to Karanga, 1940

Enemy Agent, 1940

Ma, He's Making Eyes at Me, 1940

Black Friday, 1940

Keep 'Em Flying, 1941

The Feminine Touch, 1941

San Francisco Docks, 1941

Sweetheart of the Campus, 1941

Time out for Rhythm, 1941

Secret Weapon, 1942

True to the Army, 1942

Ride 'Em Cowboy, 1942

Hi 'Ya, Chum, 1943

Hi Diddle Diddle, 1943

Lady Bodyguard, 1943

In Society, 1944

Ghost Catchers, 1944

The Scarlet Claw, 1944

Ali Baba and the Forty Thieves, 1944

The Naughty Nineties, 1945

Dangerous Partners, 1945

Sudan, 1945

See My Lawyer, 1945

Here Come the Co-eds, 1945

The Face of Marble, 1946

Variety Girl, 1947

The Paleface, 1948

Let's Live a Little, 1948

Sorrowful Jones, 1949

Fancy Pants, 1950

My Favorite Spy, 1951

The Lemon Drop Kid, 1951

Here Come the Girls, 1953

The Caddy, 1953

Casanova's Big Night, 1954

The Sword of Ali Baba, 1965

The Shakiest Gun in the West, 1968

SOL LESSER on THORNTON WILDER

HOW PRODUCER AND AUTHOR MAY WORK IN HARMONY CAN BE demonstrated by this story. I went to the Bucks County Playhouse in Pennsylvania where Wilder was acting the part of the Narrator in his own play, *Our Town*. I talked over with him the problem of transferring the play to the screen. He had never done a treatment before, but was willing to try. We worked for seven or eight days in New York. When he got through, he said he had never worked so hard in his life, but he had enjoyed it. He would take no compensation, but I finally found out from his sister that he wanted an automobile. I bought him one and sent it to him for Christmas. He was very appreciative.

I then asked him if he wouldn't work on the script, for a consideration. He said, no, that screenwriting was a different profession, but that he would be willing to comment on it. The letters we exchanged have been published by *Theatre Arts Magazine* as an example of cordiality and understanding between the author and the producer. (The screenplay was written by the late Harry Chandlee.)

The point is that a producer doesn't controvert an author's intent. Wilder was pleased with the picture and said so. There's a particular art in writing a screenplay, and it's an advancing art. Some men have the talent for understanding screen movements. Some don't. In this case, we chose well.

—SOL LESSER

15. FREUNDSCHAFT:
A MEMOIR of ERNST LUBITSCH

by Samson Raphaelson

Joel Raphaelson (son), Samson Raphaelson, and Ernst Lubitsch

I WORKED ON NINE TALKING PICTURES WITH ERNST LUBITSCH FROM 1930 to 1947, yet I never quite felt that I knew him or that he knew me. We were too much the creatures of our separate careers. I was a playwright. A play was something you worked on for a year or two, during which you managed to feed, clothe, and shelter your family, and then, if the play had the sheer soaring luck to be produced and even to survive on the stage and become a hit and pile money in your bank, something could sneak up from behind—for instance, the 1929 crash. Thus a pure, unadulterated playwright, which I was, could find himself in good company—other pure, unadulterated playwrights—when he accepted occasional employment in Hollywood, where you were paid while you wrote, week after week. Lubitsch, in contrast, was cinema incarnate. Beginning with his early years as a silent-film director—in Berlin, then in Hollywood—he had captured the imagination of Europe and America; the "Lubitsch touch" was born (*Madame Dubarry, Sumurun, The Marriage Circle, So This Is Paris*). Then, in Hollywood, with talking pictures, the "Lubitsch touch" gained in dimension, and soon he stood high and alone as the creator of a special kind of sophisticated, disarmingly warm comedy never

251

seen before or since (*The Love Parade, Trouble in Paradise, The Merry Widow, Angel, Ninotchka, The Shop Around the Corner, Heaven Can Wait*). When he died, in 1947, I mourned his loss. I stayed away from California for the next three decades, wrote on my own, traveled, "lived"—as ever hot on the trail of the future. But recently the future has been getting more and more predictable, and the past—all I have to do is turn around—has been coming alive, full of enigmas, clues, and challenges. Lubitsch comes up from under. He has been due to reenter my life, even without the reminders from today's seething film culture, because I have begun to feel that he meant much more to me, and perhaps I to him, than I've ever taken the time to realize. Looking back, I can now discern a trail, not so shadowy, of signs we gave each other outside the thousands of work hours we shared—signs of giving a damn about each other as human beings.

Lubitsch was not what a writer would call a writer, nor did he waste time trying to be. I doubt if he ever tried to create a story, a film, even a scene entirely on his own. He had no vanity or illusions about himself. He was shrewd enough to cherish writers, and he welcomed the best available, roused them to outdo themselves, and at the same time contributed on every level and in ways that I cannot measure or define. This much I know: his feel for how good a scene or a picture or a performance could be was that of a genius. Such a gift is rarer by far than mere talent, which is epidemic among the mediocre.

I try to remember what those thousands of hours we spent together were like. I knew nothing about film; he was the greatest film craftsman of his day. We always worked together in the same room. It might be his or my office in a studio building, a room in his home or mine or in a New York or Palm Springs hotel. We worked six hours a day, five days a week. There was no clash of egos, no rancor when we disagreed, sometimes violently, about a scene or a line. No matter how loudly we hollered, it was always in terms of the given task. We talked our writing. I always wrote by talking, anyway; I was no good alone with a typewriter. Fortunately, Lubitsch was a talker, too, and of course we always had a secretary with us. He wrote some of my best lines, and I supplied some typical Lubitsch touches. I did not keep score, and I never came home from work with details lingering in my mind. I had done the daily stint, earned the precious pay. The screen credit was incidental. The moment I left Lubitsch and movies, I rushed back to my "real" life — the next play, mine and mine alone. I did have a mild curiosity about seeing the finished film, but in all those seventeen years I visited a movie set less than half a dozen times, and then usually because Lubitsch wanted to change a line of dialogue. And I never hung around; there was nothing to learn by watching a three-minute scene being shot over and over.

After our first few films together, Lubitsch almost always wanted me, and I gladly came whenever it was feasible. We were an odd pair. He was short, rotund, eyes brilliant and black, hair shiny black. I was tallish, thin, nearsighted, eyes blue and bespectacled, hair brown. He was a Berlin creature — straight out of *Gymnasium* into Max Reinhardt's theatre, educated by clowning in Shakespeare and Molèire, a comic star in silent pictures at twenty-one, a world-famous director almost ten years before the advent of talking pictures. I was a Chicago product, middle-class, West Side; my goal was literary and lofty, but my youth had been misspent in four years of journalistic antics on the campus of the University of Illinois, saturated in the cultural ambience of *The Saturday Evening Post*. I soon gravitated to New York and Greenwich Village, where my culture ascended to the level of *The Nation*, *The New Republic*, and *The Smart Set* of Mencken and Nathan, and I vacillated between odd jobs reporting news or concocting advertisements and writing unsalable short stories full of integrity. I looked down on movies; to me they were all Douglas Fairbanks jumping over parapets or Rudolph Valentino looking silly. I saw two or three Chaplin films, thought they were funny, and that was that. I had seen none of Lubitsch's silent pictures and barely knew his name. I was theatre-mad, but I never dared aspire to playwriting. I had graduated from O. Henry to Maupassant, but Shaw, Molnár, George Kaufman, Eugene O'Neill, and Sidney Howard were beyond emulation. The mere concept of three successive acts — anything longer than fifteen pages — paralyzed me. I didn't know that drama was my métier until 1924, when, out of the blue, at age twenty-eight, I wrote *The Jazz Singer*, a theatre piece — heartfelt, corny, and dramatic. It hurtled me into a lifetime dedicated to never again being so shamelessly effective.

Two plays later, my first time in Hollywood, I met Lubitsch, only four years older but in his prime and, in the new talkies, greater than ever. It was late 1930 at the Paramount studios, where, married and the father of two small children, I was recovering from the 1929 crash. I was more than happy to meet him, because earlier that year I had chanced upon *The Love Parade*, which Lubitsch had produced and directed, and it was the first movie that ever caught me completely. In fact, it sent me cheering into the streets. That is what I had for him when we met—what *The Love Parade* had done to me. And it seems he wanted, for the script of *The Man I Killed*, his first attempt at tearjerking drama, someone who could write a play like *The Jazz Singer* and really mean it. At the time, neither he nor I suspected that I could write his kind of comedy.

Our work was based always on a play, always European and usually unknown here. Lubitsch would tell me briefly the general line of the plot. I never read the play, because he wanted me not to be hampered by someone else's writing. He chose material for its possibilities, material that left us free for rampages of invention in what was known as his style, a style I loved and never ceased loving—for him, not for myself. From the first, I found that a certain kind of nonsense delighted him. I would toss in preposterous ideas—"Here's a terrible example of what I mean"—while we were struggling over a scene. He encouraged such nonsense, even during the first assignment, the melancholy *The Man I Killed*, and when we got into the next, the prankish *Smiling Lieutenant*, he began actually using the stuff, to my surprise. I soon discovered that these conversational doodlings were serious business. For instance, the opening love scene of *Trouble in Paradise*, in a Venice hotel: Herbert Marshall is a master crook posing as a baron, and Miriam Hopkins is a lady thief posing as a countess. During their first rendezvous in Marshall's suite, their romance flowers when each unmasks the other. It turns out that she has pickpocketed his wallet and his watch and he has lifted her jewelled brooch and then somehow conjured the garter from under her evening dress. It was phony, incredible, and inconsistent with the image of Marshall as a supreme crook. But Lubitsch pounced on the idea, and we juggled it past all sanity. He loved my wild doodle of Miriam handing Marshall his watch and remarking, "It was five minutes slow, but I regulated it for you."

We were socially congenial, in the Hollywood fashion. My wife and I were often invited to his home, and he and his wife (the second) were invited to ours, but almost never was it merely a foursome. In Hollywood, anything less than a dinner for ten was a faux pas. I am sure we thought of each other as friends, but my private life held no interest for him, and I had little curiosity about his. As for my plays, they were fiercely my own, and he was the last man on earth I would turn to if I needed advice. I think he preferred it that way. During the long stretches when I was in the East, neither of us wrote or phoned the other, except on business. I hardly ever knew what other pictures he was making until long after they were made and I managed to see them. My wife says that we exchanged Christmas gifts when we were working together—boxes of candy or beribboned baskets of fruit and nuts.

I am not quite giving a sense of the fullness of this odd and inconsistent relationship. An example, perhaps, would be how I felt about Lubitsch's courtship of Vivian Gaye and how he gave me the news of their marriage. It was in the mid-nineteen-thirties. I had done five films with him, and I had been calling him "Ernst" since the first weeks of our first movie. (To Walter Reisch, the writer from Vienna, probably his most intimate friend, he was always "Herr Lubitsch.") He called me "Sam" and occasionally "Rafe," which I am more accustomed to. Yet underneath the informality, especially in the earlier years, I must have held him in awesome esteem. It included my concept of his male charisma. I didn't notice, for months, that he was a short man— about five feet five or six. Only when an envious Berliner mockingly compared him to Napoleon did I think of Lubitsch in terms of height. Actually, not only was he short, but his hands and feet were small, and he walked with a faintly bowlegged, lilting step. He also had a bulge at the waistline. But his remarkable face and those brilliant eyes and his true feeling for every art that went into the making of movies gave him towering stature in my eyes, and I took it for granted that he could have any woman who struck his fancy. I could not conceive of a beautiful woman in her right mind hesitating if she had to choose between, for instance, Gable and Lubitsch. Or take a society man —blue-blooded, handsome, a polo player with a yacht. Hell, take Hemingway. I could write the scene. It would be no contest.

Well, I gradually learned that he was far from being a grand vizier of love. I knew almost nothing of his first marriage and divorce; when I met him, he was unattached and freewheeling and, although not a chaser, had an appetite for and did very well with the fabulous cuties of Hollywood. But pretty soon it became clear that a wife to him meant a lady, and as

255

much of a lady as the nineteen-thirties would tolerate. He was smilingly unimpressed by glamour women (except for an occasional soupçon of awe in the presence of Garbo), and he treated other men's wives, including mine, with fond boredom. But any female with the icy look of ancestry—unmarried, of course, and not too old or too homely—made him stop, look, and listen. He wanted to marry, and I heard that he had proposed, at one time or another, to several qualified ladies, but without success. This humbly born, self-educated specimen from *unter* no Berlin *Linden,* in his art so hilariously superior to kings and dukes and earls, was touchingly modest in the presence of even an ex-lady-in-waiting to some obscure royal dowager of some distant realm—which more or less described Vivian Gaye.

I did not see Lubitsch for months after that, but one day I heard that he and Vivian Gaye were often together, and it made me, in a comfortable-bystander way, unhappy. Then, in October of 1935—I was in Palm Springs working on a play and must have missed the papers that day—someone told me they were married (something about running off to Arizona), and I readjusted my view of life, deciding that anything could happen to anybody. And, after all, the man and I merely worked together once in a while.

One day a few months later—I was still in Palm Springs, but the play was going badly—Lubitsch called me. He had a story; was I available? The next day, we lunched in great spirits at Paramount.

"What are you doing, Sam?"

"Oh, you know—a play."

"Ah. How's it going?"

"Bad. I threw it away."

"Fine, fine. I think you're going to like this story."

Back in his office, he began telling me the general idea of *Angel.* The telephone interrupted. "Yes?" His face brightened. "Hello, darling!" He spoke affectionately about domestic matters. When he hung up, his eyes became watchful and his lips curled in a naughty little grin. He said, "Maybe you heard that Vivian and I got married?"

I said, "I think I *did* hear somebody say..."

Still with that grin, he said, "Well, it's true." Then, after a moment, brisk and on his feet, "Now, where were we?"

Aging Sleuths Turn Page on Mysteries

The graying of America is spreading fast to mystery bookshelves. A genre some have dubbed "geezer lit," featuring crime-solving protagonists age 70-plus, is growing in popularity. ■ While publishers have not released sales figures, more and more mystery titles are popping up starring older characters. In *Retirement Homes Are Murder* by Mike Befeler, an octogenarian sleuth suffers from short-term memory loss. Among other novelists contributing recent titles are Cynthia Riggs (*Shooting Star*), Parnell Hall (*The Sudoku Puzzle Murders*) and Rita Lakin (*Getting Old Is to Die For*). ■ "We've just scratched the surface on so-called geezer lit," observes best-selling thriller author Harlan Coben, president of the Mystery Writers of America. "It could be the next big frontier in crime fiction." —Pat Remick

...mply complete and mail this form, or call **1-800-610-3385.**

Tell us how much money you might like to use to purchase an annuity, and we'll tell you how much guaranteed monthly income you can receive for life. Annuities can be purchased for any amount of $5,000 or more.

$ _____ $ _____ $ _____

(List up to three amounts.)

Money used to purchase an annuity will be locked into a contract. Therefore, we recommend using no more than 50% of your retirement assets (excluding your home) and keeping at least $20,000 on hand for emergencies.

Mr.
Mrs.
Ms.
_____
(please print) First Name   Last Name

Address _____

City _____ State _____ Zip _____
☐ Male ☐ Female

AARP Membership Number
_____

Date of Birth (month/day/year)
_____

If interested in a Joint Life Plan:

Spouse's First Name   Last Name
_____
☐ Male ☐ Female

Spouse's Birthdate (month/day/year)
_____

Mail completed coupon to:
AARP Lifetime Income Program.
P.O. Box 30556, Tampa, FL 33630-3556

SHB2B1

A030-04-F

I grinned back and told him where we were.

That is as near as I can come to an indication of how life was between him and me apart from our intimate existence in the more tangible world of applied imagination.

Then, in 1943, Lubitsch had a heart attack, and there were signs of reaching out, at first mainly on my side. I had last been with him in the spring of 1942, when we finished our eighth picture together, *Heaven Can Wait*—a blithe experience. Blithe because we were at the height of our productive years. (I had written *Accent on Youth*, *Skylark*, and *Jason*—a head start toward immortality, I thought; Lubitsch, pitching for the here and now, had been steadily making Lubitsch pictures with and without me.) Blithe because, separated at last from Vivian Gaye after several years of a troubled marriage, and with a four-year-old daughter to adore, he was in fine fettle. Blithe because we did our work on *Heaven Can Wait* in his Bel Air house, luxuriously at ease, me often laying aside my pipe for one of his special Upmann cigars. Blithe because we combined our individual gifts in that script and felt it was flawless. When the job was over and done, however, we parted with the usual brief handshake, knowing little more about each other than we had known before.

Jump a year, during which Lubitsch, at Twentieth Century-Fox, was bringing *Heaven Can Wait* to consummation on the screen and my wife and I, in Pennsylvania, were purchasing a farm. In the summer of 1943, leaving my family to rural bliss, I returned to Hollywood for a stint at MGM. I lived at the Chateau Elyseé, and it was there, over the radio at breakfast, that I heard the news of Lubitsch's heart attack. He had fallen down unconscious the night before at a party, in a large tent set over a portable dance floor on a large lawn at the estate of Sonja Henie. He was brought to Cedars of Lebanon Hospital, where desperate measures were being taken to save his life. The news certainly did something to me. That was thirty-eight years ago; I remember the day in patches. My wife told me later that I had called her and sounded badly shaken. I know that I did not call Lubitsch's home or the hospital and that I felt awful about it. But I hadn't seen him for a year and, as always, was not sure where I stood in his life or he in mine.

I remember the day as a long morning in my office at MGM. I arrived and got the latest bulletin from Tildy Jones, my secretary: Lubitsch was dying, if not already dead. Tildy had been with us on *Heaven Can Wait* (the working secretary was always mine), and she was continuing at my side through Hollywood thick and thin. Her news was authoritative and nearly firsthand: with nothing like my qualms, she had called the Bel Air house and simply asked for her friend, Lubitsch's private secretary, Steffie Trondle. Steffie, a dear elderly German woman who had been with Lubitsch since long before I knew him, had just returned from the hospital. She was hysterical, but also apparently in charge, talking with mad efficiency of coffins and pallbearers and, according to Tildy, referring to me as "one of the few who never let him down." (I remember those words exactly, because over the years several people have quoted them — the only precise clue to how Lubitsch felt about me. The rest of the dialogue I am improvising — as close as possible to what was said.) Tildy went on, "Steffie says that she realizes what a terrible loss this must be to you, and that you must express your grief while you feel it most, and I agree. You must write something beautiful to be printed, so that future generations will know what a wonderful man Mr. Lubitsch was."

I recall no stirrings of grief. My imagination could not, and cannot, play around death; it is all offstage stuff. I certainly was sorry he was dead. Actually, I must have felt more, because, though I had promised some work to Arthur Hornblow, Jr., an MGM producer, I could not get at it. I could not write anything, anything at all. I remember making random telephone calls, and that Tildy looked at me impatiently, perhaps reproachfully.

Then Hornblow dropped in — a cultivated and imaginative man, and one of the few producers with a fine feeling for writers — and told me to forget the assignment. He said, "Why don't you write something about Ernst while you're in this state of mind?" He left, and I turned to Tildy and tried to explain that I didn't know what to write, because, incredibly, I didn't know the man well; I didn't even know what I *felt*. The subject obsessed me, however, and I kept on explaining for an hour or so, until suddenly I said some words, then some more, and they sounded right. She got them down. The rest poured out like a scene suddenly ripe and ready. I did know him. I did feel about him. In no time at all, there was a first draft. Here it is:

Lubitsch loved ideas more than anything in the world, except his daughter Nicola. It didn't matter what kind of ideas. He could become equally impassioned over an exit speech for a character in the current script, the relative merits of Horowitz and Heifetz, the aesthetics of modern painting, or whether now is the time to buy real estate. And his passion was usually much stronger than that of anyone else around him, so he was likely to dominate in a group. Yet I never saw, even in this territory of egoists, anyone who didn't light up with pleasure in Lubitsch's company. We got that pleasure, not from his brilliancy or his rightness—he was far from infallible, and his wit, being human, had its lesser moments—but from the purity and childlike delight of his lifelong love affair with ideas.

An idea mattered to him more, for instance, than where his forkful of food happened to be traveling at a given moment. This director, who had an unerring eye for style, from the surface of clothes and manners down to the most subtle intonation of an aristocrat's heart, was, in his personal life, inclined to reach for the handiest pair of trousers and coat whether they clashed or not, to shout like a king or a peasant (but never like a gentleman) and go through life unaware of many refinements and shadings, with that clumsiness which is the passport of an honest man. He had no time for manners, but the grace within him was unmistakable, and everyone kindled to it, errand boy and mogul, mechanic and artist. Garbo smiled, indeed, in his presence, and so did Sinclair Lewis and Thomas Mann. He was born with the happy gift of revealing himself instantly and to all.

As an artist he was sophisticated, as man almost naive. As an artist shrewd, as a man simple. As an artist economical, precise, exacting; as a man, he was always forgetting his reading glasses, his cigars and man-uscripts, and half the time it was an effort for him to remember his own telephone number.

However great the cinema historian will eventually estimate him, he was bigger as a person.

He was genuinely modest. He never sought fame or coveted prizes. He was incapable of employing the art of personal publicity. You could never wound him speaking critically of his work. And somehow he never wounded his fellow-workers with his innocent forthrightness. If he only accepted you, it was because he believed you. Thus he could say, "Oh, that's lousy," and at the same time you felt his real appreciation of what you hoped were your hidden virtues. A superb actor, he was totally incapable of acting in his humble relations. He did not have one manner for the great and another for the lowly, one style for the drawing room and another for the bar. He was as free from guile and pretense as children are supposed to be, and this made him endlessly various and charming.

I am sorry I was never able to say some of this to him while he was alive.

I WAS PLEASED — MORE THAN PLEASED. IT WAS BETTER THAN A FIRST DRAFT. The real test was its effect on Tildy, a Hollywood product of a kind that I don't think exists today: about thirty, studio-bred since her teens in the silent-picture days, a virgin self-programmed to marry no one less than a thousand-dollar-a-week cinema underling, and very, very script-wise. Here my memory is clear: as I was dictating, I saw a tear rolling down her cheek. Then, after Tildy had typed it—long past lunchtime, but neither of us noticed—I read it aloud to make sure it was heartfelt yet not effusive, laudatory but judicious; and her responses were just right. At one point, she remarked that she hadn't realized how strongly I felt about Lubitsch, and of course I hadn't realized it myself. I had never before seen him defined and clear, framed and final, as by death.

A few weeks later, when I was allowed ten minutes with him at the hospital, I was deeply moved. He had to lie very still; even the use of his expressive hands was forbidden. I reassured him, mentioning John Golden, my producer on *Skylark*, a man over seventy, who was in great shape a year or two after a near-fatal stroke. Lubitsch smiled wanly. "I know, I know. But when I die, this is what I'll die of."

He did not die, and as time went on the accent of death faded. The regular life pattern took over. In the next four years, on the farm, my wife and I went through the ordeals of our children's adolescence, and I was busy with plays and stories. Lubitsch, in Hollywood, was doing his usual incomparable stuff. He probably knew I had a play on Broadway, and I must have heard of his next film, *Cluny Brown*. We were both back to normal. As for my funeral tribute, although it was now distinctly out of order I kept the two-page script—the original and a few carbon copies—where I could always lay hands on it. I reread it, and found labored adulation, inaccuracies, and a glib style. I didn't do anything about it, but I knew that if the time came I would write more truly. After all, in 1943 I was forty-seven. I was maturing. I could not quite forget the pale man on the hospital bed. My change consisted of past fragments seen anew—evidence of Lubitsch's humanity, and mine. I felt that one of us had failed the other. Maybe the original fault was mine. How did he take my obvious lack of interest in movies? True, I never received a wire from him on my Broadway openings, never felt he owed one to me. But how had he felt about no word from me on the premieres of films we had created together? In many instances, I hadn't even known they had been released until weeks later. I didn't see *Angel* until it came to Bethlehem, twenty minutes from our farm. Conceivably, all this might have chilled him. He might have opened up if I had been a total film man, ambitious to be a director myself. I doubt if there would have been envy. He was too secure in his cinema cosmos.

I began reinterpreting, finding clues in things that had passed me by before. Maybe he had tried and I had failed him. One spring afternoon way back in 1932—we were working on *Trouble in Paradise* in his Santa Monica beach house—he asked me to stay and stroll the beach with him. I was sure he had something special to say, but we walked along with small talk, and after a while he began telling me about his father—unusual, but I gave it no great importance at the time. He was very fond of the old man and maintained him comfortably in a Berlin apartment. The apartment required a housekeeper, and Papa was constantly writing for additional money and sending bills—always for repair work on the main door. It was the housekeepers; there was a great turnover in housekeepers. If they didn't yield to the old boy, out they went. If they did yield, he got tired of them after a while, and the great lover had to have a new door lock to keep a rejected sex-mad female away. Lubitsch told this with his usual glee about fun in bed and with obvious filial pride, but, looking back, I recalled a difference—some pauses, as if he were waiting for me to speak, and a watchfulness that I could sense out of the corner of my eye but that disappeared when I glanced directly at him. But I, enjoying the telling, just smiled and laughed. Then, at the end, there was a long silence. It may well have been an invitation. It was the only time he had ever asked me to stay after work. Probably he was trying to create a more intimate atmosphere and, when I failed to respond, impulsively came up with a random intimacy about his father. Why didn't I tell him about my father? Why didn't I ask for more about Ernst? Was his mother alive? How did he feel about her? How was it between mother and father? Did Ernst have brothers, sisters? We were both Jews. That was something to talk about. My family, before two American generations, had owned, or leased, or labored in vineyards or orchards near Jerusalem. How far back was his family German? And before that—Poland? Spain? Palestine? I had heard, from others, that the father had been a tailor. A little tailor in a shop? An elegant tailor, custom-fitting the rich? I resolved that, next assignment, the very first day together, we would have a fine time bandying childhoods.

I began also to reexamine some of my own behavior. Often, when talking about Lubitsch, I had said, "I love the guy." It came easily in Hollywood—a common phrase. You might say it about someone who agreed with something you said, or someone you didn't even know who did something you liked. But maybe I really cared. I recalled an evening in the second or third year of his marriage to Vivian Gaye—a dinner party. My wife and I were at the same table with Lubitsch and Vivian. I already knew—felt it, found evidence every time I saw them together— that the marriage had gone bleak. Lubitsch was out on the floor dancing, which he loved. My wife was dancing, too, and so were the others. Vivian preferred not to dance, and we were making talk. I said something about their baby girl, Nicola—that the child was beautiful and exceptionally bright, which was true. Vivian smiled and began praising the American melting pot. She believed in that melting pot, she said earnestly. Here it was not like tired old Europe. Then she said, "I'm all in favor of mixing, for instance, the blood of the aristocrat with the blood of the peasant." I lost my customary aplomb. I said, "I know exactly what you mean, Vivian. You are of course referring to Ernst and yourself—he the aristocrat, and you the party of the second part." I remember the remark well, because I was proud of my wit, and because I felt the lady had inspired it and deserved it. I also remember that we both smiled hideously at each other, pretending that nothing homicidal had been said. Then someone must have returned from dancing. I don't remember any more, but Lubitsch and I did not again work in his home until *Heaven Can Wait*, after he and Vivian had parted.

I often thought ruefully of that gauche and ungentlemanly remark, and I always attributed it to my rugged American resentment of the lady's ladyhood. It did not occur to me that it was an explosion of loyalty, to say nothing of love, for my friend, the husband. But in the years after 1943 I saw it in a different light: I hoped and prayed that my words had not added to the dolorousness of his marriage. Did that mean that I cared about the man and hadn't realized it? It was possible, but in those four years I never wrote Lubitsch or called him on the telephone. Maybe the annual Christmas card, but that is all. I was changing only in the sense that in odd moments I reinterpreted events that seemed to have other values when they happened. (I must add still another view of Vivian: All this goes back forty-five years; I was not as mellow and evenhanded as I am today; and if that episode seems in any way a reflection on the actual Vivian's character, I herewith state that I can be as wrong about fellow-humans as any man. It is quite possible that Ernst was no dreamboat in the dark mazes of matrimony, and, for all I know, Vivian may have had a prodigious sense of humor.)

I thought about Lubitsch again in a new way in 1944, after the ordeal my play *The Perfect Marriage*. Before production, the script had an extraordinary reception. It was praised high, wide, and handsome by every theatre magnifico who read it. All my other plays, especially the ones I brag about, had first been rejected, sometimes by more than a few producers. But this time there was not a single dissenting voice, beginning with my producer and friend Cheryl Crawford and fanning out to financial backers, theatre owners, and stars yearning for the leading roles. Even a Hollywood studio hailed the script with a lavish pre-production offer, which Cheryl and I, in the belief that we were outsmarting them, sneered at. Should anyone question my veracity, I have ample evidence in my files. I saved every scrap: letters from the wealthy, the wise, and the glamorous, telegrams, cajoling cards attached to boxes of flowers — every scrap except the reviews of the New York critics, which were unanimously unfavorable.

It was not exactly a box-office failure, however, perhaps because Miriam Hopkins starred in it. But she was also one of the mistakes I had made. I chose her against the advice of others, including Cheryl Crawford. Miss Hopkins did not enhance the part. I might have survived the reviews if I could have put the blame only on my not too bright choice of star. But I knew that the play itself had missed. In the past, I had learned from my failures; there always came a day, not long after, when I saw why I had missed, and that was rejuvenating. But here I remained in the dark. I learned nothing from the critics or from soul-searching. Could all those distinguished people who had loved the script be wrong? Yes indeed, they could. I longed for a god-like intelligence, and naturally I thought of Lubitsch. He and I, when going good, had the gift of catching the other on a wrong trail, thus saving what easily could be months of going nowhere, writing one splendid wrong scene after another. I found myself thinking, Just five minutes with him after I had finished that script and five minutes on the phone when we were casting—what a difference it could have made.

In 1947, when Lubitsch called me from Hollywood for *That Lady in Ermine*, I was punch-drunk from a year with a frustrating comedy about a young couple who survive the destruction of the world, and so eager for a break that I welcomed the assignment without fussing about the story. Lubitsch said, "You'll love it," and I took his word for it. I threw away the cluttered comedy script. It did not occur to me that I might bring it along and show it to him and—who knows?—get five lifesaving minutes. I did, however, take the almost forgotten funeral piece, with the vague feeling that anything might happen, and that with some cuts and careful rewriting it could be made sound and less irritatingly glib. (I abhorred "love affair with ideas.")

My wife and I arrived in Hollywood on a Sunday morning in February, called Lubitsch from our rented house, and went to his Bel Air home in the afternoon. He looked lively and fit. We greeted each other as always— two fellow-workers starting another job. We did not embrace. Unlike many Middle Europeans, he did not press lips to ladies' hands, nor did he salute males with a hug and a two-cheek kiss. We did our usual handshake, not the long granite grip and eye-to-eye contact of the true American but a sort of flap—something to get out of the way.

He had changed. He had settled into living a single life, but Nicola (now nine years old) was there, and he adored her slavishly. He had drawn

closer to a few European friends, friends steeped in the film world—
German-speaking cronies like Walter Reisch, Willie Wyler, Billy Wilder,
and Henry Blanke. And he had, probably for the first time in his life, a real
camaraderie with a lovely woman. She was Mary Loos (niece of Anita)—
young, beautiful, splendidly tall, a blue blood of California-pioneer
ancestry—whose platonic devotion Lubitsch received, to the surprise of
everyone, with gratitude and affection. And he seemed to have an
increased awareness of me as a man with a family. My wife and I felt it that
first evening when we dined with him. He asked about the school life of
our teen-age children and about life on the farm. After we told him,
however, there were no more questions. And somehow we didn't get
around to our own childhood days, then or ever. There were also changes
in his work life, and I soon found myself involved in them. Two more
heart attacks in the past year, slight ones, had somehow been kept secret,
especially from Darryl Zanuck, who revered him but might well have hesitated about giving him carte blanche on this expensive production. To
impress Zanuck, we worked on the lot, in Lubitsch's studio suite, where I
was given an adjoining office.

I did not know about any of these developments on the morning we
started work. I saw that Lubitsch no longer smoked his Upmanns but
chewed on cheaper cigars; otherwise he was in fine form, acting out every
part, selling me his approach to the original old German operetta, while
the secretary, taking no chances, was making notes like crazy. (She was
new; Tildy was living in Seattle, married, I think, to the owner of a movie
theatre.) I began finding fault the moment I saw what he was up to—just
another variation on the old Lubitsch fun-in-a-castle triangle. He thought
the stuff was great, and I thought that he was kidding himself. We had a
typical knock-down-and-drag-out hollering session.

Came lunchtime, and as we walked across the lot toward the executive
dining room—part of his design to be seen every day, as it turned out—
he looked around to be sure no one was within earshot, swore me to
silence, and told me about the two "very small, believe me" heart attacks.
He added, "And you can see, Sam, I'm taking good care of myself. I'm in
great shape. I didn't smoke this morning—I chewed on that cigar. Did
you notice?" He went on about taking walks, going to bed early, and
eating sparingly—"You'll see at lunch."

I did see. And as I watched this former trench-man diddling with a cup of consommé and an insipid slice of boiled chicken, I decided then and there to forgo my customary integrity (in those days "integrity" was in constant use by Eastern writers; so was "truth;" we tried to get them into every story, regardless of what that did to the story), and in the afternoon, after a series of properly reluctant retreats from my uncompromising position, pretended to see the light. So let it be warmed-over 1930 Lubitsch, I decided; it's still good. I rolled with it and developed everything his way —which was no cinch, and nothing to be ashamed of. I don't think I fooled him. Looking back, I believe he knew precisely what we were doing, shared my viewpoint, but preferred survival to glory. That vociferous first morning probably had scared the hell out of him.

Nothing else about his behavior—not a look, a word, a gesture— asked for special treatment. There was no off-moment when those brilliant eyes lost their immediacy and betrayed an underlying colloquy with death. Nor did I have, as I recall it, any sequel to the random stirrings toward him I had experienced when I had been three thousand miles away. Here he was; we had a job to do; his days were numbered; and there was no space for friendship fantasies in the limited workaday future.

My feeling for him, especially in the first few weeks, took a modest form. I merely wanted somehow, somewhere, at his table, at our table, or on his terrace on a weekend afternoon—I wanted to lift a glass, make a little speech, a statement. It sounds easy, but whenever an opportunity seemed to arise I realized, each time, that there was no way of doing it which would not be margined in black. Pretty soon, life was about the same as in earlier years. Lubitsch and I took each other for granted; I began privately circling around a new play idea and, in my spare time, cheating on *That Lady in Ermine* with a lady who eventually became *Hilda Crane*.

Our last day together, as it reached its end, brought a breakthrough, for Lubitsch as well as for me. It was cockeyed, somewhat demoralizing, and in some ways perhaps dramatic. The initiative, astonishingly, came from him. Fortunately, I can report in considerable detail on what led up to it. I made notes, dictated them late that same day to my wife, before packing. And the next day, on the Super Chief, I added some observations that are relevant here.

My wife's chicken soup, for instance. In the earlier years, Lubitsch had been inclined to use chicken soup, noodles, and dumplings, as lumpen metaphors for domestic felicity. But this chicken soup of 1947 — very good, but nothing sensational, my wife said, and I agreed — captivated him. He lauded it to one and all, using gourmet terms — on the level, with no mockery.

And his photograph. I had never been a collector of photographs, had never thought of asking of giving. But I saw this one lying loose on his office desk — it was during the first week of work — and I admired it. He said, "Would you like it?" I said, "I certainly would." He picked up the picture as if to hand it to me and, I thought, hesitated slightly — which is why the moment stayed with me. I recall thinking, Isn't he going to inscribe it? Does he expect me to ask? Then he said, after what I may have wrongly seen as hesitation, "Do you want me to sign it?" "Hell, yes," I said. I thanked him warmly for the inscription: "To Raph, with friend-ship, Ernst." I was not overwhelmed; it seemed a routine, cautious, adequate inscription. But I did know that, in German, "friendship" — "*Freundschaft*" — is a loaded word, carrying the privilege of using the inti-mate "*du*" instead of the formal "*Sie*" when saying "you." And he had written "Raph" (his spelling of "Rafe"), which my wife and American friends call me. Conceivably, the inscription was a signal, a message of feeling.

And then there was Steffie Trondle. Steffie is one of the many dear human beings that I failed to appreciate in the graceless interludes of my life. Over the years, I had known her only as a figure behind a desk in Lubitsch's outer office. On my way in, we would exchange descriptions of the weather and assurances of each other's good health. On my way out, she would entrust to me, itemized, a series of good wishes for my wife and children, which I earnestly promised to deliver. Now, daily at the studio, these amenities had expanded, taken on substance. Still unobtrusive, she seemed almost motherly, and I saw her as a person, but I felt no special significance in any of it. I had not seen her at all during the time of Lubitsch's 1943 heart attack. Our only contact had been Tildy's account of her hysterical telephone equivalent of a death announcement, but I doubted if she remembered much of that. Certainly she would have been astonished if I told her I had actually written a funeral piece. Her new family tone merely had meant to me: She's getting older and more chummy, and so am I.

But it turned out that she did know about the funeral piece, had known for a long time. Both she and Lubitsch! Throughout these Hollywood months in early 1947, and long before, they had known, *had read every word of the piece,* with never a hint to me—understandably, for they had got it from Tildy, from whom I had exacted a vow of silence the afternoon of that day back in 1943. I did it the instant I heard that Lubitsch was recovering. You don't want a living man to think you were in such a hurry to eulogize over his coffin that you didn't even bother to inquire if he had stopped breathing. It was more than that. I just could not bear for Lubitsch to know about it, let alone read it. Well, it seems that Tildy had broken her vow. (Tildy Jones is not her real name, by the way.) She kept her shorthand notes, which she had pledged to destroy and, purely as a lover of belles-lettres, had made a few secret copies. But she had not told anyone, not even inadvertently at lunch that first day; there was a secretarial code, a taboo protecting the inspirations of one's writer. (They might be stolen by another one's writer.) But one fine day, after I had left Hollywood, still in 1943, she ran into her friend Steffie—Steffie, who lived and breathed only for Lubitsch. After all, who had a better right to see his eulogy? Pausing only to extract a hasty duplicate of her vow to me, Tildy delivered a copy to Steffie. Whereupon Steffie, overwhelmed by my prose, and an undiscriminating worshipper of Lubitsch, went straight to her deity and broke *her* vow.

Now comes that last day, a Friday. I stopped at the studio, gathered my things, and said a fond farewell to Steffie. (I never saw her again; she died a few years later.) I drove to the Bel Air home, where Lubitsch and I had a typical windup of a typical job, leisurely checking the mimeographed script. I had long since left behind the sense of imminent death, and I had long relinquished the notion of a love statement. Only the coming evening of packing and last-minute chores was on my mind. Lubitsch, too, seemed to be taking everything in stride. No nostalgia. No "Well, Sam, this is our ninth picture together." We lunched; I don't recall whether Nicola was there. We returned to the study and, as usual, dozed for a half hour in our easy chairs. Then, I smoking a guest Upmann and he chewing his lesser cigar, we cleaned up the last sequence.

About three, we were finished, and we both got up. He seemed to be in great shape—tan, brisk, on the beam. He tilted his head a little and took a measuring look at me. Then he said, "By the way, Sam, I heard that you wrote something a few years ago when I was sick—you wrote something very nice about me, and I appreciate it."

It came more casually, part of the goodbye—a bit more than a trifle, something even to give pause, calling perhaps for a mutter of surprise and pleasure, and then out with you. I've paid my friendship dues, goodbye and good luck. But I stood there, upset. He said, "What's the matter, Sam? You worried how I heard about it? Come on, you should know how things leak in this town. So what? I'm telling you, I appreciate it."

There was something missing, and—we were still standing in the study, where we had written *Heaven Can Wait*—automatically I turned away from him, a writer with a problem, and began pacing the room. It was easy to guess that the leak had come from Tildy. He, wasting no time in petty deception, admitted it—Tildy to Steffie to himself. And then— of course! Now it came out from under, my awful suspicion: "You read it!" His guilty grin gave him away, and he told me the little story—made a humorous anecdote out of it—dwelling with wry indulgence on the broken vows of Tildy and Steffie, and on his own. "Please, Sam, don't ever tell Steffie I said a word!"

As he went on, I found myself visualizing that piece of writing through his eyes, and its defects became scarifying. My God, it was all about him; he was the subject matter—his *life*, total and complete. Was that the best I could or would do, once he wasn't there to pass judgment?

All he seemed to care about, however, was getting the whole thing over with, and he became serious and brisk. "What's the difference?" he said. "I *liked* what you wrote, Sam. I really appreciated it." This from the man who time and again, through the years, when I had drudged over a scene and he had read it would say, "Sure it's good. But good isn't enough—you know that. For *us*, it has to be *terrific*." And here he "liked," he "appreci- ated." It was sinister. It was ironical. The man hated me.

I had to have it out. "It's only a first draft!" I cried, and I floundered on in fragments, saying and not saying and almost saying that I positively would have seen the inadequacies of those two pages the very next day if he had been dead according to expectation. "You know damn well the jumps I can make from the first or the second or third version," I said. I threw his words back at him—"You *liked*, you *appreciated*"—accusing him of insulting my intelligence. I practically called him a monster for waiting four years to tell him, if he truly did "appreciate" and "like" what I'd written, and a double monster for speaking now. I dared him to be honest and specify the defects; I challenged him, betting I saw more than he did; and somewhere along the line he laughed at me, and I laughed, too. Of course, it was funny, but part of the laughter came from my relief at discovering that he was not in the least squeamish about his own death or any of the chapel-and-cemetery high jinks it would beget—that to him the whole subject was comic. I laughed, but I returned to what I was really trying, in my writer's pride, to say: that when and if he did die, that piece would be corrected, perfected, illustrious, accurate—a true monument.

It got to the point where, according to my notes, he said earnestly, "I believe you, Sam. I am satisfied absolutely that if I drop dead tomorrow you'll do a polishing job that I would rave about if I read it in advance."

He was not smiling, nor was I, and suddenly we were looking at each other in a very familiar way. I was thinking, "My God—he and I together—right now—it would take just an hour, that's all!" And I saw in his eyes exactly the same thought.

Inevitably, that is what happened. We started working on the piece as if it were a speech in a film. No, it was not like that. I'll come to it. I pause only to caution against false expectations. Let it be clear that this is not heading into a big scene, climactic, transcending the literal truth. (I don't remember whether it occurred to me then, but today I suspect he was suddenly smitten with the fear that—behind his back, as it were—I might do a lousy rewrite job.) Well, I kept standing there, probably looking untrustworthy, and suddenly he was up on his feet and around the desk. "Listen, Sam," he said, "this is different from the way we work on a *scene*," and he vigorously argued that here I would not be condemned for literary lapses, that these very lapses, in a person of my taste, were the stammering, decisive evidence that the heart, not the mind, was speaking. As for the inexactitudes about himself, he said, "Who can object? It's your opinion."

The matter had become undisguisedly personal and important to him —much more so than it could be to me. After all, it was his funeral. I saw the point and had no trouble agreeing with him. He was making sense. However, for the record, I carefully reminded him of his own ample critical observations. He dismissed them, reminding me in turn of my ironclad belief that in creative work if you go for the whole truth, honoring every crumb, you're a clerk, not an artist. I accepted that, too, even if it did not exactly apply. But still he wasn't sure of me. "Promise me, Sam," he said, "that you won't change a *single word.*" I promised at once, of course. I was on the verge of volunteering a vow, but I refrained; vows were a dime a dozen that day. Anyway, he believed me at last, and all was well.

It was nearly five o'clock when we said a brief final goodbye, both having been thrown off schedule and fretting to get things done. However, as I drove in my rented car to our rented house, I was aware that I most likely would never see him again, and that this last hour had been truly cockeyed, running aslant in all directions, full of implications that might take on meaning in time. I tried to memorize highlights—phrases, expressions on his face, my own thoughts at a given moment. At home, my wife agreed that our packing—everything—could wait, and I dictated to her all I could remember. I couldn't figure out, and I still can't, whether somewhere toward the end his "I appreciate" had been transmuted into "It's terrific!"

I heard the news of Lubitsch's death over the radio on the farm in Pennsylvania. That was in late November of the same year, and I made sure I sent flowers, telegrams, and letters. I was immersed in a series of short stories, and there was little else I could do until sometime in December, when a letter came from Richard English, editor of *The Screen Writer*. He was publishing a symposium of tributes to the Master and would I write one. English gave a brief report on the funeral. It was impressive and without pomp. Lubitsch rested not in a formidable crypt but out in the open—a simple tombstone, uncrowded, accessible, and pleasing. English admired the eulogy by Charles Brackett, and he enclosed the text. He also dwelt glowingly on Jeanette MacDonald's rendition of "Beyond the Blue Horizon," adding that it was too bad she hadn't sung it that well originally for Lubitsch in *Monte Carlo*.

271

I kept my promise to Lubitsch and sent the untouched first draft—untouched except for a brief obeisance to Brackett's graceful and scrupulous eulogy. Otherwise not a comma or a period was altered. I did hesitate about the little postscript in which I regretted not having made my sentiments known to the deceased while he was alive. Lubitsch and I had overlooked that item. I decided to take my promise literally, and launched the dissembling postscript intact, not even revising its sloppy wording. I knew then and there, of course, that I was thus proclaiming myself a liar if ever in the future I should find occasion to write what I am writing now, in 1981, when, had he lived, Lubitsch would have been almost ninety and, in my opinion, most amenable.

SAMSON RAPHAELSON'S CREDITS:

FILMS:

The Jazz Singer, 1927

The Smiling Lieutenant, 1931

Trouble in Paradise, 1932

One Hour with You, 1932

Broken Lullaby, 1932

Caravane, 1934

The Queen's Affair, 1934

The Merry Widow, 1934

Caravan, 1934

Servants' Entrance, 1934

Dressed to Thrill, 1935

Ladies Love Danger, 1935

Accent on Youth, 1935

Angel, 1937

The Last of Mrs. Cheyney, 1937

The Shop Around the Corner, 1940

Skylark, 1941

Suspicion, 1941

Heaven Can Wait, 1943

The Perfect Marriage, 1946

Ziegfeld Follies, 1946

The Harvey Girls, 1946

Green Dolphin Street, 1947

That Lady in Ermine, 1948

In the Good Old Summertime, 1949

Mr. Music, 1950

Bannerline, 1951

Main Street to Broadway, 1953

Hilda Crane, 1956

But Not for Me, 1959

THE EPSTEINS and "CASABLANCA"

AT THAT TIME, INGRID BERGMAN WAS "OWNED" BY DAVID SELZNICK under the terms of a long contract, and she could be pried away only by the lure of a good story that would advance her career and her box-office value to the Selznick organization. In the words of Julius Epstein, "Jack Warner summoned my brother Phil and me and said we had to go to Selznick and talk him into letting us have Bergman, and that David would want to know every detail of the screenplay. We said we didn't know what to say, but Warner told us to make up something, anything, just bring back Bergman! So Phil and I were ushered into Selznick's office, and I got things started by saying it was a romantic melodrama with a sinister atmosphere. Dark lighting and a lot of smoke ... Selznick slapped the desk top and said, "That's all I need to know, you've got Bergman!"

Mike Curtiz started giving out the incomplete script to various colleagues on the lot. Inevitably, their reactions varied, and Mike's attitude towards the story shifted with the changing winds. When I protested that some of his suggested changes were illogical and out of character, he would answer impatiently in his Hungarian idiom, "Don't worry what's logical. I make it go so fast, no one notices!"

—HOWARD KOCH, 1979

FAULKNER at MGM

THE EARLY THIRTIES AT MGM WERE MARKED BY THE IMPORTATION OF authors from every field of writing. Those who proved inept as "constructionists" or dialogue writers did not stay long, but it was said that if anyone could sign his name to a contract he was sure of an annual salary of at least $100,000 — for two weeks. Those who were retained were men and women who brought proven talents with them. P. G. Wodehouse was able to write several Jeeves stories while waiting, on salary, almost a year for a studio assignment. Writers noted for their individual creativity were dazed by the material on which they were told to work. Dorothy Parker's biting wit and unsentimental compassion were considered by one producer as ideal assets for adapting that early wave of a flood of soap operas, *Madame X.*

William Faulkner's advent at MGM made an impression long remembered. We had been friends since 1929, when he came to New York for the publication of *The Sound and the Fury.* His speech was always slow, partly because of his natural Southern drawl and partly because of a conversational gambit he habitually employed. Before answering a question he would exhale a long, meditative puff from his straight-stemmed pipe; then, as often as not, he would contemplate the bowl for a few seconds more.

When he first met Thalberg, Bill was asked if he was familiar with MGM productions. "Ah don't believe Ah know which pictures are yours," Bill replied. "Do you make the Mickey Mouse brand?"

"No," Thalberg replied icily, "we make some shorts, but we want you to familiarize yourself with our big features and the work of our leading stars."

Bill said he'd be happy to do so. A production room was placed at his disposal where he could privately enjoy the latest masterpieces of Lana Turner and Norma Shearer. Actually he was ignorant of the work of both. Ten minutes after Bill entered the production room he dashed out, almost colliding with another writer. The anguish on Faulkner's face made the latter ask: "What's the matter?"

For once, Bill did not puff on his pipe before pronouncing his Impression of MGM epics: "Jesus Christ, it ain't possible!"

—MARC CONNELLY

16. FAULKNER and the PYRAMIDS:
HAROLD JACK BLOOM

1972

William Faulkner by Carl VanVechten

THIS WAS WILLIAM FAULKNER'S FIRST EXPERIENCE IN A HOLLYWOOD studio, but it was far from his last. After MGM he put in a stretch at Twentieth Century Fox during the '30s, when he received a co-credit on the screenplay of *The Road to Glory*, which Howard Hawks directed in 1936, and on which his collaborator was Joel Sayre. In 1937, his credit on *Slave Ship* is that of the author of the screen story.

When asked about such projects, Faulkner once said, "I'm a motion picture doctor. When they run into a section they don't like, I rework it and continue to rework it until they like it. In *Slave Ship*, I reworked sections. I don't write scripts. I don't know enough about it."

Nunnally Johnson, who spent many years at Fox, both writing and producing, recalled, "Faulkner ... worked on a script for me once but I never thought for a moment that he had the slightest interest in either that script or anything else in Hollywood. Howard Hawks kept bringing him out here for reasons that I can only guess at. It may be that he simply wanted his name attached to Faulkner's. Or since Hawks liked to write, it was easy to do it with Faulkner, for Bill didn't care much one way or the other."

The simple fact was, Faulkner may have disliked Hollywood and screenwriting, but he constantly needed money to support his family in Mississippi and to enable himself to continue writing. In the early '30s, his novel *Sanctuary* was sold to Paramount, as would be his future works, *Pylon*, *The Sound and the Fury*, and *The Reivers*. But his writings did not produce sufficient income, and Faulkner would continue to return to California.

One of his longest stints beneath the California palms was in the early '40s, when Hawks brought him out to work on *To Have and Have Not* and *The Big Sleep*. On the first picture, he shared a credit with the veteran screenwriter Jules Furthman, and on the second, the two writers were joined by Leigh Brackett. Faulkner's tour of duty at Warner Bros. was long and frustrating, and he was finally able to persuade the studio to release him from the arduous job of screenwriting.

But in 1955, after all the years of low-paid frustration at the studios, the drawling, soft-spoken, pipe-smoking gentleman from Oxford, who'd served with the British Royal Flying Corps in World War I, and who'd scratched out a meager living writing literary masterpieces ever since, earned himself yet another screen credit.

In Leonard Maltin's review, it is listed as *Land of the Pharaohs* 1955:

> "Talky, fruity spectacle about the building of the Great Pyramid, filmed on an epic scale." Howard Hawks claimed that neither he nor his writers, William Faulkner, Harry Kurnitz, and Harold Jack Bloom, "knew how a Pharaoh talked" and it shows. "Still worth catching for great revenge ending and campy villainy by Joan Collins."

An epic story of Egypt and the pharaohs? Collaborated on by William Faulkner, who would go on to win the Nobel Prize for Literature?

Almost half a century later, one must ask: How did such a film ever come to pass, and why did the gentleman from Oxford participate?

"In 1954 he was 53 years old," said Harold Jack Bloom, the third member of the triumvirate who'd provided the screenplay. "He done a good deal of writing in Hollywood, usually with his good friend, Howard Hawks. They got along very well. They liked to talk about fishing or hunting. They rarely talked about films. Faulkner, who never went to the movies, didn't really consider the movies anything either to like or dislike.

"He agreed to work with Hawks because he just liked Howard as a person...and Hawks felt he was getting a great talent for very little money."

Which was?

"$500 a week. I know, because that's what I was getting."

That was all? It does seem rather puny.

"He considered it found money," said Bloom. "It was the Christmas season, this gig started early in December and went to January, and Hawks arranged for Faulkner to have all his expenses paid, as well. He called Faulkner in Oxford, told him to fly over to Europe, and then to a villa in Stresa [Italy], where I joined them...and we worked together for ten weeks."

How did the notion of a historical epic based on the pharaohs ever come to pre-production?

"It was my premise," said Bloom. "That was the reason I was hired to be there by Hawks. What I'd come up with was a story about a pharaoh who wanted a tomb that could not be robbed. So he hires a Greek architect, one who was a slave who'd been captured; the defense the Greek had devised beforehand had so impressed the pharaoh that he hired the architect to design this proposed pyramid...So soon the architect is in charge of some twenty thousand people, building the pyramid."

By the wildest stretch of the imagination, it seems incredible that Howard Hawks would consider Faulkner an apt writer for such historic extravagance.

"That's not how Hawks worked," said Bloom. "He thought his friend Faulkner was a very talented man, which was certainly true...a talent which could be secured reasonably...Perhaps I'm doing Hawks an injustice, but I think he was impressed by being in Faulkner's company...And don't forget, he'd have Faulkner's name on the screen. Pretty prestigious."

And how did Faulkner feel?

"He had no respect at all for films. He didn't consider anything about the movies as an art form. He felt that doing anything in films was getting money for nothing, and he certainly wanted the money. He said to me once, 'I'm getting paid to have a vacation.' And I guess he was absolutely right. You see, on this job, Faulkner never did any actual writing. He simply sat in on our story conferences."

By that time, had Kurnitz arrived?

"Right at the beginning," said Bloom. "Harry was the most brilliant man I think I've ever met. Not only brilliant, but the wittiest... So the three of us sat there, Harry at the typewriter and we went to work. Harry could write twenty pages a day. Compulsively. And Hawks liked that, believe me."

"If it weren't for Harry, I would have gone crazy on that whole project, because it was a truly spooky adventure, believe me."

Spooky?

"Here we were in this villa. It was December in Stresa, which is as off-season as you can possibly get. The only reason the villa was even open was that a friend of Hawks' owned it! Opened it just for us. Four of us and Howard's wife... and two servants, and we were the only population of Stresa, which is in the northern Italian lakes! Cold, very cold, but beautiful. A very spooky arrangement..."

"Especially for me," says Bloom. "Don't forget, Hawks was 56, Faulkner was 53, and we celebrated Harry's 45th birthday later... and here am I, the kid... 29. And I'm surrounded by these veteran campaigners; remember, I was really a neophyte. I'd written a couple of pictures, and some TV scripts, but this was big time stuff... I was only there, remember, because the whole Egyptian thing was my premise! See, I'd never met Hawks before; my agent brought us together in Paris when he was looking for a springboard... What a strange mish-mosh we were... Faulkner, Kurnitz, and Harold Bloom."

"The thing I found out about Hawks was, he felt that writers were necessary... and that was all. If we could give him twenty or twenty-five pages a day, he could find one or two of some value. He used to say to me, when I turned in four or five of my own pages, 'Well, you're not giving me any choices.' And of course, my attitude was that I had made those choices *before* I gave him the pages! But he didn't understand he was getting a distillation of what I'd done for him... And we had plenty of arguments about that. Meanwhile, Harry kept giving him his twenty pages."

The two writers worked separately?

"Sure, we took different scenes. We'd leapfrog each other, and then we'd have a meeting, every day, with Hawks and Faulkner. We'd talk about what had been written, and we'd throw stuff out, or save something, and get a new idea or two."

Was Faulkner a contributor?

"Very recalcitrant. Only offered something when prodded. And remember, he ended up with not just a screen credit—but the *first* screen credit! But that's what Hawks had hired him for in the first place, as window dressing, so to speak."

Did he ever contribute anything at all, or did he just sit there and comment?

"Well, the premise I'd come up with," said Bloom, "was a very socially oriented one. I suggested that the Egyptian dynasties were destroyed by the building of the pyramids. That the very nature of the building of the pyramids was to create an army of twenty or thirty thousand people which had to be fed, clothed, and housed for twenty years … and that army produced a group of influential merchants. Those were the people that the royalty had to pay to maintain that huge army of workers … And the merchants became very, very wealthy, and pretty soon they became politically powerful. So, in a sense, the building of the pyramids contributed as much as anything to the destruction of the Egyptian dynasties!"

An interesting premise, indeed. How long before that premise was dumped?

"It didn't last very long," said Bloom, with a smile. "Hawks kept the premise that I had, about the fact they'd hired this Greek architect. But as for Faulkner, he kept pooh-poohing our seriousness about the whole thing. He more or less wanted to do a pirate picture with togas."

Seriously?

"Absolutely," says Bloom. "The people would be dressed as Egyptians … but the nature of the picture would be with pirates jumping around, swashbuckling, and lovely maidens in pantaloons … insane cliché stuff like that!"

He truly was sneering at the project, wasn't he?

"The word is patronizing," remembers Bloom. "He felt this was much ado about nothing, and his attitude was 'What the hell difference does it make?' He didn't really like movies; he thought that the making of a movie taken seriously was just fuss and feathers."

Even after his own works had been adapted into films?

"I asked him once about how he felt about movies, and he told me he never saw them!" says Bloom. "Told me 'I never go to 'em!' And that's when he told me another thing... 'I've stopped reading,' he said. 'Except to go back and re-read certain classics.' And when I asked him why, he said, 'If I read contemporary things, I can't concentrate on what I myself am doing... This happened as I got older,' he told me. 'In the last five years or so...'"

It wasn't the first time that Faulkner had been taken away from his serious writing to do so-called film work, which he obviously despised doing.

Back in 1943, when he'd been under contract to Warner Bros., he'd spent a most frustrating time working on various projects and killing time in the afternoons with fellow writers, such as Eliot Paul and A.I. Bezzerides—whom I had once found on a warm day, sitting in an office at the Writers Building, engaged in a game of lotto.

"Well... they were doing a job... like lettuce pickers," commented Bloom. "Prominent in their own field of prose, they didn't take screen-writing seriously. I take it seriously because it's always been my major field. I think screen writing is damned important work. But these guys usually felt being assigned to do a rewrite of some script was a step down on the ladder.

"But I have to admit, Faulkner wasn't a bit hypocritical about this Egyptian job. Didn't hide behind any pontification. Came right out and said, 'That's why I'm here; I'm being paid to have a vacation by Warner Bros.!'"

Ten weeks, at a mere $500 a week?

"Yes, but remember, we were living on studio money, so he banked the whole $5000! See, Hawks moved us up from the villa at Stresa to the St. Moritz Hotel... And the first night we arrived, we went to the restaurant, and I discovered that Faulkner was a wine fancier. Asked the sommelier if he had a particular wine. 1937 Romanee Conti. The guy was very impressed and said they might have some. Faulkner said, 'Find out how many bottles.' The guy came back and told us it was eleven. And Faulkner bought all eleven bottles...on the spot, with Warner Bros. paying for it."

A sweet sort of revenge, indeed.

"And we had one each night. For eleven nights. And in those days, they charged $40 a bottle. They would be about three times that amount now. He didn't care. He knew a lot about wine and food...He'd spent a good deal of time in Paris. He loved Paris.

"...One night he got a little drunk, maybe drunker than usual, and he started wandering around St. Moritz, thinking he was in Paris and wondering why certain places had closed and what had become of his old friends. Things like that...Of course, he'd usually start very early. Three in the afternoon, he'd ask for a martini, and he'd say, 'It's 5 PM in Moscow...' The first few times, we laughed, but later on, we smiled politely."

And how did the script progress?

"Well, Faulkner sat around, but he didn't offer much. Fact is, he was very withdrawn; never gave of himself voluntarily. You'd have to drag everything out of him...At best, he was a counterpuncher in his conversation; never originated anything," says Bloom. "Liked to smoke his pipe and be the wise old man...well, after all, we're talking about a 53-year-old."

That's old?

"It was to me," he said.

What about the ladies?

"Loved young ones, especially the adoration which went along with them, when they spotted him and recognized who he was...Then he'd open up a little and bask in their adoration."

And what about his relationship to you and Kurnitz? Was he ever hostile?

"No, no," said Bloom. "Must've been because he didn't consider me to be that important...And his attitude towards Harry was pretty much the same."

Kurnitz, even after all these years, is still remembered for his flashes of wit. Did Faulkner enjoy it?

"Well, being Harry, he started out by making jokes...or trying to. And particularly, when we were having dinner, in a group, at St. Moritz, and there were plenty of those parties, believe me. Harry, of course, would be the raconteur, the life of the party.

"But when we were among ourselves, Harry's attempts to make jokes with Faulkner faded very rapidly, because the only response Harry would be getting would be from me. Whereas Faulkner treated Harry like a clown. Actually, if anyone said something funny, Faulkner treated him as if he were an entertainer...and indulged him."

Back to the Egyptian spectacle, of the Greek architect and the pharaoh. Did Faulkner actually write any of it?

Bloom shook his head. "Nothing."

Notes on paper or anything?

Bloom sighed, "Actually, he never wrote a line."

So what did Faulkner and Hawks discuss, while you and Kurnitz were busy turning out script pages?

"Oh, they went on talking about hunting and fishing...for hours. Different guns and different lures for fishing...which one was best for certain fish, that sort of thing. But it's funny," Bloom mused, "I always had the feeling that Hawks was doing this to curry favor with his pal Bill Faulkner...and the even funnier thing was, I don't think Faulkner was being fooled by it, because he was just as carefully patronizing his pal Hawks!"

While pocketing the salary, on which he could write yet another book?

"That's about right."

The same process by which Faulkner had turned out other master-pieces.

"Once we finished the script, I left. Harry may have stayed on a couple of weeks longer. And Faulkner hung around until his ten weeks were up ...and got paid, and I suppose he took it all back to Oxford."

And did Bloom ever see Faulkner after the script was turned in? Or hear from him?

"Nope. Never again. I tried, but nothing happened. No response. But you know, we weren't exactly friends. He was a very withdrawn man, kept to himself a good deal. Actually, he didn't permit people to become his friends...He'd call people by their second names...something like the way the British refer to each other. I was Bloom, and Harry, he'd call

Kurnitz, and that was it. But Hawks? He was Howard … After all, they'd been buddies for thirty years. He didn't mind if we called him Bill … but we always remained last named.

"He'd show up each day, always dressed very conservatively, never casually. Tweeds, that sort of thing. Well groomed, clean shaven … obviously very vain about his appearance. Always the gentleman. One day we started talking about writing and how he'd chosen it as his profession … and he brought me up short. He said, 'I'm not really a writer, Bloom. I'm a farmer who writes.'"

But even at that time, when he'd become such a major literary figure, both in America and Europe? With books which sold well — certainly not like his early days, when a Faulkner novel rarely if ever went past its first printing.

"Matter of fact," said Bloom, "before I went to Strega to work on this film, and after I came back, all my friends were very, very impressed by my association with him. Remember, he was a French cult figure … like Chaplin, or Jerry Lewis, very big time. And they stay with their loyalties. But to him, it seemed writing was not a profession in itself … And certainly not screenwriting."

He shakes his head, thinking back two decades. "It was an amazing experience. How could it not be? Imagine me, a young guy, starting out, working with two such people, and sitting around having daily conferences with Howard Hawks, another legend … And then, when we finished work after the day hours, there was all that St. Moritz social life. And my agent, Charlie Feldman, another Hollywood legend — he was representing Faulkner, so he'd show up, and there was a lot of nighttime action. And there I am, mingling with all sorts of socialites … dancing with amazingly beautiful girls … having a ball. And working the next day on a picture with Harry Kurnitz … and *William Faulkner?*

"That has to be a once-in-a-lifetime experience!"

REVIEW: "THE LAND OF THE PHARAOHS" 1955 [FROM THE WARNER BROS. STORY, 1980] "Director Howard Hawks employed 9,787 extras to appear in one of the many spectacular scenes in this epic, and visually, at any rate, he emerged with a stunner. He was less successful in his deployment of scenarists. William Faulkner, Harry Kurnitz and

Harold Jack Bloom, whose screenplay, although literal enough, was basically commonplace…"

THIS POSTSCRIPT MIGHT WELL BE TITLED "THE EGYPTIAN RASHOMON."

In 1956, after Hawks' film was released, three French cineastes, Messrs. Jacques Becker, Jacques Rivette, and Francois Truffaut came to interview director Howard Hawks for *Cahiers du Cinema.*

Hawks was extremely anxious to discuss his latest film, *The Land of the Pharaohs.* In discussing the origin of the picture, he presented the following history: "It then occurred to me that the building of the pyramids … demonstrated what man is able to create with his bare hands, from sand to stone. This kind of story appeals to me tremendously. We thus wrote our script on this one theme; the construction of a pyramid."

Cahiers: "What part did William Faulkner play in the development of the scenario?"

Hawks: "He collaborated with Harry Kurnitz [sic] in the writing of both story and screenplay. As always, he contributed enormously. He's a great writer; we are very old friends and work easily together. We understand each other very well, and any time I need any sort of help, I call Faulkner. He has done three or four scenarios for me, but he has also helped me on many others. The story of *The Land of the Pharaohs*, because his imagination was challenged by these men, their conversations, the reasons for their belief in a second life, how they happened to achieve these tasks for their belief in a second life, how they happened to achieve these tasks for beliefs we would find it difficult to understand today, such as the slight importance attached to the present life in comparison with the future life, the rest that was to be assured to the pharaoh where his body would be secure … for eternity … for all these reasons, Faulkner was the man for the assignment; he has an affinity for these ideas. They are what he is made for."

ALL THE PRINCIPALS IN THIS EPISODE ARE GONE NOW.

However, it certainly seems that Mr. Faulkner, the dapper pipe-smoking gentleman farmer, who brought the Warner paychecks home to Oxford after his ten-week tour of duty sitting in with Harry Kurnitz and

Harold Jack Bloom, and returned to his own work, has had the last word — or is it words?

"I decline to accept the end of man. It is easy enough to say that man is immortal simply because he will endure; that when the last ding-dong of doom has clanged and faded from the last worthless rock hanging tideless in the last red and dying evening, that even then there will be one more sound; that of his puny inexhaustible voice, still talking. I refuse to accept this. I believe that man will not merely endure, he will prevail. He is immortal, not because he alone among creatures has an inexhaustible voice, but because he has a soul, a spirit capable of compassion and sacrifice and endurance."

Those were his words upon receiving the Nobel Prize.

So what if he couldn't write screenplays!

AUTHOR's NOTE: REGARDING FAULKNER's ACCEPTANCE OF HIS Warner Bros. salary, as he spent the weeks in St. Moritz drinking expense-account vintage wine and waiting out the ten-week assignment —

A Warner salary was nothing new for Faulkner. He had spent considerable time at Warner Bros., working for Hawks on *To Have and Have Not* and *The Big Sleep*, also at $500 a week. Quite a bargain, considering how successful both pictures were at the box office.

But during the war years, Faulkner was back in Burbank, working on various projects that were never to be made. One such dead end came with *The DeGaulle Story*, a pretentious piece which dealt with wartime France, then divided between Marshal Petain's government and the burgeoning resistance movement of pro-DeGaullists.

Hardly the sort of subject one would suggest Faulkner take on.

It was early in 1943. I was at the studio, temporarily assigned, as were the rest of us G.I.'s, to the filming of Irving Berlin's wildly successful soldier show *This Is the Army*. That was when I first encountered Faulkner.

He had an office upstairs in the Writers Building. He came and went, quietly puffing on his pipe, working on the projects to which he was assigned, almost anonymous. Somewhat naïvely, I could not believe such an enormously talented author did not merit more attention than, say, Peter Lorre or Hugh Herbert — but he did not.

One evening I was invited to a small party in Hollywood, and there was Faulkner. He was escorting Meta Wilde, his new lady friend. When I told him how much I admired his writing, he nodded politely, sipped his drink (he'd had quite a few), and puffed on the pipe. The fact that someone recognized him for the fine writer he was may have gratified him, but under these circumstances, while he sweated out his days at the studio, it may have been bittersweet.

A few days later, I managed to unearth a copy of one of his books, in its dust jacket, in a Hollywood Boulevard used bookstore. None of Faulkner's early books ever sold well.

The price? I believe it was $2.

I brought it to the studio the next day and found my way to his office in the Writers Building. When I asked his secretary if I might see him, she shook her head. "He's very busy now," she said. I explained this wouldn't take long, just a moment or two, for him to sign my book. She went inside and consulted with him; then she ushered me in.

Three men sat around a table. Through the haze of tobacco smoke, I could make out Faulkner and a round-faced bearded middle-aged gent. He turned out to be Eliot Paul, a successful author of detective stories (he eventually was called in to do "additional dialogue" on *Rhapsody in Blue*, the biography of George Gershwin). The third man, burly and unshaven, was A. I. Bezzerides. He'd written *They Drive by Night* and was working on *Action in the North Atlantic*.

Was this a story conference?

Not precisely. On the table was a board; on Warner time, these three were playing lotto.

"I didn't mean to interrupt," I said, and proffered my Faulkner first edition for a signature. Would he oblige? "No problem," smiled Faulkner, and carefully inscribed it.

"Why didn't you bring one of *my* books?" asked Paul.

"I'll go find one," I promised, and next day I picked up his marvelous work, *The Life and Death of a Spanish Town*.

"What about *me?*" demanded Bezzerides.

"I'll look," I promised. But I never did find one of his.

To this day, I have never forgotten the sight of our future Nobel Prize winner, seated at a lotto table, puffing on his pipe.

Anything to avoid wasting his talent on his current Warner Bros. assignment. The fate of which, I am certain Faulkner must have known, was to end up on some dusty Warner story department shelf — yellowing, forgotten — and unread.

William Faulkner's Credits:

Films:

Flesh, 1932

The Story of Temple Drake, 1933

Today We Live, 1933

The Road to Glory, 1936

Slave Ship, 1937

Submarine Patrol, 1938

Four Men and a Prayer, 1938

Drums Along the Mohawk, 1939

Gunga Din, 1939

Northern Pursuit, 1943

Air Force, 1943

To Have and Have Not, 1944

Mildred Pierce, 1945

The Southerner, 1945

God Is My Co-Pilot, 1945

The Big Sleep, 1946

Deep Valley, 1947

Adventures of Don Juan, 1948

Intruder in the Dust, 1949

Land of the Pharaohs, 1955

The Long, Hot Summer, 1958

The Tarnished Angels, 1958

The Sound and the Fury, 1959

Sanctuary, 1961

The Reivers, 1969

Tomorrow, 1972

Rose for Emily, 1982

Kaki bakar, 1995

Two Soldiers, 2002

Harold Jack Bloom's Credits:

Academy Award Nominations:

The Naked Spur, 1953

Films:

Arena, 1953

The Yellow Tomahawk, 1954

Land of the Pharaohs, 1955

Behind the High Wall, 1956

Foreign Intrigue, 1956

You Only Live Twice, 1967

A Gunfight, 1971

SIDNEY LUMET on PADDY CHAYEFSKY

"In the early days of television, when the 'kitchen sink' school of realism held sway, we always reached a point where we 'explained the character,'" recalled Sidney Lumet. "Around two thirds of the way through, someone articulated the psychological truth that made the character the person he was. Chayefsky and I used to call this the 'rubber ducky' school of drama. 'Someone once took away his rubber ducky away from him, and that's why he's a deranged killer.' That was the fashion then, and with many producers and studios, it still is.

"Chayefsky used to say, 'There are two kinds of scenes; the Pet the Dog scene, and the Kick the Dog scene. The studio always wants a Pet the Dog scene so everybody can tell who the hero is.'"

—Sidney Lumet

17. THE COLONEL FADES OUT:
JACK WARNER

Julius and Philip Epstein

SINCE JACK WARNER HAS PRESENTED ALL OF THE HOLLYWOOD SCRIBES and pharisees herein with a title for this book, it seems only proper that he be accorded some recognition, here in the next-to-closing, eleven o'clock chapter.

On second thought, knowing Warner, he would certainly have demanded a line above the title, so it would read, "Jack L. Warner Presents!" And throwing us all out of his office if we did not immediately agree.

Bette Davis might defy Jack, but very few others tried it more than once.

Some years back, at a Warner studio function, Jack rose to make a speech. He rambled on and on, interspersing his remarks with typical Warner witticisms, some amusing, most merely tedious. ("Jack would rather tell a bad joke than make a good picture," was Jack Benny's rueful assessment, and having made *The Horn Blows at Midnight* for Warner, Benny certainly knew such truths.)

Flash forward a few years, after Warner had died, to a commemorative dinner sponsored by the Friends of the U.S.C. Libraries. A prestigious evening—the title was The Colonel: An Affectionate Remembrance of Jack L. Warner.

After dinner, the evening was replete with duty laughs. On such a night devoted to good works, as the guests rambled down Hollywood's favorite street, Memory Lane, it would have been bad taste indeed for anything as elusive as the truth to be spoken.

So it was highly significant that the largest belly-laugh would come when the late beloved writer Julius Epstein, who had with his twin brother Phillip turned out literally dozens of scripts for Warner's most successful films, turned around to peer up owlishly at the large portrait of a grinning J. L. that dominated the festivities.

"That's Jack, all right," commented Epstein. "I remember that expression on his face; it's exactly the way he looked before he told you you were fired."

The audience roared, and then applauded. Nobody needed to tell that crowd of Hollywood veterans, actors, writers, songwriters, even a few surviving producers that there was more, much more to be said about J. L. On Memory Lane, there are no unpleasant neighborhoods.

Long before this night, I had learned the essential Hollywood rule: You take a man's money, you dance to his tune. And if you come to the place where you can't stand the heat any longer, the door is always open, pal, close it on the way out.

My father, Jake Wilk, had worked long and hard for that smiling gent hanging above us that night. He'd begun as J. L.'s Eastern story editor in January 1929 and stuck it out until early 1952. For twenty-three years he'd taken the Colonel's shilling, through good times and the Depression, World War II and its aftermath; week after week he brought home that weekly Warner paycheck which fed us, housed us, and educated me and my siblings in style.

The trouble with legends is that they have a bad habit of hardening into what passes for truth. So much of what has been written down about Hollywood in those so-called golden years is simply fan-magazine puffery, now being marketed to cineaste-types, who thrive on a steady diet of legends. And now we are being inundated with the truth—biographies that roll back the curtain to reveal it all, down and dirty, the dirtier the better. Which of your childhood legends was really a lesbian? Which one specialized in orgies? Who was a closet sadomasochist, a drunk, or a child molester? Check it all out at Barnes and Noble over caffe latte.

There have been books about Warner and his brothers, one by Jack himself, assembled by quondam historians who haven't a clue about what it was really like out in Burbank. Self-appointed psychologists do dissertations on what they can find in the Warner archives out in Wisconsin. But those of us who were around during the Warner years, and who can still remember what it was truly like, have perhaps a small obligation to pass on some of the truth—in case anyone in the future really cares.

From the age of nine, I was a Warner brat. Other kids spent their Saturday afternoons playing baseball, or at scouts, or shoplifting at Woolworth's. Not I. I hung around Warner projection rooms. In the darkness I studied at Warner Academy, learning from such teachers as Jimmy Cagney, Eddie Robinson, George Arliss, Joan Blondell, Paul Muni, Bette Davis, and Lyle Talbot. I laughed at Joe E. Brown, studied music with Harry Warren and Al Dubin, and learned about female anatomy from the Busby Berkeley girls. It was a prep school from which only a fool would wish to graduate.

The years passed, and I made it to college. Summer jobs were hard to come by, but my father had the clout to finagle one for me; through the reliable magic of nepotism, I found myself hired at $15 a week, to serve as an office boy in the Warner publicity department out in Burbank—hardly a sentence to Devils Island!

Jack Warner turned out to be a jovial, dapper man, with a pencil mustache and a ruddy complexion. He had his own private masseur, a huge man named Abdul. Jack dressed in what we called "sharp" clothes and was given to rattling off in his high, piercing voice a constant stream of so-called jokes, material he'd picked up at vaudeville houses, or wherever comics gathered. At our first meeting on a studio street, he said "Okay, kid, what do you know about real estate?" When I, the new kid on the block, replied, "Nothing much, Mr. Warner," he shook his head. "No, no, kid! You're supposed to say *lots*!" And so it remained, thereafter.

If you hung around the writers and the publicity men, you could hear all the classic lines about Warner. It was the acerbic Wilson Mizner, who ended his days on the Warner payroll as an "idea man" for story lines (someone was assigned to follow Mizner around the lot and jot down his comments for later use in screenplay dialogue) who once remarked "Jack Warner has oilcloth pockets—so he can steal soup!" Even Warner may have chuckled at that one, but it's certain he wasn't at all amused by the next Mizner nifty, which went "Making a deal with the Warners is like fucking a porcupine—it's one hundred pricks against one!"

Yes, Warner was tough, he was difficult, but he was also shrewd, and like so many of his producer contemporaries, he was a gambler. If he wasn't an original thinker, he was sharp enough to latch on to talent, both in front of and behind his cameras, and to exploit it for whatever it was worth. He fought with them all—not only Bette Davis, Cagney, Bogart, and all the rest. But remarkably, it took meek and soft-spoken Olivia De Havilland who finally challenged J. L. in a courtroom, to break the yoke of those oppressive seven-year exclusive-service contracts, by which all those Hollywood feudal lords kept their talented serfs in legal chains.

Gamble though he would, J. L. wasn't at first eager to take plunges into what the business regarded as "classy" ventures. These days it's simple to hold commemorative Warner celebrations on Turner Classic Movies, and trot out the jewelry from the vaults, such masterworks as *The Life of Emile Zola, Watch on the Rhine, The Letter,* or *Dark Victory.* But in the days when my father would propose such projects from the Eastern office, his was often a lone voice in the wilderness; the immediate response from Warner and his Burbank yes-men was that the public didn't want such elegant stuff. Rapid-fire detective stories, sure, Cagney shoot-'em-ups—they were sure-fire at the box office. But as for these historical epics? Never mind that George Arliss had been a hit in *Disraeli.* As one hard-bitten Warner wag, Hal Wallis, put it, "Every time Paul Muni parts his beard to peer down another microscope, this studio loses another million bucks."

Not that Warner was hesitant to take bows for *Pasteur,* for *Dr. Ehrlich's Magic Bullet,* for *Black Legion,* an honest film which attacked neo-fascists in the Midwest, for the bold *Confessions of a Nazi Spy.* He could also bask in the reflected glory of such "classy" ventures as *The Petrified Forest,* which brought him Humphrey Bogart, and *The Maltese Falcon,* bought for peanuts in 1931, remade once more since then and now a film classic.

Not that he always kept his temper. When John Huston took his production of *The Treasure of the Sierra Madre* down to Mexico, far from studio interference, and the rushes arrived daily in Burbank, Warner would screen them. For day after day, he was treated to the sight of a grizzled, perspiring Bogart wandering through the desert, searching endlessly for water. One day, Warner had had enough. "If that bum doesn't find water soon, I'll go broke!" he cried.

It was that same peculiar mix of classy-cum-dreck, that successful pousse-café in which excellence co-existed layer by layer with profitable schlock, which was Warner's formula for survival. From the early silent days of Rin-Tin-Tin and John Barrymore, then through the sound film, brought to the brothers by their own Sam Warner, through the blackest years of the Depression, there was always a measure of substance to balance off the easily forgotten Warner shadows.

Came Pearl Harbor, and J. L. answered the call. Jimmy Cagney as George M. Cohan in *Yankee Doodle Dandy* couldn't enlist, but Warner became a Lieutenant Colonel in "Hap" Arnold's Air Force. His specific assignment was to set up a motion picture studio in which the Air Force could produce its own training and propaganda films. He did a fine job; he found the old Hal Roach studio in Culver City, a comedy factory languishing unused and unwanted. He negotiated a lease for it, then recruited and moved in a cadre of carefully picked production people, all of whom would go to work and staff Fort Roach. Wags may have dubbed the First Motion Picture Unit as "The Flying Typers," but General Arnold was well satisfied with its results.

Mission accomplished, the Colonel returned to civilian life. Hollywood rumors had it that J. L.'s nose was out of joint because the Air Force never gave him a full Colonel's status, while his ex-chief of production, Darryl Zanuck, received a pair of gold oak leaves from the Infantry.

But J. L. made an end run on all the other studios. He bought the rights to Irving Berlin's smash hit soldier show, *This Is the Army*, and made a deal to turn over all the profits of the picture, which would end up being millions, to Army Emergency Relief. Such patriotic largesse brought him back to where he wanted to be, on top of the heap.

All through the wartime years, he kept production going for an audience that was starved for entertainment. He may have been short of leading men, but he could and would make do with Bette Davis, Sidney Greenstreet, Peter Lorre, and Dennis Morgan (another utility type who'd inherited the mantle of Lyle Talbot). When Henry Blanke produced *Old*

Acquaintance with Bette Davis and Miriam Hopkins, the search for a leading man equal to the two stars was difficult, to say the least. Finally, the role was filled with an actor named John Loder. At the preview, someone rushed up to J. L. and raved at Bette Davis' performance. "She was great," agreed J. L. Miriam Hopkins, as well. "Also terrific," agreed J. L. And as for John Loder? J. L. shrugged. "Victory casting," he said.

Within the Burbank surroundings, pasha-like, Warner ruled. The studio was his personal factory, and he ran it efficiently. One of his major requirements was that every employee punch a time clock, no matter whether he be a back-lot crew member, a star, or as highly paid a team of writers as Julius and Phillip Epstein. There came the famous day when the Epsteins rebelled against this nine-to-five ukase, maintaining that creative types do not keep such hours. "Why not?" demanded Warner. "Executives can come in at nine, bank presidents can come in at nine, why in hell can't you come in at nine?"

A week or so later, the Epsteins delivered the first thirty pages or so of their new screenplay to Warner, with a note attached. It read. "Dear J. L., Have the bank president finish this."

The argument persisted. One evening, the new Epstein comedy was taken out of the studio for a top-secret preview at a neighborhood Los Angeles suburb.

Afterwards, as always, the post-mortem was held upstairs in the manager's office. "This is a piece of crap!" raved Warner. "The worst you've ever done!"

"I don't understand it, Jack," said Julius Epstein, "We came in every morning at nine."

Warner was not amused, nor was he to be dissuaded. "I want my money back!" he told the Epsteins.

Phillip shrugged. "Sorry," he sighed. "I took it and used it to build a new swimming pool. However, if you're ever in the neighborhood and feel like a dip ... feel free."

At Warner's Angelo Drive mansion, a truly impressive place, the walls were hung with Renoirs, Degas, and other such fashionable Impressionists. If the establishment wasn't quite as lavish as, say, Hearst's San Simeon or Mr. Huntington's Library in Pasadena, it wasn't exactly a raised ranch, was it? Across rolling greenswards was an Olympic-size pool, and then, the private tennis courts where Warner could demonstrate his athletic superiority. Jack was equipped with a regular opponent for the weekends, a pleasant chap named Solly Baiano, who had once been a crack tennis player. Now he was a Warner talent scout, respected for his sharp judgment.

For years Solly participated in a regular weekend drama; for years, his boss always seemed to beat Solly, even though it was well known Solly was by far the better player. On and on the ritual continued; his boss firing bad jokes and tennis balls across the net to Solly. Solly laughing dutifully and somehow managing to miss return shots.

But one weekend, Solly must have come to the end of his tether. Perhaps J.L. had made one bad joke too many. Some sort of a veiled insult? ("Hey Solly, you know the sound spaghetti makes when it hits the plate? It's *wop!*") Whatever the cause, on that memorable Angelo Drive afternoon, Solly forgot himself, and in front of Warner's guests, beat his boss badly.

Retribution was swift. When Solly arrived at his office the next Monday, he found a pink slip waiting. After all these years as a loser, he'd actually lost.

In the home, Jack and his wife Ann entertained guests at formal dinners; stars, celebrities, directors, and producers of the A list, all sharing tables with a sprinkling of the international white-trash set, most of whom had taken refuge in Southern California for the duration.

Writers? Rarely, if ever. The caste system still applied. The Warners would be delighted to entertain some celebrity playwright from New York, say, but none of his hired-hand schmucks from the studio. And at the head of the table, there sat J.L. throwing out a steady stream of gags. It mattered not to him if his guests were famous or eminent for their intellect. Everyone came under his verbal blasts. Was he not, after all, the same host at a luncheon years back to honor Albert Einstein, where he remarked, "I don't know a hell of a lot about your theory, Al, that relativity stuff, but I sure know about relatives … I've got 'em all over the place!"

And when he'd entertained Madame Chiang Kai-Shek at another formal luncheon, was it not J.L. who'd risen after dessert to say, "And now that we've all finished eating, Madame, can we send you out with the laundry?"

During those war years, the Warner emblem appeared at the start of many truly important films, movies with definite sociological impact on the audiences they attracted. Perhaps today, such films as *Action in the North Atlantic*, on which John Howard Lawson shares a screen credit, or *Pride of the Marines*, written by Albert Maltz, or *Watch on the Rhine*, with its script by Lillian Hellman and Dashiell Hammett, may have less of an impact than they did in their own time, but they, among several others of the same ilk, were important enough to cause Bosley Crowther, the critic of *The New York Times*, to announce that Warner Bros. "combined good citizenship with good picture making." This sentiment was proudly emblazoned on the Burbank studio walls, in letters large enough for every passer-by to notice.

Ironically enough, years later, when the congressional witch hunts were launched and questions were raised concerning Communist influence on picture-making, it would be Warner Bros. where many instances of such "infiltration" would be cited, with the names of writers who had been employed by the studio cited over and over again.

Warner's response? He had been an unwitting dupe, a part of a gigantic political conspiracy, and since he was far from the only producer who had been taken in by these infiltrators, how could he be held responsible?

Half a century later, those films still hold up, examples of what screen-writers are capable of when they are allowed to do their best work.

Years passed. The Justice Department caused the studios to divest themselves of the vast theatre chains that had, for years, constituted the monopolies for the major studios. Television began to draw away some of the audience which had for so many years supported the studios. But if the ship was sinking, nobody in California was worried. One night, Warner was a guest at a typical Hollywood party, one of those opulent affairs complete with canvas tent in a Brentwood garden, a dance band playing, the catering by Chasen's, with caviar and vintage champagne, and with a crowd of the A-list (only New York playwrights, no locals).

Warner beamed at the crowd of bejeweled ladies and their sun-tanned escorts. He turned to one of his tablemates. "My boy," he remarked, "*these* are the good old days."

Jack left the running of the studio behind for a few years and took a sabbatical in the south of France. He enjoyed the good life for a while, but eventually his brother Harry insisted that he return to California; the studio couldn't operate properly without Jack calling the shots. When Warner returned, one of his friends informed him that Ronald Reagan, who had spent years at Burbank making all sorts of films there and who had served as the adjutant during the war years at Fort Roach, was about to make a run for the governorship of California. Warner thought for a moment and then shook his head. "No, no," he said. "Jimmy Stewart for governor ... Ronald Reagan for his best friend!"

In 1956, Warner Bros. made a deal to sell all their pre-1956 product to a newly created releasing company. The Warners took a large chunk of cash; the head of the purchasing company took possession of a huge backlog of films, good, bad, and indifferent.

For Warner stockholders it was, to say the least, a very poor deal. The price paid for that library of films was vastly less than what Warner Bros. might have made by hanging on, as did MGM, to its assets. For the past forty-odd years, those Warner pictures have been run and rerun—in art houses, in Europe, on television, and on cassettes—churning out profits everywhere, except to the Warner stockholders.

Towards the end, J.L produced some very "classy" pictures: *A Star Is Born*, *My Fair Lady*, *Who's Afraid of Virginia Woolf*, and *Camelot*, which he always referred to as "Costalot."

The schlock side of his product was still there, but now it was all for TV. The department that he had set up earned hefty profits during the late '60s on an assembly line set-up that made the old Warner movie department—wherein Bryan Foy could grind out pictures in two and three week schedules—look like a Rolls Royce factory. Day after day crews put together episodes of *77 Sunset Strip*, *Cheyenne*, *The Roaring '20s*, etc., by the truckload. "They shoot so much film," one old Warner hand remarked, "that we're wearing out the equipment!"

As Warner grew older, he became less belligerent and less anxious for the confrontations he'd enjoyed over the years. In the old days, he would roar across his desk at anyone who dared to cross him. Now, he had become unable to indulge in such rough-and-tumble brawling. Where once he had ordered people off his domain, now he was even unable to face firing people. Diminutive Steve Trilling had been J.L.'s trusted aide for more than three decades. One Friday afternoon, Warner left, ordering

Steve to keep a close eye on the studio while he was away in New York. Monday morning, Steve arrived in his office, and on his desk blotter was a pink slip.

When Warner finally retired from active production of films, he would dabble in various ventures, one of which would be a Broadway musical based on the life of the late mayor, James J. Walker. The show was less than a smash hit, and after a few weeks of disappointing business, one of the authors, Mel Shavelson, called Warner and suggested they put up the closing notice to save money—most of which was Warner's.

Warner demurred. "Let the show stay open," he said.

Why would he want to do that?

"Well, if we close the show," said Warner, "who would I have dinner with?"

And for once, he was not making a joke.

Warner died, leaving an estate estimated to be valued at over fifteen million dollars. A playwright named Shakespeare, the same whose play, *A Midsummer Night's Dream*, was made into a Warner film in 1936 (classy yes, but most unprofitable) once wrote, "The evil that men do lives after them. The good is oft interred in their bones."

J. L. would probably have said, "Another schmuck—with a quill pen!"

In this case, he would have been right. J. L. is interred, warts and all, and by now very few remain who remember his transgressions. But his good deeds? They survive—on videotape, on DVD, on discs—morning, noon and night, when they start out "Jack L. Warner presents…"

And if you were a man who lived to make movies—almost as much as you liked telling people you knew a woman who lived with cats, Mrs. Katz—well, that's not a bad way to leave 'em. If not laughing, applauding.

And whether or not he actually did call his writers schmucks, let's refer to Howard Koch, one of his very best. When Koch had finished the screenplay for Warners' very successful film *The Letter*, and shooting was completed, Koch joined director William Wyler, Bette Davis, and others for a wrap party at which Koch generously sprang for champagne.

"How Jack heard about it, I don't know," recalled Koch, "but the studio was a small world and as my secretary said, 'Everybody knows everything here.' Jack's remark was a typical Warner evaluation. 'Where does a three-hundred-dollar-a-week writer get off giving a champagne party?'"

FINALE? ONE MORE.

Warner was once confronted by one of his directors during the HUAC hearings; the director complained that he'd been blacklisted. "There's no blacklist!" insisted Warner, "and you're not on it!"

Hal Wallis and Jack Warner by Edward Sorel

18. DOUBLE FEATURE:
EVAN HUNTER and ED MCBAIN

May, 2000

Evan Hunter by Dragica Hunter

Should you be discussing screenwriting with Evan Hunter, the two of you are not alone. You are also talking with Ed McBain and Matthew Hope.

Hunter is a master of the art of beginning a story, carrying it through the middle, and bringing it to a conclusion. He has demonstrated this considerable gift some fifty-four times now, as Ed McBain, who is the documentarian of the 87th Precinct, and whose police stories have amassed him a worldwide audience of passionate devotees, who snatch up his latest works as rapidly as his publisher can deliver them to your local bookstore.

McBain's Matthew Hope stories add up to thirteen more volumes. And as Evan Hunter, he has produced twenty novels.

One of his latest works, *Candyland*, was a joint venture. Evan Hunter had written the first half of the book; Ed McBain had completed it. Very few authors can boast of having collaborated with themselves!

Over the years of his remarkable career, Hunter has also written TV episodes, "long-form" two- and four-hour TV scripts, and he has also had quite a few encounters with Hollywood producers. Back in the 1950s, his novel *The Blackboard Jungle* was made into a very successful film by Metro. "My novel, *not* my script," he comments dryly.

Why dryly? This pattern is a familiar one for playwrights and novelists who encounter film studio logic. "They buy a good story from you, but they somehow cannot believe you'd be the right person to adapt it for the screen," he remarks. "Go figure."

Some years later, Hunter did write the screenplay for Alfred Hitchcock's classic horror thriller *The Birds*, which was based on the Daphne DuMaurier novel. That assignment came to him after he had written several episodes for Hitchcock's TV series, *Alfred Hitchcock Presents*. For years now, film audiences have been shocked by Hitchcock's terrifying vision of birds attacking human beings; cineastes constantly pay homage to the master's frightening work.

So shouldn't Hunter feel satisfied with such an homage to his work on the screenplay for *The Birds* as well?

"No," he says, all these years later. "...I was never happy with the final script. Hitch made changes that annoyed me, without ever consulting me."

And that is that. Case closed.

Hunter's next experience with writing for the screen came when Columbia bought the screen rights to his novel *Strangers When We Meet*. "Once again, the same old ball game," he recalls. "They buy my novel for a picture, but they don't think I am the right choice to do the screenplay. It's because I am a novelist. But would you believe, they go and hire another novelist to adapt my novel?...Which doesn't make too much sense, does it?"

Are we going to spend any of his valuable time trying to derive any sense out of Hollywood studio logic?

"No," agrees Hunter. "Absolutely not. Anyway, they wanted Kim Novak to play the lead in the picture, and I happened to meet her on one of my publicity trips out to L.A. She told me she loved my book—but she hated the screenplay this novelist, Norman Katkov, had done. And she immediately asks me if I'll do the rewrite...at the time, she was very close to the director, Richard Quine. So one thing led to another...Believe me, I wasn't too happy following another author on my own story—but when I read his script, I realized he had taken my book and thrown it away! Why do they always throw the original work away?" He shakes his head. "It must be because they have no respect for what they bought, don't you think?"

Once again, who has an answer for that question?

"Anyway," he continues, "from reading that script, I could see what needed to be done. Why not? I was the author, wasn't I?... So I agreed to do the rewrite Columbia wanted, and what I turned in to them seemed fine for everybody. They went ahead and made the picture... from *my* script!"

When the picture was completed, the Columbia executives liked the final version. So much so that Hunter was called into a meeting at the summit with the head of the studio, a long-time Hollywood veteran, Sam Briskin, who had taken over the position after the death of the legendary Harry Cohn.

"Briskin asked me, 'So, what are you writing *next?*' And I told him I had an idea for another novel, *Mothers and Daughters.* He wanted to know what it was about, and so I told him, what I had in mind was three generations of American women... in a long story. That's all I had. Briskin nodded and said, 'Sounds good. We'll buy it. Have your agent call me.'"

Hunter grins. "Believe it or not, they bought it! Sight unseen!"

Thus bearing out the classic Hollywood rule... *when you're hot, you're hot.*

"So, I wrote the novel, and it was published... and can you believe this? Columbia hired somebody else to write the script." He shakes his head in disbelief. "They never even *asked* me to take a crack at it."

And what became of the saga of three generations of American women, a subject which would seem to have been a solid basis for any number of the female leading ladies of the '50s and '60s?

"Terrible script... good book," remembers Hunter, grimacing.

Then he shrugs. "But you mustn't let those guys out there get to you, especially if you're a novelist. I just keep on going, writing my books. That's how you keep your sanity.

"Once in a while, I'd agree to try writing for television. During the '60s and the '70s, I would occasionally do what was called 'long-form' — those were two- and four-hour scripts. I found them interesting to write; it gave me room to plot a story... And there wasn't too much interference from the guys at the networks." He grins. "Who knows why? Maybe they were scared of me. By that time, I'd developed a pretty decent reputation as a novelist who could tell a good story—all by himself.

"There are a few other novelists who seem to have been able to avoid running into trouble with movie producers," he muses. "Take Donald Westlake—he's a very good writer, and he was able to write the script of his own work *The Grifters*, and nobody fooled with it, and it came out as a damn good picture, remember? It's already become a cult film.

"But you have to know this; Donald is a guy who'll simply walk away if he doesn't agree with what the studio people want him to do. He'll just say, 'Sorry, fellas, I don't want to do what you're asking for—I don't agree, so you can take it on from here yourselves, without me.' And he leaves."

And what about another major contemporary detective story writer, Elmore Leonard?

"Well, Dutch is a guy with his own very particular style," says Hunter. "The way he writes dialogue, the scenes he plots, which don't seem to follow each other in any particular order... those wonderful characters who keep on popping up here and there, unexpectedly... and you never know exactly where the story is going or how... All of that is marvelous.

"I think it was Quentin Tarantino who was first able to imitate Leonard's particular style in *Pulp Fiction*," muses Hunter. "You have to remember, up to then, Leonard had tried writing various scripts... and they hadn't quite worked. It wasn't until they did his *Get Shorty* that they were able to crack that unique Leonard code.

"But it has always seemed to me that if they'd just shot Leonard's novels *the way they were written*, they'd have found it much easier to transfer those stories to the screen."

There is no doubt that Hunter/McBain, along with Leonard, Westlake, Tony Hillerman, and others, each must be classified as the truly creative writer: one who works solo, creating his own characters, spinning out his stories in a unique style, a writer who is totally responsible for the work that emerges.

So the question that follows is why are studio people so insecure when it comes to hiring such recognized talents to do their own adaptations for the screen?

"Well, the author is a necessary evil, but once he's done his job, and they've paid him for the rights, you get the feeling that they want him to go away and to leave *them* alone to turn his work into a screenplay," says Hunter. "Part of it has to be ego, of course. They feel they can improve his work."

Which brings us to the classic Hollywood writer's complaint, author to producer and/or director: "Where were you when the page was blank?"

"You know," muses Hunter, "maybe it's because the author thinks differently. When a novelist does his own adaptation, it probably does retain some of his depths and shadings, which is what he brought to the story in the first place...And I happen to think that's a good thing."

He shrugs. "Obviously, out there, they don't."

Over the years, Hunter has answered the siren call of various other producers to work on projects he did not originate and with varying results.

"I worked on one picture called *Fuzz*—awful," he remarks. Case closed.

"And then, along with Larry Turman—good producer, the guy who did *The Graduate* and *Great White Hope*—he got me into something I really enjoyed doing. Larry called me up and asked, 'What do you know about gangs?' I said, 'Everything.' He said, 'Okay, what do you know about *L.A.* gangs?' I said, 'Nothing.' 'Okay, so why don't you come out here and research them with me for a picture?' he said.

"This was a few years back; there were no white gangs out there then, only blacks and Chicanos...so I went out there and spent some time with Larry, and we dug around until we had enough material to present a story idea to United Artists...They sat and listened, and I couldn't believe it, but they told us they wanted it.

"We'd concentrated on the Chicano gangs. Okay, that meant I had to do the script. And if I say so myself, it was a damn good script!"[3]

What happened then?

Hunter's screenplay of the Chicano gangs disappeared into that particular limbo that is defined by anyone who has been there as Development Hell.

Usually followed by silence.

Hunter returned to his novels.

[3] The film Hunter was referring to is *Walk Proud*, based on his own *A Matter of Conviction*. Released by Universal, 1979.

"Years later, the thing surfaced again—this time with a young actor, Robby Benson. He'd read it and liked it. Which got us back into business. So I did the inevitable rewrites—this time to beef up the Romeo and Juliet aspect of the story…and believe it or not, the picture got made."

With what results?

Hunter grimaces. "We ran into a real problem. In the interim, somebody else had made a picture about the L.A. gangs—how about *that* for timing! And when that other picture hit the theatres out there, there were riots! The gang kids went in and tore up the theatres, remember?

"So when it came time to release *our* picture, the film people were very, very nervous…Who can blame them?" He shrugs. "It did not play in too many locations."

Once again, Hunter/McBain returned to the 87th Precinct and its people.

"Then, a couple of years later, I get a call from Richard Dreyfuss—he came out of the blue and wanted to talk to me about an idea he had for a movie. No script—just an idea. It was about cops, and he knew I had a good background in their world…Would I listen to his idea? Sure, why not? So we met and talked, and Richard had himself a very seductive premise—the title was *The Last Cop*.

"It needed fleshing out, of course, but his hook was great. It took place in a seaport, a coastal town; the mob is planning a big score, they're bringing in an entire shipload of drugs. So, in order to make sure the stuff gets into the country safely, they systematically buy off all the members of the local police force, one by one…Until only one guy is left…One cop and he's honest. He won't sell out!…And that part, of course, is the one Dreyfuss wants. Surprise.

"I liked the idea a lot," says Hunter. "We talk some more, and pretty soon we have enough to take it in to one of those events they refer to as a 'pitch meeting.' It's at a company called Touchstone, we go in, we sit down, and we tell the guys the premise. And guess what? They like it. 'So, how does it end?' asks the guy in charge." Hunter grins. "'I don't know until I write it,' I tell him, which I can immediately tell does not go over too well.

"'Look,' I tell him. 'I have written almost forty 87th Precincts, and I never knew until I was actually working down to the end of the story what the hell the ending was going to be. So, if I can't figure out the end of *this* one . . . I better quit, right?'

"...The guy says, 'I hear you. We'll be in touch.'

"Dreyfuss and I walk out of the office, and we're convinced we have blown it at Touchstone . . . Silence . . . and then, believe it or not, they call us up and say, 'Go!'

"...Okay, so after all the time it takes, everything is settled, and we have a deal, I go to work on the script . . . and it ends up with the ship pulling into the harbor at night, none of the cops are there excepting for our hero . . . He's the one who hasn't been bought off—he won't give in . . . And the boys come up to him, and *whammo*—they toss him off the dock into the water! They *kill him!*. . . And then the crew begins to unload the cargo of drugs from the ship!

"We send in the script, and then we start to hear screams from the Touchstone guys. '*You killed him!* You killed the *hero!*'

"There's a lot of arguing back and forth, and finally, I get a call, and they say, 'We're going to have to put another writer on it, do you understand?'

"So I say, 'Do I understand that you're putting another writer on it, *or* do I understand *why* you're putting another writer on it?'

"To this, they don't have too much of an answer. So I finally say, 'Look, I've come nine yards—don't you think I can come *ten?*'

He sighs. "No, they do not agree. They finally tell me, 'What you are saying is that in our society, today, drugs are all powerful—nobody can withstand them.'

"'Exactly!' I say. '*That's precisely what I am saying!*'

"It's no use. I guess what they must have figured was, 'If we give in to him, he won't change his vision . . . and we cannot make that movie. No way!'"

And another project went on the shelf.

Ironically enough, in 2001 there would be the film called *Traffic*, which earned rave notices, awards, and attracted audiences to theatres . . . which postulated precisely the same premise that Touchstone turned down.

What is the basis of all this confusion? And why does it customarily take place in California film works?

Is it because the writer who sits and creates his novel or his play thus becomes the owner of the copyright to said work and can avoid changes to it? Whereas, the writer who accepts a film assignment, and signs a contract to do so, has, since the very earliest days of the studios, automatically signed away the copyright to the work he has done for hire?

And can only sit in conferences and argue and listen patiently, while executives and their hirelings suggest endless changes?

"Correct," sighs Hunter. "The movie is not ours. It belongs to the studio. But when you come right down to it, if you postulate that the author should own the copyright to the picture—don't you have to ask about all the other elements that went into creating it? The producer, the director, the designer—don't *they* all have some sort of claim to the final work?"

He shakes his head sadly. "So how could we ever go in and claim that we, only the writers, have the copyright? They'd never give it to us…"

Ah, but there are historic instances when the studios *have* given in to such a claim. For example, take the case of Edna Ferber, that very prolific author whose agent, Leland Hayward, decided Ferber's successful novel *Saratoga Trunk* was such an important property for a film that he would not sell it outright. What was Hayward's proposal? He stipulated a seven-year lease to whichever studio obtained the rights to the Ferber book, at the end of which time, the buyer would relinquish any and all rights to Ferber…and she would retain the copyright throughout those seven years.

A bold and daring notion, one which caused enormous resentment among the studio moguls; how did Hayward dare to rock the boat in such an outrageous manner? None of this leasing—to buy is to *buy!*

"Did they give in?" asks Hunter.

Yes, indeed. Kicking and screaming and cursing; but Hayward had the guts to stand fast. He got his lease deal from Jack Warner, who in turn leased a property for Gary Cooper and Ingrid Bergman for seven years.

"Okay, fine," says Hunter. "But I'll bet you one thing—Edna Ferber didn't do her own script."

True enough, she didn't.

"That's it." says Hunter, triumphantly. "They don't trust the author. I've sold a lot of my books—there's one I've written called *Love, Dad.* It's gone through three complete rewrites. They've changed the title, they've changed the entire damn story; it's been reworked so often, they've totally forgotten why the hell they bought the book in the first place."

Also a hardly new take on the Hollywood pattern.

One need only consult the memoirs of the late R. C. Sherriff, the talented British playwright who wrote the classic *Journey's End*, in which he relates his experience some seventy years ago, in 1930, when he first journeyed to California to work for Universal out in San Fernando Valley.

According to Sherriff, he was asked to try his hand at a script based on H. G. Wells' *The Invisible Man*, to be directed by the legendary James Whale. "There were many others who had tried," Sherriff reported. "I was given a stack of scripts, one worse than the next. It seemed no one had any idea of how to transfer Wells' novel to the screen. In each draft, the various writers had all gone further and further away from the original story."

Might he read the original Wells novel?

Alas, nobody at the Universal story department seemed to have it anywhere in the files.

Sherriff thereupon drove downtown to Los Angeles, found himself a second-hand bookstore, purchased an old copy of *The Invisible Man*, took it home, and read it. "A marvelous story," he reported.

He sat down at his desk to spend the next few weeks adapting Wells' novel into a screenplay, remaining faithful to the original story.

Does anyone need to add the sardonic twist to the end of this story? Everyone who read Sherriff's screenplay was delighted with it. "Overnight, I became the hero of Universal!" he reported. James Whale directed Claude Rains in the original filmed version; the picture was a great box office success.

Seventy-odd years ago. Has anything changed so much since those early pioneering days at Universal City?

Nothing, perhaps, save the ownership of Mr. Laemmle's studio.

"I can give you another horror story," says Hunter. "One that's gone on for almost seven years. They bought a book of mine called *Criminal Conversations*—optioned it and as usual put some writer to work on it. He was the first of *five*.

"For six years they've been having scripts written ... Of course, they've never asked me to try doing it … After all, I'm only the author. So last year, they called up and said they were tired of renewing the option on my book … so guess what? They've decided to *buy it*."

And why have they never asked the author himself to try to adapt the work?

"Who knows?" shrugs Hunter. "Maybe it's just that I'm too old. You and I both know, the entire business is run on the theory that anyone over thirty is over the hill. I mean, just look at that ridiculous episode a couple of years back, when Disney hired some girl specifically to write scripts because she was nineteen—and they figured she'd be perfect to write scripts for the nineteen-year-old audience? Isn't that incredible? As if none of *us* has ever been nineteen!"

And one must add the ultimate irony, which was that the girl Disney hired was actually twenty-nine and had passed herself off as a teenager in order to get the job.

"What does that tell you?" says Hunter, shaking his head. "And I'll bet you—if you went into a pitch meeting and threw that whole episode as an idea for a comedy, the producer would shake his head and tell you it was too far-fetched.

"…But I can give you another horror story, one which just happened to *me*. One of my books, *King's Ransom*, was made into a Japanese film by Kurosawa, the great director. It's called *High Low*. Martin Scorsese saw it and thought it would make a good picture here, so he bought the rights to do it in English.

"So far, this project has been through three writers, the last one being David Mamet … When he finished, he informed them he wanted to direct it. But I'd never heard anything more until the other night, in New York. I was at the theatre, and during the intermission, I happened to run into one of the producers. I asked her what was happening with the project, and she said, 'Well, we're looking for another writer.'

"'So why don't you ask *me*?' I said. 'I'm a writer, I do that sort of thing,' I reminded her. 'Oh, you *do*?' she asked. And then she said, 'Oh yes, that's right, isn't it!'"

An anecdote that is not only ridiculous, but which serves as a comment on the status of all of us writers, correct?

"I guess so," muses Hunter. "And if you're going to be a writer in

322

Hollywood, you *should* learn how to direct. At least that way you have some measure of control over your original work."

Exactly the same sentiments of Billy Wilder, who expressed them some two decades earlier.

"I mean, look at that picture *A Perfect Plan.* The guy who wrote it also directed it, and I thought he did a damned good job. And so did Lonergan, with *You Can Count on Me.*"

And let us not forget the excellent screenplay John Irving provided the director of his own book, *Cider House Rules.*

"Maybe," mused Hunter, "it's because we bring more respect to the work than some outsider does. Dammit—it's *ours.*

"…But I have to admit," he concedes, "there are a lot of times if somebody suggests I could do the job adapting my own work, I've gotten to the point where I turn them down. Because it means spending two years or more of your life, working on a rehash of something you've already given birth to…Look, you write a novel, you bring it in, you drop it on the publisher's desk, you're finished. Nobody calls you up in a couple of days and says, 'Hi there, we've passed your book all over the office, we've all read it, and we've assembled quite a few notes—we'd like you to think about them for *changes*…okay?'"

Amen.

On the other hand, hasn't Hunter been working on the script for a future Broadway musical, an adaptation of the film *The Night They Raided Minsky's?* And how long has he been involved in that endeavor?

"Only a couple of years, so far," he admits. "But I keep on turning out the books as well." He smiles. "But nobody ever said writing a musical was easy…If it were easy, everybody would be doing it, right?"

And let us not forget the contract for writing said Broadway musical, which specifically retains for Hunter the rights to the libretto he has written.

"Yeah, that does make it worthwhile," he agrees.

Meanwhile, he alternates between the works of Evan Hunter, and for his huge audience of 87th Precinct fans, Ed McBain—who continues to turn out his mysteries.

And what if some film producer was to call up tomorrow and broach the subject of his working on a screenplay?

Hunter shakes his head. "Not a chance," he says. "I keep telling you, it won't happen. I'm too *old*."

Every author should be so old. And at the top of such form.

Evan Hunter/Ed McBain's Credits:

Films:

Blackboard Jungle, 1955

The Mugger, 1958

Cop Hater, 1958

The Pusher, 1960

Strangers When We Meet, 1960

The Young Savages, 1961

The Birds, 1963

Mister Buddwing, 1965

Last Summer, 1969

Every Little Crook and Nanny, 1972

Fuzz, 1972

Without Apparent Motive, 1972

Walk Proud, 1979

LARRY GELBART on "THE NOTORIOUS LANDLADY"

RICHARD QUINE WAS UNHAPPY WITH THE WRITER, REWRITER ACTUALLY, OF the suspense comedy. The original writer on the project had been Blake Edwards. Quine was in a bind. He needed new pages, lots of them, and he needed them the day before yesterday. His actors were assembled and he had to start shooting right away. Jack Lemmon was the male lead, and Jeanne Moreau apparently not being available, Kim Novak was his leading lady. The third star was Fred Astaire, in a nondancing role. (But then, I, the once-and-never future Fred Astaire, was also involved in a nondancing capacity.)

The work went well. I thought so. They thought so. At least, they thought to tell me they did. I was enjoying the sensation of actually working in a motion picture factory that used to ship the boy I had been fresh dreams and fantasies for my Saturday afternoon delectations. I dined alongside famous faces in the studio commissary. I met other writers. Important writers, writers who actually knew how to do what I was only beginning to know. I met S. N. Behrman, for Christ's sake.

I was having a very good time. I know you're way ahead of me, so just let me connect the dots for you.

One day, working on the last few scenes of the script, I heard gales of laughter coming from the office next to mine, the office of the producer of the picture, Fred Kohlmar. Putting a drinking glass to our common wall, a primitive but time-tested way of eavesdropping, I soon realized that the laughers were Kohlmar and Richard Quine. There was a third laugher in the room. It was S. N. Behrman. What the three men were enjoying so heartily was Behrman's rewrite of a portion of my rewrite—the one they kept telling me was going so well. Without informing me, Behrman had been working behind me, improving my improvements, with Quine billing and cooing in his ear

I was a young, trusting writer when I listened in on the wall to the everyday run-of-the-mill betrayal going on behind it. I was also a good deal older and smarter by the time I put my glass down. Also, really crushed.

I've had similar experiences since, when I'm on the other side of the drinking glass, when I'm rewriting somebody else's rewrite. It's never pleasant, either way.

—LARRY GELBART, *Laughing Matters*, 1998

CODA

DEAR GRIFFIN:

I'm still waiting for you to call. You said you'd get back to me. My answering machine is on all the time, so you can't say that you called but I wasn't in. I told you my idea, you said you wanted to think about it, and you said you'd get back to me. My agent said that was a good sign, the part about getting back to me. I've waited long enough. You lied to me. It's obvious you have no intention of hiring me. In the name of all the writers in Hollywood who get pushed around by executives who know nothing more about movies than what did well last week and have no passion for film, I'm going to kill you.

—MICHAEL TOLKIN, *The Player*, 1992

INDEX

334